SHATTERING
THE CHRISTIAN
LOOKING GLASS

Order this book online at www.trafford.com
or email orders@trafford.com

Most Trafford titles are also available at major online book retailers.

Note for Librarians: A cataloguing record for this book is available from Library
and Archives Canada at www.collectionscanada.ca/amicus/index-e.html

Printed in Victoria, BC, Canada.

ISBN: 9781-4251-8395-0 (soft cover)
ISBN: 9781-4251-8396-7 (eBook)

*We at Trafford believe that it is the responsibility of us all, as both individuals
and corporations, to make choices that are environmentally and socially sound.
You, in turn, are supporting this responsible conduct each time you purchase a
Trafford book, or make use of our publishing services. To find out how you are
helping, please visit www.trafford.com/responsiblepublishing.html*

*Our mission is to efficiently provide the world's finest, most comprehensive
book publishing service, enabling every author to experience success.
To find out how to publish your book, your way, and have it available
worldwide, visit us online at www.trafford.com*

 www.trafford.com

North America & international
toll-free: 1 888 232 4444 (USA & Canada)
phone: 250 383 6864 ♦ fax: 250 383 6804 ♦ email: info@trafford.com

The United Kingdom & Europe
phone: +44 (0)1865 487 395 ♦ local rate: 0845 230 9601
facsimile: +44 (0)1865 481 507 ♦ email: info.uk@trafford.com

10 9 8 7 6 5 4 3 2 1

TABLE OF CONTENTS

Catholic Christians are so imbued with their Church's rendition of Christ and his messages that they instinctively, viscerally reject any suggestion that any part of the Jesus story might be untrue. This reaction was never so evident as when I and my wife were on a cruise ship in the Mediterranean a few years ago. Before the cruise I had read *Holy Blood, Holy Grail* by Baigent, Leigh, and Lincoln and had become curious about the book's message after viewing a prime-time television program critiquing it. One evening during dinner I mentioned the book to a fellow passenger. I tactfully, casually, non-threateningly raised, purely as a topic for friendly conversation, the book's speculation that Jesus "may" have been married to Mary Magdalene. My listener, sitting across from me, was visibly shocked. He stared at me with eyes wide open, as if I had just told him I had thrown the ship's captain overboard, and said softly — straight-backed, chin up, but quite politely not to offend me — "Well, people believe different things."

And that was that! End of conversation. There was no engagement in a friendly theoretical discussion of the relationship between Jesus and Mary Magdalene. The conversation was abruptly ended. His silence made it clear that to even suggest that Jesus had had carnal thoughts or, perish the thought, had copulated with the Magdalene was unthinkable. This passenger, a devout Catholic, spoke not another word to me for the rest of the cruise, avoided even looking at me for fear, I suppose, that our eyes would connect and the heretical beliefs to which I had referred would somehow magically insinuate themselves into his mind. Or perhaps my remark, in challenging his unchallengeable faith, had resurrected in him deeply hidden doubts about it. Who knows?

Had he been wholly confident in his Christian beliefs, he would have calmly cast aside my statement and chided me for my ignorance and foolishness. But he was clearly shaken by the very idea that Jesus might not be the person the Church had led him to believe he was. The impact of what I had said literally left him speechless.

When my wife asked a neighbor friend, a Catholic, if she intended to see the movie *The Da Vinci Code*, the friend replied resolutely, perfunctorily, and without elaboration, "No!" My wife then asked if she had read the book. Again "No!" That was it. My wife knew at once by the woman's curt replies and her withdrawn expression that any further discussion would be viewed as antagonistic and rude. This incident made clear that this woman's faith in her religion, like that of the man on the cruise ship, was so frail that both the book and the movie posed a viable threat to their beliefs. Neither of them had sufficient knowledge or conviction to dispute the contention, however absurd the notion might appear to them, that Jesus and the Magdalene were not only man and wife but together had begat a child. The reactions of these two people were the well-known one of compulsive denial: "I don't want to talk about it!" Why? Because that discussion frightened them.

These episodes not only demonstrated how inept most Christians are in defending their religious faith when it is challenged, they also revealed how superficial that faith can be. By that I mean Christians for the most part are ignorant of their Faith's substance and history. They, of course, know the arresting story of Jesus' birth, mission, miracles, crucifixion, and resurrection. That's standard. But that's about all they know. Indeed, as foolish as it may sound, they know more about Hollywood celebrities and contestants on *American Idol* than they do about the origins of Christianity and the Bible. But it's not foolish at all. It's the reality of the Catholic laity. Christians revere the Bible, but few of them read it. According to surveys, twelve percent of self-identified American Christians think Noah's wife was Joan of Arc. One-quarter do not know what is celebrated on Easter. Eighty percent of born-again Christians believe it is the Bible that says, "God helps those who help themselves." Actually, it was Ben Franklin.[1]

Unlike most Protestants, most (90 percent?) of the Catholic Faithful, even those who attended Catholic schools, are biblically illiterate, which is understandable, because attendees in the past at Catholic schools, even colleges, rarely studied the history of the Gospels and who wrote them. Things may have changed; I don't know. But they didn't change for my wife. Although she attended Catholic all-girl schools from kindergarten through college, not once in all those seventeen years did she *study* the Bible. The nuns and priests, of course, quoted the Bible to recount Jesus' life, teachings, and sufferings, but there was never a concentrated probing examination of the Christian Scriptures and their origins. Instead, her religious education focused on the catechisms, the lives of the saints, and the Church's miracles...pure unadulterated mindless indoctrination. Even today she can recount in detail the story of almost every saint who is honored with a Saint's Day, much to my never-ending amazement. "How do you remember this stuff?" I ask her. To which she replies, "It was drummed into me year after year in school. How can I forget?"

My wife's ignorance of the Bible wasn't a question of her intelligence or her reading habits. She was a star pupil, loved reading, was bright and inquisitive, and was valedictorian of her college graduation class, but studying the Bible wasn't required, so she never developed an interest in it. Indeed, as Mary Faulkner, who holds a Master's degree in religious education from Scarritt Graduate School explains in *Supreme Authority*[2], "Prior to the Second Vatican Council in 1962, Catholics were not encouraged to read the Bible...Private interpretation was forbidden because the Church worried about deviation from its own carefully packaged doctrine. Reading the Bible was considered Protestant, which was reason enough to avoid it."[3] (Even biblical scholars can be humorous!) Instead, the Catholic Faithful over the centuries obtained their limited knowledge of the Bible in judiciously apportioned, carefully orchestrated snippets at Sunday Mass...and still do. Thus, they have only sufficient understanding of biblical themes, characters, and stories to meet the Church's ordained minimum — you could say "maximum" — requirement for true believers.

The fact is, until 2004, I was a carbon copy of them. Like most Catholics, I had never read the Bible and was totally ignorant of its history, who wrote it, when, who the New Testament authors were, and where they came from. But I never felt any need to. It had been an article of faith since I was a child that "whosoever believeth in Jesus shall have everlasting life". It was enough that I "believed" in Jesus...and I did. I was a devout believer...and *still* am...that he was God's messenger of salvation beyond death. Concerned forty years ago at my confirmation about my lack of knowledge of the Catholic Church and its doctrines, I posed the question to the young priest who was instructing me. He assured me that belief in the Nicene Creed was all that was required to become a Catholic. He explained that one needn't believe in the miracles, the saints, or what have you. The Creed said it all. I was relieved, because I had never read the Bible, and fortunately for me it wasn't necessary. It wasn't important.

There was, however, one niggling question that had nagged me over the years. At first I shunted it aside as inconsequential. After all, the Creed was everything; all the rest was secondary. The question was: Why would an all-loving, all-merciful, limitlessly omniscient God create souls and place them on Earth, knowing, as He must *in advance* no less, that certain of those souls would commit unpardonable sins and be condemned to the torturous fires of Hell for all eternity. It was counterintuitive and made no sense at all to me. But I let my uncertainty ride, as I had other things to think about and deal with: making a living and being a good husband to my wife and a good father to my children. Meanwhile, as I said, I attended Mass, crossed myself, genuflected, recited the Creed and the Rosary, sang the hymns, listened attentively to the priests' homilies, prayed, and left Mass each Sunday comfortable in the sure knowledge that I was a good Catholic and a good Christian. Not perfect, to be sure, but good...good enough I was certain to go to Heaven when I died.

Then one day, purely on impulse, I offhandedly posed that still nagging question to an elderly but intellectually keen priest whose expressed knowledge of Catholic doctrine I admired and trusted. "Why, Father, would an all-loving, all-merciful, limitlessly omniscient God create souls and place them on Earth, knowing in advance as He must, that certain of those souls would commit unpardonable sins and be condemned to the torturous fires of Hell for all eternity?" The priest lowered his voice, almost conspiratorially, and said, "Phil, it's one of the great mysteries."

Mysteries? Mysteries, my eye! It made no sense! If God is pure love, as the Church avers, how could He create souls knowing in advance the ones who would fail the test and spend eternity suffering in Hell? According to decrees of the Vatican Council, God has eternal and infallible foreknowledge of human actions.[4] Moreover, the Church teaches that God is pure love. Certainly pure love can't create evil people or condone ever-lasting punishment in Hell. The priest's answer to my question unsettled me and left me in a minor quandary. Still, undaunted, I continued to attend Mass regularly with my family, sing the hymns, say the prayers, celebrate the Eucharist, and be in every way a faithful Catholic. But that all changed with the shocking disclosure of the pedophile scandals.

I had had personal experience as a twelve-year-old with a pedophile who ran the Boy Scout Troop I was in. On a camping trip I watched spellbound one morning as, smiling lecherously, the troop chief slid his hand under the blankets of one of my friends and began fondling his genitals. My friend's eyes bugged out. He looked at me almost pleadingly as if to say, "What's he doing?" Neither he nor I knew what to do. When moments later the pedophile left our cabin for breakfast as if nothing had happened, neither my friend nor I spoke, nor did we say a word to each other or to anyone else about this puzzling and disturbing episode thereafter...ever! When in 2004 I read of priests' sexual assaults on boys and girls, the memory, the images, of that long-ago incident in our Boy Scout tent came vividly alive, as did my abhorrence of these sick priests and their vile acts. Yet I, like millions of Catholics, viewed the assaults as incidental. All priests weren't pedophiles, and all pedophiles weren't priests. Moreover, a few bad priests, a few bad apples, didn't desecrate the entire Holy Roman Catholic Church. So I, like millions of Catholics, continued as usual attending Mass, participating in the sacred rituals, and contributing to the offertory.

At the same time I, again like millions of Catholics, was deeply troubled by the Church's handling of its pedophile priests. For years, centuries even, the Church had kept mum about their transgressions, shifting them from one parish to another, exposing other innocent children to abuse, and bribing parents with large sums of money to ensure their silence. Incidentally, the parents who took the money are in my mind as guilty as the pedophiles for, by keeping silent, the parents became a party to further sexual assaults. Still I remained loyal to my Faith.

Then one Sunday at the end of Mass my parish priest enjoined the congregation to "Pray for the priests!" Everyone in the congregation knew he was referring to the pedophiles. I was instantly so incensed that he didn't also ask for prayers for the priests' *victims* that it took monumental self-control not to stand up and scream, "What about the victims, Father? What about the victims?" In retrospect I suppose I should have, but I was not yet equipped intellectually to vocally challenge the Church's handling of these crimes. Nevertheless, I have never again attended Mass!

Why? Because it suddenly dawned on me like an epiphany that Holy Mother Church's all-encompassing preoccupation has always been to protect itself, not its parishioners, not its faithful adherents. Protection — preservation — of the Church was the Vatican's pre-eminent concern. Everything else was subservient to that solitary objective. Everything!

According to a July 15, 2007 *Associated Press* article, the U.S. Catholic Church since 1950 had paid out a total of more than $2 billion to settle pedophile claims. Two billion dollars! What is more, says a July 17, 2007 article in *USA Today*, "Some church leaders, including Los Angeles Cardinal Roger Mahony, have fought victims' law suits with a ferocity that seems more suited to a corporate boardroom than to a religious institution." As I was to learn through my research, no matter how heinous the crime committed by any of its monks, brothers, nuns, deacons, priests, monsignors, bishops, archbishops, cardinals, or popes, the Church over the centuries has tended to cover up their misdeeds as best it could and has forgiven and blessed the perpetrators (thank you very much), because the Church must above all endure...and with it, of course, the Church's power and control over the world's Catholics numbering today one billion.

I was abysmally ill equipped at that time to challenge the Church. I, like most every other Catholic, knew next to nothing about the Church, its origins, and its history and had never questioned either its doctrine or authority. But a new day had dawned for me. I began probing and questioning these factors in earnest. I started buying and reading books and magazines on the history of Christianity and the Catholic Church and the history of the Bible and Church dogma and was frankly appalled at my ignorance. I was, moreover, ashamed for having given my allegiance to a religion about which I knew so little.

My research led to a cataclysmic, life-changing perception when I began reading the actual history of the Church, the Bible, Jesus, and the Ever Virgin Mary. The Church wasn't at all what I had believed it to have been, nor was Christianity, nor was the Bible. The biblical accounts of Jesus' life and death were riddled with contradictions and inconsistencies, in some cases outright myths, even lies. My Faith collapsed, but only in regard to the Church. I perceived that the profound teachings attributed to Jesus had nothing at all to do with the Catholic Church as *an organization* and that one didn't have to be a member of the Church, in fact any Church, to believe in Jesus' teachings and to live one's life guided by them. It was that realization that propelled me to write this book. I'm not going to try to impress you with my awesome academic credentials of biblical scholarship, since I have none. My undergraduate degree in economics is wondrously superfluous. I do contend, however, that I'm one hell of an analyst whose research skills have been honed to a fine edge over the years. So when it came to researching the Bible, Christianity, and the Catholic Church, I must immodestly say I was at the top of my game. I also viewed this book as an opportunity to do readers a favor and save them the years it would take them to go through all of my manifold research materials. I have therefore extracted from these materials only those passages that are specifically relevant to the issues I address.

I have tried to keep the tenor of this book light, adding bits of humor (at least I think it's humor) here and there, with a not-so-subtle touch of irreverence, to make it entertaining, readable, as well as informative. But don't let my perhaps lame attempts at wittiness mislead you. This is a deadly serious treatise about a deadly serious subject. And to relieve any concern you may have, I am not going to belabor the book's subject. What I have to say doesn't require a lot of verbiage...just the necessary amount of words to express what I believe needs to be expressed.

Incidentally, although over the past several years I have read a dauntingly large number of books, articles, and Internet materials related to the subject of this book, you will note that I cite a number of sources frequently. The reason is that I found these particular texts the most thoroughly researched, informative, well reasoned, and relevant. Most of the other material I researched was, I regret to say, either boring, tedious, confusing, digressive, annoyingly redundant, unashamedly biased, or simply unhelpful.

And please don't impulsively label me a slobbering wild-eyed anti-Catholic radical, even the anti-Christ, or some crackpot who has the outrageous audacity to belittle, ridicule, and slander the teachings of Jesus. On the contrary, I venerate those teachings. They are profound wisdom with which to pattern our lives, to bring peace and happiness to the world, to triumph over the evil that humans perpetrate not only on others but on themselves. Jesus' teachings are wondrous guides to a "good" life, "good" in the sense of being spiritual and God-serving. If you want to live a happy life, enjoy a happy marriage, raise your children responsibly and productively, be in all respects a "good" person, then let Jesus' teachings be your guide.

Nevertheless, you are probably incensed that I, this "miscreant", have the brazen insolence to criticize Holy Mother Church and by implication her family of Protestant offspring. Indeed, the devout Faithful will undoubtedly relish condemning me to Hell or burning me at the stake (a favorite, long-standing Christian tradition, as you know) for my *sins*, which is a wholly appropriate starting point for this book.

That said, I think it fitting to issue a mild warning. As Bette Davis, standing on a stairway in the movie *All About Eve* famously announced to her guests, "Fasten your seatbelts, everyone. It's going to be a bumpy ride!"

CHAPTER 1

The Garden of Eden

Let's begin by turning our attention to the story of the Garden of Eden. If, like most Christians, you think this tale in Genesis with its Tree of Knowledge of Good and Evil is unique, think again. It's as old as human civilizations. Similar legends were told all over the world hundreds of centuries before there was any sacred literature among the Hebrews. The basic story of the Garden of Eden was anciently known in Nubia, Phoenicia, Chaldea, Babylonia, Assyria, India, Persia, Etruria, China, Egypt, and Greece.[1]

Greece

The ancient Greeks boasted of their Golden Age when sorrow and trouble were unknown. Epimetheus received a gift from Zeus (God) in the form of a beautiful woman, Pandora. She brought with her a vase, the lid of which was by command of God to remain closed. The curiosity of her husband, however, tempted him to open it, and suddenly there escaped from it troubles, weariness, and illness from which mankind was never afterwards free.[2]

Persia

The Persians supposed that a region of bliss and delight called Heden (sounds like Eden, doesn't it), more beautiful than all the rest of the world, was the original abode of the first men, before they were tempted by the evil spirit in the form of a serpent, to partake of the fruit of the forbidden tree Hom.[3]

India

The Hindu legend approximates that preserved in the Hebrew Scriptures. Siva, the Supreme Being, desired to tempt Brahma, who had taken human form and was called Swayambhura — son of the self-existent. Siva dropped from heaven a blossom from the sacred fig tree. Swayambhura, instigated by his wife, Satarupa, endeavored to obtain this blossom, thinking its possession would render him immortal and divine. But when he grasped it, Siva cursed him and doomed him to misery and degradation. The sacred Indian fig is endowed by the Brahmins and the Buddhists with mysterious significance as the "Tree of Knowledge".[3]

China

The Chinese have their own Age of Virtue, when nature furnished abundant food, and man lived peacefully, surrounded by all the beasts. There was a mysterious garden where grew a tree bearing "apples of immortality" guarded by a winged serpent called a Dragon. Partly by an undue thirst for knowledge and partly by increasing sensuality and the seduction of woman, man fell. Passion and lust ruled in the human mind, and war with the animals began. In one of the Chinese sacred volumes, called the Chi-King, is written:

> All was subject to man at first, but a woman threw us into slavery. The wise husband raised up a bulwark of walls, but the woman, by an ambitious desire for knowledge, demolished them. Our misery did not come from heaven, but from a woman. She lost the human race...The world is lost. Vice overflows all things like a mortal poison.[3]

Some artful believers will contend that the seeming consistency of these many tales "proves" the truth of the story. Sorry, people, but "consistency" by itself has never proven anything.

The Short Story of Adam and Eve, from Genesis

After God created the first humans, Adam and Eve, and had settled them nicely inside the Garden-of-Eden paradise, they impudently, willfully disobeyed Him, goaded by a serpent into tasting a fruit from the Tree of Knowledge of Good and Evil. God became incensed. Instead of throwing away the mold and starting over again, as one would expect an indescribably intelligent, limitlessly powerful god to do, God threw a holy tantrum and evicted Adam and Eve from the Garden, condemning them...and all humans after them...to lives of struggle, suffering, and death. Death was the epitome of His curse because there had been no death in Eden.

It was all Eve's fault, of course, women being the weaker, more mischievous sex. God had forbidden Adam and Eve to eat the tantalizing fruit of the Tree of Knowledge of Good and Evil. Why He placed this bewitching tree in the middle of the Garden in the first place isn't at all clear, since He, as Creator of the Universe, would surely have known of its irresistible nature. The only reasonable explanation is that He wanted to test His human prodigies' love for Him and their loyalty, self-discipline, and obedience. Why else? Even so, He surely could have foretold the future and known that Eve would cave in. All that logic aside, as luck or God would have it, a talking serpent, a rarity in Nature to be sure but apparently not in the Garden, tempted Eve to sample the fruit...which she did. Licking the sweet juice from her fingers, she offered it to Adam. Like any dutiful, unsuspecting soul mate, he took a bite, and the world's never been the same.

Outraged at this wanton display of disobedience, God vented his anger first on Adam:

> (Genesis 3:4) "Cursed are you among all animals and among all beasts of the field."

Having put Adam in his place, God turned his divine invective on Eve:

> (Genesis 3:16) "I will greatly multiply your pains in child-bearing, in pain you shall bring forth children." And if that weren't punishment enough, He added, perhaps as a mean-spirited afterthought: "Your desire shall be for your husband, and he shall rule over you."

I can't help but think that the Jewish theologians in Babylon who allegedly wrote and edited Genesis three thousand years ago threw in that last curse on Eve because the women of their religious community (perhaps their own wives) were getting too uppity. Well, it's possible! Incidentally, do you get from this scene the same impression I do, that God was exhibiting some strangely human emotions. They seem, at least to me, quite out of character for an all-powerful God of the Universe. Indeed, they come across as nothing more than the reflection of the beliefs, biases, and pent-up emotions of the men who wrote Genesis. More about God's "humanness" later.

But God wasn't through with Adam:

> (Genesis 3:17-19) "Cursed is the ground because of you; in toil you shall eat of it all the days of your life; thorns and thistles it shall bring forth to you; and you shall eat bread till you return to the ground, for out of it you were taken; you were dust, and to dust you shall return."

The full significance of God's kicking Adam and Eve out of the Garden of Eden was not fully articulated in the Christian Church until Aurelius Augustinus (born in 354, died in 430 at the age of 76), better known as Saint Augustine, penned his monumental interpretation of what became known as the one and only "Original Sin".

Augustine wasn't just any run-of-the-mill follower of Jesus. In addition to being the bishop of the Christian Church in Hippo Regius (modern Annaba, Algeria) on the north African coast of the Mediterranean, he was one of the leading and most respected Christian theologians of the 5th century and remains so today in the Catholic Church. Indeed, his theological and biblical scholarship formed the veritable cornerstone of the Christian tradition. The Stanford Online Encyclopedia of Philosophy[4] describes Augustine as "one of the towering figures of medieval philosophy whose authority and thought came to exert a pervasive and enduring influence well into the modern period, even to the present".

Just for the record, in case you're wondering, Augustine did not invent the concept of Original Sin. Paul, in his Letter to the Romans written some three centuries before Augustine was born, addressed Original Sin at some length, although not by that name. Paul explained that by one person's act — Adam's disobedience — God imposed sin and death on us all. Moreover, renowned biblical scholar Elaine Pagels, historian of religion at Princeton University, observes in *Adam, Eve, and the Serpent*[5] that, long before Augustine came to grips with Original Sin, "most Jews and Christians had agreed that god gave humankind in creation the gift of moral freedom, and that Adam's misuse of it brought death upon his progeny". Thus all humans are sinners and condemned. Indeed, we Christians are taught from an early age — and reminded each Sunday lest we forget — that we are downright sinners, born with Adam's Original Sin stapled to our souls and thus destined to commit sins throughout our lives. So every time we peer into a looking glass — in a bathroom, in a store, or for women a make-up mirror in their purses — we see a sinner! Ergo, the title of this book.

The *New Advent Online Catholic Encyclopedia*[6]: By the early 5th century the theory of Original Sin had become the focus of a bitter theological debate within the Church over the teachings of Pelagius, who vociferously and insistently denied the existence of Original Sin. In reaction, the Council of Carthage in 418, reportedly attended by two hundred Christian bishops including Augustine, ended what became known as the Pelagian Controversy, proclaiming that death did not come to Adam from a physical necessity but through sin. True or not, this canon became a lasting article of faith binding on the universal Church.

> (Not a great deal is known about the life and career of Pelagius, reportedly a perverse character who had the courage to challenge what he believed was wrong-headed dogma. He was born circa 354 reputedly in the British Isles. An ascetic, he was called a "monk" by his contemporaries, though there is no evidence that he was associated with any monastic order. History lost track of him after the Council of Carthage.[7])

The Council of Carthage's decision that sin was the cause of Adam's death was significantly influenced by two famous Latin works that Augustine wrote in 412, "On the Merits of Sinners and Their Forgiveness" and "On the Spirit and the Letter," which skillfully argued among other things the case for "the existence of original sin, the necessity of infant baptism, and the impossibility of a life without sin". As the *New Advent Online Catholic Encyclopedia*[8] explains, greater "clarity" was given to these disputed questions, thanks to Augustine's efforts, resulting in the Church's "first impulse...towards a more careful development of the dogmas of original sin and grace".

The reference to "a more careful development" is of special note because it's an admission that during the Church's first four hundred-some years its declarations about what became known as Original Sin were sloppy, poorly thought out, and even misleading. The Church therefore was in dire need of a coherent dogma on Original Sin that would stand the test of time. Augustine saved the day, for he professed that Adam's sin was forevermore passed magically through Adam's sperm to all of humanity, both male and female, permanently corrupting us, leaving us, in Augustine's words, "with an inherently evil nature," which automatically merited God's continual punishment. Although no one in those days, of course, knew anything about genes or how they passed human characteristics from one person to another, Augustine apparently assumed from his knowledge of the breeding of animals and how human offspring exhibited the physical characteristics of their parents that sin could likewise pass from one generation to the next. Thus Original Sin, thanks to Augustine, became for the Church the defining characteristic of humanity.

Digressing for a moment, I think it's relevant to this treatise to put into perspective Augustine's personal outlook on sex, which, says researcher and writer Helen Ellerbe in *The Dark Side of Christian History*[9], he believed was intrinsically evil. "Who," Augustine wrote, "can control sex when its appetite is aroused? No one!...This diabolical excitement of the genitals" is evidence of Adam's original sin which is transmitted "from the mother's womb, tainting all human beings with sin and leaving them incapable of choosing good over evil or determining their own destiny". Augustine, who lived the latter part of his life in a celibate monastic community, clearly had an obsession, a deep psychological problem I would say, with sex which, I suggest, skewed the conclusions he drew regarding his concept of Original Sin. It's no wonder then that the Catholic Church today, reflecting Augustine's slanted preoccupation, appears overly sensitive to and obsessively concerned about the celibacy of priests, the role of women in the Church, adultery, cohabitation, masturbation, and sex in general. Although I grant that human society has always had a fixation on sex, it understandably became a paramount concern of the Church because having sex is the single major distinction that separates the clergy from the laity.

According to Christian dogma then, we human beings are, inexplicably, not what God intended us to be. As retired Episcopal Bishop John Shelby Spong related in *The Sins of Scripture: Exposing the Bible's Text of Hate to Reveal the God of Love*[10] concerning the penalty we all incurred because of Adam, "We are fallen sinners, willfully disobedient creatures" who, having been banished from God's presence, deserve His divine wrath. "Not only were we fallen, but we had no power to rescue ourselves from our self-inflicted wounds."

Now I ask you, if we humans were indeed not what God expected, why didn't He go back to His drawing board and redesign us into the loving and lovable children He wanted us to be in the first place? Surely He wasn't powerless to change us. It just doesn't make sense. If He has the power, as Christian Creationists believe, to create a three-legged zebra with a flick of His "fingers", He would also have the power to give the zebra a break and provide it a fourth leg. But, of course, Christian dogma doesn't have to make sense to the Faithful. That's what Faith is all about. As the saying goes, ours is not to wonder...or question...why. Moving on, it is the uncontested idea of our worthlessness, wrote Bishop Spong, that has convinced Christians over the centuries that "human beings are fallen, baseborn, and in need of rescue. If there is no rescue, we are doomed."

In the mid-1700s, explains Ellerbe in *The Dark Side of Christian History*[11], a New England Calvinist by the name of Jonathan Edwards elaborated on this theme, although "elaborated" hardly does justice to his extreme fanaticism. Edwards averred that a human is "a little, wretched, despicable creature; a worm, a mere nothing, and less than nothing; a vile insect that has risen up in contempt against the majesty of Heaven and Earth". Thank you for sharing, Jonathan!

"How," continues Bishop Spong[12], "these doomed humans are to be properly punished in order to be saved becomes a major theme, perhaps the major theme, in Christian theology. If one begins with a faith journey in which the human is defined as a fallen creature deserving of punishment, then the faith system will surely develop a cure for the accepted diagnosis. That is the doorway through which the human sense of guilt and its corresponding need for punishment entered the tradition and found therein a compatible dwelling place."

All this talk about what woeful creatures we humans are stems, of course, from Augustine's profound doctrine of Original Sin, whose impact on Christian dogma was far-reaching, permanent, and monumental. Like a fast-spreading, uncontrollable contagion, Adam's sin, according to Augustine and the dutiful Church, continues to infect us all, making all of us sinners at birth..."wretched, despicable creatures" to quote Edwards. As a consequence of this first sin, reaffirms *New Advent*[13], we humans bear "the hereditary stain with which we are born on account of our origin and descent from Adam". In 418, lest the Catholic Faithful have any doubts, the Church put its magisterial imprimatur — the Vatican's formal stamp of approval — on the doctrine of hereditary transmission of Original Sin, however illogical that doctrine was. So it's official: We're all sinners! And there's no escaping it!

Given the fact, corroborated by Genesis and more particularly Augustine, that we are congenitally wicked sinners, our souls must somehow be wiped clean of all sin before we can enter purified through the Gates of Heaven...which I suppose makes sense, but only if you believe we're all sinners from birth and that those Pearly Gates are permanently closed to "sinners". The scriptures, according to the Church, make this perfectly clear. And to no one's surprise the early Church fortuitously provided a convenient and, certainly from the Faithful's point of view, wholly satisfactory way out of this dilemma through the creation of two holy sacraments.

> The Church, by the way, will insist that it was Jesus, not the Church, who created these sacraments. Proof that these sacraments are owed to Jesus lies solely in how one interprets the statements attributed to him in the New Testament. They are, I don't need to tell you, open to different interpretations. The Church selected the interpretation that validated its dogma.

The first sacrament was **Baptism**, which washes souls clean of Original Sin and any sins committed *before* baptism. I address the subject of baptism in Chapter 2. The second was **Penance** (i.e., Confession or more recently Reconciliation), in which sins committed *after* baptism are forgiven. I comment on penance in Chapter 3.

The impact of the doctrine of Original Sin went far beyond the sacraments of baptism and penance; it fundamentally influenced all of the Church's dogma. The beliefs concerning Jesus' mother are a notable example. The evolution of the dogma relating to the Ever Virgin Mary demonstrates how the theological tenets flowed, seemingly logically, from one to another, one century to the next, like a sequence of waterfalls in a surging river:

> The Council of Nicaea in **325** proclaimed, after much acrimonious debate, that the son (Jesus) was of the same divine substance as the father (God).[14]

> The Council of Constantinople in **381** resolved the prolonged controversy that ensued over the Nicaea proclamation (not all Christians at that time believed in Jesus' divinity) and established once and for all both the divinity of Jesus and his fully human nature.[15]

> The Council of Ephesus in **431**, accepting that in Christ there was one divine person — fully God and fully human — proclaimed that Mary was therefore the Mother of both God (Jesus' divine person) and the fully human Jesus.[16]

> The doctrine that Mary had been born, lived, and died free from Original Sin — how could the mother of God possibly have been

otherwise? — was not officially ratified until **1854**, when Pope Pius IX declared, as a matter of Church dogma, that Jesus' mother "at the first instance of her conception was preserved immaculate from all stain of Original Sin, by the singular grace and privilege granted her by Almighty God, through the merits of Christ Jesus, Savior of mankind".[17]

In due course, the First Vatican Council in **1869** confirmed that, because Mary's soul was of necessity free of Original Sin and without the inclination to evil — it being accepted without question that God would not have chosen her to birth Jesus had her soul been so tainted — the semen which spawned her life could not have carried Adam's evil seed. Therefore her birth must have been by Immaculate Conception.[18]

> *New Advent*[19] explains that "the germ [semen], in whose development and growth into the Infant Jesus Mary cooperated, was [impregnated] not by any human action, but by the Divine power attributed to the Holy Ghost." However, *New Advent*[20] confesses that "no direct or categorical and stringent proof of the dogma [of the Immaculate Conception] can be brought forward from Scripture." Therefore, the entire dogma from beginning to end is conjectural, i.e., there's not an iota of proof that it's true.

Pope Pius XII proclaimed in **1950** that, because Mary's soul had been free of the pernicious effects of Original Sin, upon her death her body would not have decayed in a tomb. It thus became official Church doctrine that her body had been assumed intact with her holy soul directly into Heaven[21] — despite the fact that there is nothing in the Bible about the Virgin Mary's bodily assumption. That belief, like all of the doctrine surrounding Mary, is a purely theological construct.

> Actually Mary's assumption had been a common Catholic belief for many centuries. Explains Gary Greenberg, New York City attorney and president of the Biblical Archaeology Society of New York, in his scholarly treatise *101 Myths of the Bible: How Ancient Scribes Invented Biblical History*[22], "There had, after all, been an approved cult of the Assumption since the early Christian Church."

In **1964** Pope Pius XII proclaimed Mary Mother of the Church.

> The Pope's proclamation merely made her assumption official...while not coincidentally serving at the same time as the initial, and so far only, demonstration of the Church's then newly enunciated doctrine of papal infallibility. Also, as a practical matter — the costly and unrewarded search by the Crusades for the Holy Grail still a vivid memory — the declaration conveniently precluded any search for Mary's remains on Earth. That development has surely been disheartening to the throngs of the world's money-hungry relic hunters, any number of whom are still searching for Noah's Ark.

The Dogmatic Pyramid

Beginning in the 1st century, believers in Jesus set about constructing, piece by arduous piece, what in the centuries to follow would become a gigantic edifice of dogma, whose assemblage was, according to the Church, guided as always by the ever-present but unseen and incomparably wise Holy Spirit. It could not have been otherwise if this dogma were indeed God's dogma. In the same way that pagans carved deities out of stone and wood and then, enacting the omega of absurdities, fell on their knees and prayed to their own lifeless creations, the Catholic Church, having over the centuries figuratively sculpted its mountainous dogma from bits and pieces of ideas and beliefs, endowed that sculpture with godlike truth.

This dogma today spans the entire realm of Christian theology, from virgin birth to ascension into Heaven, from grace to free will, from salvation to Hell, from baptism to extreme unction, from miracles to limbo, from indulgences to excommunication, and so on. As theological questions arose over the centuries, the Church, as required, provided answers, some quite logical, extrapolated from previous declarations, others strained and conjectural, and some in hindsight manifestly preposterous. All of the tenets, the bricks with which the edifice of dogma was built, are bound permanently and tightly together by the cement of unyielding, undying faith. The entire structure — and it is gigantic — rests like a humongous inverted pyramid on a single precept: belief in Adam's fall into sin in the Garden of Eden.

But what if the story of the Garden of Eden were untrue? Then the entire inverted theological pyramid, balanced precariously upon that single tenet, would come crashing down like Humpty Dumpty's irreparable great fall off his wall, destroying the foundation of the Church's teachings and its authority to represent and speak for God. In the worlds of engineering, science, and computers such a disaster is understandably called a "catastrophic failure".

The Problem with Genesis

As you may not know, unless you're one of the relatively few lay Christians in the world, outside the confines of biblical scholars, with any discerning knowledge of the Bible, there are basically two contradictory narratives of creation in Genesis. These contrasting stories stem from two separate theological schools which scholars have labeled J and P. I won't discourse on the meaning of "J" and "P" or their differences, since their contrasting substance is irrelevant to this discussion. What is relevant is where these two schools came from, namely, Egyptian mythology.

Greenberg in *101 Myths of the Bible*[23] explains that J's roots go back to Creation teachings in the ancient Egyptian city of Heliopolis, then one of Egypt's most influential religious centers.[24] P, on the other hand, adopted the Creation philosophy associated with the Egyptian city of Thebes, the political and religious capital of Egypt during the time the Israelites are believed to have resided there. "Theologians concerned with the need for biblical consistency," writes Greenberg, "simply ignore the differences [between the P and J accounts of Creation] and treat the two stories as part of the same cycle. Scholars, on the other hand, willing to acknowledge the contradictions, simply accept that the two stories have different origins and that subsequent editors attempted to integrate the two separate accounts into a single narrative. Generally but pointedly overlooked is that both sources originate from separate *Egyptian*, not *Jewish*, traditions."[25]

If you think this statement is farfetched, then go and read some of the plethora of books about the history of the Jewish and Christian Faiths and the origins of the Bible, both Old and New Testaments. I promise the more you read about these histories from a variety of different authors' perspectives, the more you will come to appreciate the thin reed upon which Christian doctrine on the origin of humans rests. But do yourself a favor. Avoid texts written by ultra-conservative Christian theologians and clergymen. They rarely give you an objective view, being, as they are, intellectually and professionally chained to Church doctrine, which puts them automatically in an uncompromising, biased, defensive posture.

Of course, my having said that will immediately deter the devout Christian — my principal intended audience — from venturing anywhere near such an undertaking. The fear of having one's religious beliefs dented, in the worst case torn asunder, will be enough to discourage their even opening one of these books. You know how it goes. They're in a bookstore. They glance at a book's dust cover, take note of its subject, perceive its heretically threatening nature, instantly throw up that invisible mental shield that protects one's religious beliefs, then move quickly on in search of a book that poses no threat. Any popular novel will do nicely as a replacement.

Evolution: The Heart of the Matter

What it all comes down to is the question of humankind's origins. Christian doctrine for the past two thousand years has been inextricably wedded to the belief that human life began in the Garden of Eden in the person of Adam, who, as related in the above story, was uniquely created by God and then ungratefully turned his back on his Creator...the infamous "fall from grace" known as the Original Sin. For Christian doctrine to retain its integrity, there *must* be Original Sin. That being the case, humans must necessarily have originated with Adam, or so the "logic" follows. The three tenets — Garden of Eden, Creation of Adam, Original Sin — are bound inextricably together. There's no way around it.

According to *New Advent*[26], whose texts hold fast to the Church's traditional doctrine on human origins, Adam was the head of all humankind, the historic father of the human race, the father of all according to the flesh. To believe otherwise is to contravene the very foundation of the Christian Faith, namely, and I apologize for repeating myself, that humans, being of Adam's spawn by direct descent, are inherently sinful and therefore require salvation — by the Church no less — through belief in Jesus, lest when they die they be pitched body and soul into the abyss of Hell.

As I'm sure you're aware, according to Charles Darwin's famous — or infamous, depending on your beliefs — theory of evolution, *Homo sapiens* evolved, as God ordained, like every other organism on Earth, i.e., gradually over hundreds of millions of years through the dual processes of random mutation and natural selection. Believers in mainstream Creationism, which holds that Adam, the first human, the father of humanity, was created just 10,000 years ago, keep their eyes, ears, and most particularly their minds hammered shut, lest the truth of humankind's Darwinian evolution seep in and contaminate their beliefs. Driven as they are by religious zeal and fundamentalist belief in the absolute truth of the Bible, the veritable Word of God, the arguments of Creationists in defense of Creationism distort the incontrovertible scientific facts. What Creationism reveals is not the truth of humankind's origins but the reckless ignorance of Creationists. If you are a hidebound Creationist and are offended by my criticism, I invite you to close this book and no longer be offended. But if you're courageous, pry open your mind and keep on reading.

In order to believe that we ascended from Adam, whom the Church calls "the first human", one must ignore science...all science! The science of biology, the science of physics, the science of medicine, the science of human behavior, and so on. Just put them out of one's mind along with that *man behind the curtain*. And to my utter astonishment and regret a huge number of people do. We can put a man on the moon, send deep-space probes to the planets, photograph the components of atoms with x-rays, develop vaccines to protect us from any number of lethal diseases, perform astonishing medical healings, predict weather patterns, develop methods for increasing the production of food, and accomplish a hundred thousand other amazing, purely scientific feats every year, yet modern, highly sophisticated methods of dating fossils using the most advanced technology are, Creationists contend, "unreliable". No, my confused but sincere friends, it is Creationism that is unreliable.

According to an appalling *2007 USA Today/Gallop poll*[27] of American Christians, "63 percent in the poll said Creationism, the idea that God created humans in their present form within the past 10,000 years, is definitely or probably true". Other surveys produce somewhat different results, but the bottom line is, I regret to say, that a significantly large percentage of Christians mindlessly believe in Creationism's 10,000-year-old Earth. Perhaps this book will cause some of these sadly misinformed or stubbornly resistant Faithful to re-examine their beliefs, but I seriously doubt it, Faith being what it is.

What these Faithful willfully and necessarily choose to disbelieve is that science has proven the mechanism by which humans evolved. It is a process powered and directed by the engine of continuous minute random genetic mutations in deoxyribonucleic acid (DNA), which contains the genetic instructions in chromosomes for the biological development of cellular life. Evolution by natural selection is therefore an indisputable fact...a fact that effectively nullifies the doctrine of Creationism.

The late Michael Crichton, renowned novelist and doctor of medicine, wrote a succinct and engaging description of the evolution of humans in his novel *Prey*[28]:

> The first life shows up four billion years ago as single-cell creatures. Nothing changes for the next two billion years. Then nuclei appear in the cells. Things start to pick up. Only a few hundred million years later, multi-cellular organisms. A few hundred million years after that, explosive diversity of life. And then more diversity. By a couple of hundred million years ago there are large plants and animals, complex creatures, dinosaurs. In all this, man's a latecomer: four million years ago, upright apes. Two million years ago, early human ancestors. Thirty-five thousand years ago, cave paintings.

The Catholic Church's position on humankind's evolvement from earlier primates according to Darwin's theory of evolution "by gradual descent" has been traditionally negative and unwavering. "The proofs of the descent of man's body from animals," says *New Advent*[29], "are inadequate, especially in respect to paleontology."

The Church's linking the origin of man with Adam is — forgive my stridence — patently ridiculous, yet the Catholic Church has no alternative but to stick with its

2,000-year-old tradition and continue preaching about Adam as the progenitor of the human race. How could the Church's position be otherwise? Its rickety doctrine on humanity's congenital sinfulness rests wholly, resolutely, and contentedly on the belief in the claim that Adam was the first human, and a sinful one to boot. If he wasn't, the entire theology implodes, and the Church's *raison d'etre* vanishes as quickly as you can snap your fingers.

That was the very issue that, according to an item in *USA Today* of February 7, 2007, prompted Bishop Boniface Adoyo, leader of Kenya's popular and powerful evangelical Christian movement, to call for a boycott of an exhibit displaying fossils of one of humankind's oldest relics: the most complete skeleton of a prehistoric human ever found — the 1.6 million-year-old Turkana Boy. Said Adoyo, "These sorts of silly views [about human origin] are killing our faith." Indeed.

So what conclusion can be drawn from the gradual evolution of humans from earlier species? Only one. And you'd best tighten your seatbelt for this.

THE GARDEN OF EDEN IS A MYTH!

Please forgive the theatrics. I simply want you to fully appreciate the degree of my contempt for those Christian theologians and biblical scholars who ignore — DELIBERATELY DISREGARD! (there's no kind way to say it) — what should be obvious to the most casual observer, namely, that *there never was a Garden of Eden*. Says Bishop Spong, "Though most educated people in the world today dismiss [the Genesis story of Creation] as a myth not to be [viewed as historical fact], that story has nonetheless continued to set the tone for the way [Christian] religious systems relate to human life."[30] In short, says Spong, the story of the Garden of Eden is "a bad myth, a false myth, a misleading myth".[31]

Strangely, the minds of many biblical scholars seem to leave them witless when they write about sin, salvation, Hell, etc. As intelligent academicians, they know rationally that the roots of these subjects stem from the biblical account of the Garden of Eden, which they also know — but may be unable to acknowledge because of their professional circumstances — is pure legend and myth.

For example, the science disciplines have proven beyond any doubt that the Earth was not created in six Earth days as claimed in Genesis. Scientist-Christians have strained — in vain, I dare say — to force-fit Genesis' six days figuratively with the actual physical processes by which Earth was created over three billion years ago. If that makes you happy, be my guest, but in case you haven't noticed, the Creator of the endless universe certainly didn't need to rest on the "seventh day"! These are nothing but mythic tales intended to guide the thinking of illiterate, uneducated, unsophisticated people, as the dogmas of ancient religions always did...and some modern religions do today.

What is most revealing is that so many of these same scholars begin their published analyses of the Bible with a halfhearted disclaimer of one sort or another regarding the Holy Book's veracity. For example, Jay Haley in his masterful, thought-provoking essay *The Power Tactics of Jesus Christ*,[32] wrote, "Questions can always be raised because of doubts about the objectivity and authenticity of the Bible. The view offered here will take the gospel writers at their word". In other words, "The Bible story of Jesus may be a total fiction, but I have this intriguing theory to disclose about Jesus' motives and objectives, and the Bible is the sole source of my information."

New Advent's text on Adam makes a similar disclaimer: "To what extent these chapters [of Genesis] should be considered as strictly historical is a much disputed question, *the discussion of which does not come within the scope of the present article*" [italics added]. What a cleverly slick but nonetheless transparent way to circumvent the real issue, which is the veracity of Genesis. The text then goes on to say, "Be that as it may [i.e., pay no attention to that *man behind the curtain*], it will be pertinent to the purpose of the present article to examine the main features of the two-fold Creation narrative with special reference to the origin of man."

What these writers are really saying is, "Let's save the delicate and problematic discussion of whether the Bible stories are fact or fiction for another day, so we can move on to our analysis, which is what we're all really interested in. After all, studying and writing about esoteric subjects like the Garden of Eden is what we do. It's how we maintain our standing both among the Church's theologians and in the publish-or-perish academic community." These writers completely ignore Genesis' flimsy, imaginary foundation, then proceed to discuss the implications of the story of the Garden of Eden as if there were no uncertainties about its actuality. This anomaly apparently doesn't concern them, since they are writing primarily for other biblical scholars who observe the same convention.

Some analysts of the Bible circumvent the issue of whether the Bible is fact or fiction by treating it, not as history, but as a piece of literature. It's tantamount to saying, "Here's what the Bible says. And here's what it means for you, the Faithful. Whether or not it's historically true doesn't matter." As a Catholic priest once said during one of his homilies, "A story can be untrue but also true." In other words, a Bible story can be a total myth, but it's moral can be true. Indeed, the same can be said of Grimm's fairy tales. In truth, it's a crafty way to sidestep the issue of the Bible's veracity, but it's worked for the Christian churches for centuries, so why not.

If the Garden of Eden never existed, then there never was an Adam, there never was an Eve, God did not create Eve from one of Adam's ribs, there never was a talking serpent (as far as I know, snakes have never talked except in fables), and there never was a Tree of Knowledge of Good and Evil. Earth to Christians! These stories are wholesale ancient myths! If you earnestly believe these tales, then I've got several hundred bridges to sell you. Moreover, you must also be an ardent believer that Santa Claus, Goldie Locks, the Pumpkin Fairy, Thor the God of Thunder, Superman, the Cat Woman, and Spiderman are real living people. Oh, and just to be on the safe side, you must also believe in the reality of Mother Nature. I would never dream of overlooking her. As we all know, it isn't wise to make Mother Nature angry!

Let me summarize:

ADAM AND EVE NEVER EXISTED!
GOD NEVER CURSED THEM!
THERE WAS NO ORIGINAL SIN!
HUMANS ARE NOT BORN SINNERS!

So there's good news today! You are not a born sinner after all!

That being the case, there is also no Final Judgment. That's a mind-stopper, isn't it. If we don't commit "sins" during our stay on Earth, then there's no basis for a "judgment" after death. We are born free of sin, and we die free of sin.

Unfortunately, simply saying this doesn't free devout Christians from their dilemma. Even if they accept, on the one hand, that the Genesis story is a myth, as it surely is, they are, on the other hand, required by their Faith to believe we are all born sinners and are destined to be "judged". Yet the two beliefs are wholly contradictory and incompatible. You can't have it both ways. So the Faithful throw up their hands, put the dilemma behind them, and dutifully go to Mass, all the while studiously ignoring that *man behind the curtain.*

One Last Thought

According to Genesis 2:28, "be fruitful and multiply" was the first divine command that God, before He lost His temper, issued to Adam. The Church has used this command for centuries to impel faithful Christian married couples — even many today! — to perform as well as they could like rabbits, breeding large families, because the Church said to do otherwise was a sin...even when over the ages birthing child after child strained or ruined a family's finances, destroyed the mother's health, and in countless cases resulted in her death. In years past I can recall people upon observing a large family entering church for Mass say, either admiringly or derisively, I could never tell which, "There's a good Catholic family." And "good Catholics" they were, for the Church's position has always been and remains that the purpose of sex is primarily — but not solely — the procreation of children. One all-important benefit of this policy, surely never ignored nor perhaps admitted publicly by the Church, was increasing the number of Catholics in the world, as history has long proven there is strength in numbers, which not coincidentally also provided a fruitful and dependable source of both money and priests. As I said in the Forward, protection and preservation of the Church have always been the Church's pre-eminent concerns. As a corollary, the Church has used the divine directive to be fruitful and multiply as one of its arguments against unnatural birth control. Yet the truth is God never gave such a command. It's a myth just like the Garden of Eden.

CHAPTER 2

The Quietus of Baptism

The sacrament of baptism, says *New Advent*,[1] "is the door of the Church of Christ and the entrance into a new life. We are reborn from the state of slaves of sin into the freedom of the Sons of God [meaning baptism bestows on us Free Will with all the unavoidable risks and punishments of its misuse]. Baptism incorporates us with Christ's mystical body and makes us partakers of all the privileges flowing from the redemptive act of the Church's Divine Founder". As Jesus is reported to have said in John 3:3, "Unless a man be born again of water and the Holy Spirit, he cannot enter into the kingdom of God." Thus, according to the Church, baptism cleanses one's soul of Original Sin and absolves one of any "actual sins" committed before baptism.

New Advent, showing off its erudition, calls "actual sin" *ex parte actus*, which phrase you can use to impress your Christian friends. I don't recommend using it with non-Christians, because in all likelihood they've never studied Latin, so they'll have no idea what you're talking about. Come to think of it, neither will your Christian friends.

It may interest you...or not...to know that descriptions by early Christian authors of Christian baptism are indistinguishable from descriptions by early Pagans of Pagan baptism. As Timothy Freke, an authority on world mysticism, and Peter Gandy, who holds a Masters degree in classical civilizations, inform in *The Jesus Mysteries: Was the "Original Jesus" a Pagan God?*[2] "As long ago as the Homeric hymns...ritual purity was the condition of salvation. People were baptized to wash away all their previous sins." Baptism then was a central rite in most of the ancient religions in which the initiate was cleansed and exonerated of all previous sins and figuratively "born again". It will therefore disappoint many Christians to learn that the revered rite of baptism is not, contrary to general belief, unique to their religion but has, like the Garden-of-Eden myth, been around for millennia.

By the way, one of the more interesting riddles of Christian dogma, based as it is on the Christian Scriptures, is how Jesus qualified <u>at all</u> to be baptized by John the Baptist, seeing as how Jesus was divine, the Son of God, sinless, and inarguably in possession of a free pass into Heaven without being challenged or judged at the Pearly Gates. Curious! I know, I know. Jesus' allowing himself to be baptized was a purely symbolic gesture...a demonstration and example for Christians to follow. Perhaps. Perhaps not. The *New Advent* encyclopedia and a plethora of other scholarly works devote a great many words — too many, if you ask me — to offer a plausible explanation for this seeming incongruity. So in the end, as always, we are left to conjecture. But if the Garden of Eden was a myth, then there is no Original Sin, and we don't need to be baptized to cleanse our souls. If we are not born sinners, then baptism has no effective purpose other than a diverting ritual to welcome a new soul to Earth and into the Christian Church, much as tourists arriving in Hawaii are welcomed with "Aloha". Writes Spong[3], "Baptism, the sacramental act that washes away the inherited stain of Adam's original fall into sin, becomes inoperative."

> It may delight my Christian detractors to know that Bishop Spong and I are in deep trouble. *New Advent*[4] reports: "The Council of Trent declared anathema upon anyone who says that baptism is not necessary for salvation." Spong and I will take our chances.

If Adam's fall is a giant myth, then so is our unavoidable destiny as lifelong sinners. Therefore we're not only <u>not born sinners</u>, we're also <u>not lifelong sinners</u>.

I realize this conclusion doesn't square even in a hundredth of a millimeter with Christian beliefs, indeed it crashes into them at a thousand feet per second, but the conclusion is inescapable. Everything about the tale of the Garden of Eden is a myth! Everything!

CHAPTER 3

On Forgiveness

As Alexander Pope observed, we humans are destined to "err" from time to time. Some, many, of these errors violate the Ten Commandments and other acts the Church has defined as sins. This being the case, when we err, that is, "sin", why can't we simply look up into the sky and meekly, sincerely ask God to pardon our "wickedness"? It ought to work. After all, according to the *Encyclopedic Dictionary* in my Bible, "Jesus proclaimed the unlimited forgiveness of sin by God to all who turn to Him. Regardless of the immensity of the sin, the mercy and forgiveness of God are infinitely greater." Note the words "unlimited" and "infinitely". That's more than a lot. Moreover, biblical scholars are unanimous in describing God as "perfect in his love and forgiveness". Faulkner in *Supreme Authority*[1] states that "God is a loving and warm image." In deference to my New Age readers, I would also mention that renowned psychic Sylvia Browne says, "Jesus preached and expounded on a loving God, a God who was forgiving and kind." I could name a hundred other authoritative sources, but the conclusion is always the same: God is limitlessly merciful, kind, and forgiving.

So why can't we appeal directly to God, bypassing any priestly intermediary? Well, regrettably we can't, because the Church, which claims to know a lot more about this than we do, insists that the Roman Catholic Church alone is the one and only path through which forgiveness can be granted. Faulkner[3] explains: "Not even in its muscular Holy Roman Empire days did the Catholic Church wield such power...over the consciences of its members century after century as it claimed for itself sole authority to forgive sins in God's name."

If the Church is indeed the only path to God's forgiveness, how did the Church acquire this unique power and authority? The answer, which I'm sure you don't know if like most Catholics you are unread on the Bible, was Jesus' famous alleged consigning to His twelve disciples in the Gospel of Matthew the power to do anything. Anything!

> Matthew 16:19: [to Peter] "<u>Whatever</u> you bind on Earth shall be bound in Heaven, and <u>whatever</u> you loose on Earth shall be loosed in Heaven." [my underlinings]

No other "whatever" statement is present in the Gospels. None.

The Gospel of John reports that Jesus bestowed on his disciples the power to forgive or not forgive sins, the implication being that Heaven (God) would sanction these acts. But John says nothing about a "whatever" power.

> John 20:23: [Jesus to his disciples] "Whose sins you forgive are forgiven them, and whose sins you retain are retained."

The Gospel of Luke says nothing about the disciples being given the power to forgive or not forgive sins, and nothing about any "whatever" power. Luke's quotations from Jesus speak only of people forgiving each other and echo similar statements in Mark and Matthew.

> Mark 11:25 — When you stand to pray, *forgive anyone* against whom you have a grievance, so that your heavenly Father may in turn forgive you your transgressions.

> Matthew 6:9 — If you forgive *others* their transgressions, your heavenly Father will forgive yours. But if you do not forgive others, neither will your Father forgive your transgressions.

> Luke 6:37 — *Forgive* and you will be forgiven.

> Luke 17:3 — If thy brother sins, rebuke him. And if seven times in the day he sins against thee, and seven times in the day turns back to thee, saying, 'I repent,' *forgive* him.

Without its "whatever" power the Catholic Church would never have developed further than a new-caught baby fish floundering in the bottom of a rowboat. Without that power the Church had no more authority than a group of lowly shepherds herding sheep in the fields around Palestine. Prior to the dissemination of the Gospel of Matthew, the early believers could rant and proclaim all day long, but when challenged about their authority, the best they could have said was that it derived from their irrevocable belief in Jesus' divinity, nothing more. That being the case, imagine how the "whatever" power emboldened and empowered the early believers. Now when challenged, they could cite Jesus' bestowal of the "whatever" power upon his disciples as the mighty, one and only God's sanctioning of their Church. The bestowal would have changed everything!

"Whatever" is an incredibly boundless term that empowered the Catholic clergy over the centuries that followed not only to forgive sins but to determine dogma, ordain priests, canonize saints, condemn heretics to death, rule against women becoming priests, outlaw contraceptives, annul marriages, grant indulgences, torture "sinners", burn them at the stake, and make a thousand other momentous decisions binding on the Faithful, day in and day out, century after century. Significantly, the "whatever" statement in Matthew lacks any qualifiers or caveats; it's unconditional and unlimited. According to Jesus' reported bestowal, whatever the Church's decisions might be — good or bad! helpful or harmful! holy or sinful! — they are automatically endorsed by God in Heaven. It literally takes your breath away.

I vividly remember the many times Matthew's text about the "whatever" power was read aloud during Mass. Every time I heard it, I, surely like every other member of the congregation, shifted the focus of my eyes momentarily from the reader to the celebrant priest and marveled, half in wonder, half in fear, at the awesome power this man and his ecclesiastic colleagues around the world wielded over the Faithful. Imagine possessing the power to condemn sinners and to decide the punishment they deserve. Think how clergymen have used and abused this power over the centuries to manipulate and terrorize people.

Spokesmen for the Church will argue, no doubt, that it's only common sense that Jesus bestowed the "whatever" power on his disciples with the certain understanding that, if they used it for evil, either the power would be withdrawn or evil decisions would be nullified. Well, they would have to say this or something like it. But I don't see any statement in Matthew that Jesus meant the "whatever" power to be qualified in any way. Moreover, whether or not the "whatever" in Matthew was *subliminally* caveated by Jesus is irrelevant to my point, which is that the Church has never recognized or acknowledged any caveat...and still doesn't.

In which year each of the four Gospels was written is, as you probably can guess, it being two thousand years ago, a matter of conjecture among knowledgeable, respected biblical scholars. Be that is it may, there is general agreement (there will never be total agreement) that Mark was penned between 68 and 70, Matthew 70-90, Luke 80-90, and John 90-110. What is significant in these dates is the number of years between each of them and Jesus' death in 33: Mark 35-57 years, Matthew 37-57, Luke 47-57, and John 57-77.

What is supremely curious then is that Mark, the earliest Gospel, written some thirty-five years after Jesus' death, makes no mention of Jesus conveying the majestic power referred to in Matthew. Biblical scholars accept as fact, as noted in Freke's and Gandy's *Jesus and the Lost Goddess: The Secret Teachings of the Original Christians*[4], that large parts of Matthew (which Church tradition holds was originally written in Greek) are an explicit copy of Mark right down to the same Greek particles. [By the way, "tradition" means "long-established beliefs", which I hasten to point out are not for that reason either facts or true.] If the author of Matthew knew about this historic whatever-you-decide-is-okay-with-God power, why didn't the author of Mark? It seems implausible that this stunning episode in the lives of the disciples came to light only **after** the Gospel of Mark was written. Is it conceivable that for some thirty-five years after Jesus' death followers of his teachings knew of the granting of this awesome power but inadvertently failed to communicate this remarkable event to Mark's author?

How's this for an improbable scene? A friend of Mark's author, after reading his gospel, tells him, "Hey, buddy. You forgot to mention Jesus telling his disciples that whatever they bound on Earth was bound in Heaven, and whatever they loosed on Earth was loosed in Heaven." To which the author replies, "Y'know you're right. Gee whiz! I forgot to include that. Is it important?" !!!???

Would the author of Mark have known about the "whatever" power if Jesus had bestowed it upon the disciples? Let's examine this question.

Communications among Christian Communities

In those days, communication was primarily by word of mouth. There were no newspapers, and only a tiny fraction of the population was literate. Thus the first stories about Jesus circulated orally from person to person, from town to town, from one group of Jesus' followers to another. These recountings gradually evolved among those few who could read and write into written form as letters and essays... and the tender roots of the New Testament were born.

Bart Ehrman, the James A. Gray Professor and Chair of the Department of Religious Studies at the University of North Carolina, in *Lost Christianities: The Battles for Scripture and the Faiths We Never Knew*[5]: "One of the distinctive features of early Christianity ["early" being in the 1st-century after Jesus' crucifixion, say, the 50s onward]...was its literary character. Literature served to provide sacred authority for Christian belief and practice, to defend the religion against its cultured despisers, to unite local communities of believers...to encourage the faithful in their time of suffering, to instruct them how to live, to entertain them with accounts of heroes of the faith, and to warn them against enemies within, promoting some forms of the faith and denouncing others. With the partial exception of Judaism, no other religion of the Roman Empire was so rooted in literary texts." The early Christian communities, writes Ehrman in *Misquoting Jesus: The Story Behind Who Changed the Bible and Why*[6], were thus unified by an unusually wide range of literature produced, disseminated, and read by their members. It was through these communications that Jesus' teachings were originally shared, recorded, and collated.

It's reasonable therefore to assume that the author of Mark, obviously an intelligent, literate person, would have been not only a recipient of these writings but an originator as well. The granting of the "whatever" power to the disciples would have been big news and would certainly have been reported by both word of mouth and missives through the communications channels linking the Christian communities during the thirty-five years after the crucifixion. In which case I profess that the author of Mark would surely have known about the "whatever" power, if Jesus had granted it to his disciples.

Why would followers of Jesus not speak and write about something as astounding as this power, especially as it pertained to forgiveness of sins, something humans yearned for, a safe and foolproof avenue to salvation? It's like a *New York Times* journalist writing about a family's financial plight, while failing to mention they had just won a multi-million-dollar lottery. The granting of this power would have been exciting news, a stupendous event. Indeed, it still is today…which is why the Vatican mandates that the story of Jesus' bestowal of this wondrous power be read once each year to every Catholic congregation in the world! Word would have spread like wild fire among Jesus' followers. "Did you hear that Jesus gave his disciples the godly power to forgive sins so we can be sure of going to Heaven?" To which the listener would surely have replied, "Praise God, that's wonderful!"

Imagine you were living in Jerusalem in Jesus' time and heard from a friend that Jesus' disciples could by the power of God forgive sins, ensuring untrammeled passage through the gates of Heaven. No one else had ever had that power. Would you yawn in boredom? Would you stay at home calmly working in your garden? Would you go to a neighbor's house to trade gossip over a cup of wine? Are you kidding? You'd grab your friend's shoulders and joyfully demand to know if it were really true and, if so, where these disciples were. Surely had the author of Mark been informed of this great news his gospel would have reported it in view of the "whatever" power's immense significance for the promotion of the Christian cult. But the Gospel of Mark is strangely silent.

It's possible then, but <u>exceedingly unlikely</u> over the some thirty-five years between Jesus' death and the writing of the Gospel of Mark, that for some peculiar reason this particular story, however sensational, never reached the ears of its author. It's also possible — I would say, <u>exceedingly likely</u> — that the Gospel of Mark doesn't report the bestowing of this mighty power because the bestowal never happened! I repeat: NEVER HAPPENED! This means that between the time Mark and Matthew were written the story of the disciples receiving this power conveniently, magically surfaced.

Here are the four Gospels' citations and non-citations of the "whatever" power:

	Years Written	
Mark	68-70	does not mention the "whatever" power
Matthew	70-90	cites the "whatever" power
Luke	80-90	does not mention the "whatever" power, cites the need to forgive one another's sins
John	90-110	does not mention the "whatever" power, cites the power to forgive or not forgive sins

The "whatever" power, being the <u>sole source</u> of the Church's spiritual and temporal authority, is the crucial keystone component of Christian doctrine, so let me recapitulate to ensure your complete understanding:

> The absence of any reference in Mark to the "whatever" power is strong evidence that its author had never heard of it. If he had, he surely would have cited it in his gospel, given the power's huge import for the fledgling Christian Faith.
>
> It strains credibility to believe that the story of the "whatever" power, which appears first in Matthew, suddenly came to light after the writing of Mark, that is, some 35 to 37 years after Jesus' reported crucifixion. The only reasonable conclusion (I'm open to alternative explanations) is that someone, perhaps the author of Matthew himself, concocted the story after Mark was circulated.
>
> It seems likely that neither Luke nor John had ever read or heard of the "whatever" power until perhaps the Gospel of Matthew was circulated. If that were indeed the case, neither of them apparently assigned any credibility to the story, because neither mentioned it.
>
> Luke and John did, however, report Jesus' instruction to his disciples to forgive sins, but their descriptions differed significantly. Luke's gospel spoke only of the need for all people, not just the disciples, to forgive other people's transgressions against them, and Luke doesn't mention Heaven sanctioning or not sanctioning this forgiveness. John's account, emboldened perhaps by Matthew's forgiveness theme, empowered the disciples to forgive or not forgive sins with the certain implication that Heaven would sanction the disciples' decisions regardless.

Embattled Zealots

"Few quotations preserved by history are as powerful as (Jesus' bestowing the *whatever* power)," observes Faulkner in a remarkable understatement in her book, *Supreme Authority*[7]. Imagine the immense authority with which Jesus' alleged pronouncement empowered his disciples. Indeed, it was an empowerment they would have welcomed with open arms and surely made every effort to publicize, because those followers of Jesus who were the early vanguard of the Roman Catholic Church were struggling at that time to promote their beliefs in direct competition with Judaism, Christian Gnosticism, and mighty far-flung Paganism.

Contrary to what many agenda-driven histories of Christianity contend, spiritual life in the Roman Empire at the time of Jesus' death had not waned, allowing Christianity to step into a void, establish a foothold, and immediately bloom. Charles Freeman, a British historian and specialist on the ancient world and its legacy through history, wrote in *The Closing of the Western Mind: The Rise of Faith and the Fall of Reason:*[8] "Christianity did provide for important spiritual needs, but it was only one of many movements that attempted to do so and was by no means the most sophisticated." As for the Pagan masses, the advent of Christianity was initially unheralded, unseen, and unheard.

Dr. J. P. Moreland, Professor of Philosophy at the Talbot School of Theology at Biola University in La Mirada, California is quoted in an interview in *The Case for Christ*[9] concerning the emergence of the Christian Church: "It began shortly after the death of Jesus and spread so rapidly that within a period of maybe twenty years it had even reached Caesar's palace in Rome." I trust that Moreland, being the distinguished scholar he is, had good reason to make this statement, but I have three good reasons to challenge it.

First, as far as I have been able to determine, there was no organized religion called "Christianity" at the beginning, only the "Jesus cult" as many scholars — not Jesus' early followers as far as is known — have dubbed it. Freke and Gandy in *Jesus and the Lost Goddess*[10] write that the initial followers weren't even called "Christian". Laurence Gardner, a Fellow of the Society of Antiquaries of Scotland and the Jacobite Historiographer Royal of the European Council of Princes, states in *The Magdalene Legacy: The Jesus and Mary Bloodline Conspiracy*[11] that scholars, based on Acts 11:26, believe the term "Christian" was first used in Antioch in 44, a decade or so after Jesus' reported crucifixion. It was in Antioch where the new religion gained its first frail foothold.

Secondly, notwithstanding Moreland's artful description of the rise of Christianity, it did not burst onto the scene as a discrete and identifiable religion that grew by leaps and bounds. Bernard Simon points out in *The Essence of the Gnostics*[12] that, according to Origen, a revered Christian scholar of the 2nd century, only a small number of Christians were in evidence in the first two centuries...so few that the 2nd-century history of Rome by Dion Cassius never mentioned either Christians or Christian Churches. I hasten to acknowledge that these disparate followers were in all likelihood communicating with each other, but not as unified members of a bona fide church as we understand the term today, that is, an organized institution with agreed upon beliefs and an internal hierarchy of clergy.

Strictly speaking, there were no "original Christians" early on, just a loose patchwork of followers of Jesus with different experiences of life and thus different mindsets, all rendering their own unique versions of his story. Ehrman in *Lost Christiani-*

ties[13] speaks to the remarkable diversity of early Christian beliefs: "During the first three Christian centuries, the practices and beliefs found among people who called themselves Christian were so varied that today's differences among Roman Catholics, Primitive Baptists, and Seventh-Day Adventists pale by comparison."[14] Jesus himself was a "Jew" not a "Christian".

If Christianity — Moreland called it a "church" — spread so rapidly even to Rome, why did historians of the time not mention it? I discuss this puzzling omission below under Man or Myth.

Thirdly, for the first three centuries, followers of Jesus who believed he was "literally" a flesh-and-blood human were a fringe sect, known to modern biblical scholars and academicians as "Literalist" Christians. The movement to which Moreland apparently refers as "reaching Caesar's palace in Rome" was not that sect of Literalists which would evolve into the Catholic Church. The movement that reached Rome was composed primarily of Gnostic Christians. Gnostic Christians — those individuals who believed Jesus was, like every other deity in the ancient world, an eminent heroic but still mythical figure — were far more numerous.[15] Because Gnostics did not believe Jesus was a real person, they would not qualify in today's terminology as "Christians". Says Stephan A. Hoeller in *Freedom: The Alchemy of a Voluntary Society*[16]: "Theology has been called an intellectual wrapping around the spiritual kernel of a religion. Most religions are strangled and stifled by their wrappings. Gnosticism did not run this danger, because its world view was stated in myth rather than in theology. Myths, including Gnostic myths, may be interpreted in diverse ways...Still, such mythic statements tell of profound truths."

Gnostic Christianity spread rapidly throughout the ancient world. Freke and Gandy in *The Laughing Jesus: Religious Lies and Gnostic Wisdom*[17] write that by the 3rd century Gnostic Christianity reached from Spain to China. In Egypt, Syria, and Asia Minor the first Christians on record were all Gnostics. Tertullian (155-230), a Literalist church leader and prolific author of early Christianity, bemoaned the fact that Gnostics fill "the whole universe". That Gnosticism was, at least briefly, in the mainstream of Christianity is witnessed by the fact, noted in Simon's *The Essence of the Gnostics*[18], that in the year 140 one of the most influential Gnostic teachers, Valentinus, lost by a small margin election to the post of Gnostic Christian Bishop of Rome.

From the start, Jesus' spiritual message spread only sporadically from village to village, gaining new believers a few at a time here and there along the way. These scattered fragments of the "Jesus cult" were not a Church per se but rather a collection of small disparate groups dotted throughout the Middle East founded independently by an assortment of evangelists, each of whom preached his or her* own individualized version of the "Good News".[19] In fact, as Ehrman relates in

Misquoting Jesus[20], "The theological diversity was so extensive that groups calling themselves Christian adhered to beliefs and practices that most Christians today would insist were not Christian at all."

*Contrary to what the Church has long led people to believe, women played a vital role in the early Church. There is a whole genre of books on the subject, so if you're interested, investigate them.

As one might expect from this situation, these groups lacked cohesion or anything recognizable as an ecclesiastical structure. Historian Paul Johnson in *A History of Christianity*[21] observes that, struggling for decades to survive in competition not only with heretical insiders and Jewish outsiders but with the mostly Pagan world at large, a newborn church emerged only gradually "amid confusion, controversy, and schism".

At that time (the 2nd century), says Ehrman[22], more than ninety percent of the population of the Roman Empire was Pagan, worshipping thousands of different Gods. Most of these Pagan religions had no particular creeds or rules of behavior. One simply prayed to one's array of gods respectively for health, bounteous crops, prosperity, good fortune, victory in battle, etc.

Most people today — brainwashed by centuries of Catholic teachings — view Paganism as primitive and barbaric. In point of fact, say Freke and Gandy in *The Jesus Mysteries*, Pagan spirituality was the sophisticated product of a highly developed culture expressed through "vibrant and mystical religions called The Mysteries".[23] The Mysteries had flourished for many centuries throughout the ancient Mediterranean, inspiring the greatest minds of the Pagan world such as Plato, Socrates, Heraclitus, and other famous Greek philosophers who regarded the Mysteries as the very source of civilization.

The ubiquitous figurehead of the Pagan religions was a "dying and resurrecting godman" known by different names in different countries — Osiris in Egypt, Dionysus in Greece, Bacchus in Italy, Attis in Asia Minor, Adonis in Syria, Mithras in Persia.[24] His mythic forms were many, but he was everywhere essentially the same figure, whose collective identity was Osiris-Dionysus.[25]

The Mysteries involved two elements: the Outer Mysteries and the Inner. The Outer were for the illiterate, uneducated masses who worshipped their respective godmen without fully understanding the beliefs that lay at the heart of the Inner Mysteries. It was probably (who knows?) these illiterate and uneducated people whom the evangelists of Jesus' teachings initially targeted and who became the seedbed in which the tree of Christianity took root. Those more literate individuals educated in the Inner Mysteries, which held sacred knowledge known only to those who had undergone a rigid process of initiation, were a much smaller and certainly a more resistant target audience.

While the Outer Mysteries were ceremonial form without content, the Inner were highly structured and profoundly substantive. Through understanding the allegorical myth of the Mystery godman, initiates in the Inner Mysteries became aware that, like the mythical godman Osiris-Dionysus, they, too, were "God made flesh," an immortal Spirit encased in a physical body. They learned the mystical meaning of the Outer rituals and myths, a process that brought about the initiates' spiritual enlightenment and transformation. They were taught that they were all sons and daughters of God and that, through sharing in the symbolic death and resurrection of the mythical godman, they were spiritually reborn and experienced their own eternal essence. By understanding the myth of the sacrificed godman, they were resurrected into their true immortal, divine identities.[26]

This was heady stuff — an elaborate, sophisticated, highly spiritual dogma far from what the Catholic Church defensively and slanderously labeled...and still may today...primitive and barbaric. For the followers of Jesus, competing with the Inner Mysteries was like butting their heads against a stone wall. It was a tough sell, which is why the disciples probably focused initially on followers of the Outer Mysteries. Nevertheless their recruitment efforts would not have resulted automatically in droves of Pagans switching their allegiance to the Christian god. Pagan devotion to and dependence on its traditional centuries-old deities would not have been cast aside so easily, as the populace was tightly wedded both culturally and religiously to its traditional gods, whose pervasive presence permeated deeply into the fabric of everyday Pagan life.

What the leaders of the newborn Jesus cult needed was some practical means — a mechanism, a hook — not only to recruit Pagan followers but to secure their loyalty and retain their followership. The power to forgive sins would have been just the ticket. No other religion at that time offered the extraordinary *promise* — not just the hope, but the *promise* — of salvation and eternal life in the hereafter. This incentive was something different, novel, and intriguing.

"Join us!" the Jesus Faithful would have said to those individuals who were curious about his message but still devoted to their Pagan deities. "Forget your silly Pagan gods. They promise you nothing. They are mythical and worthless. The divine Jesus, the only true godman, the true living Son of the One and Only God, gave us the power to forgive your sins. We can save you from the horrors of Hell. Come join us. Join our group. We can promise you eternal life in Heaven." Like the advertisements we see on television for pain killers that promise quick results, Jesus promised salvation...a ticket to Heaven...a way out of this miserable, painful, awful world. All one had to do was believe in Jesus and one got a free ticket to Heaven.

What a deal! What a promise! What a come-on!

The crucial importance of the "whatever" power to the Jesus movement is evident in the order in which the books of the New Testament were arranged by its assemblers in the 4th century. The four Gospels came first, but not in the chronological order of their writing. The first book was not Mark, the earliest, but Matthew. The other Gospels followed in chronological sequence. If chronology had determined the order of the canon, Paul's letters, of course, would have come first, as they predated the Gospels. But the letters did not relate Christ's life and miracles, so they were placed last as supplemental texts.

Why would the assemblers of the New Testament take Matthew out of order and place it first? The answer is obvious. Of the four gospels, Matthew contained six emphases that best articulated the cornerstones of Christian doctrine:

1. Matthew related Jesus' birth and life as the fulfillment of earlier Jewish prophecies.

2. It contained the lengthiest elaboration of Jesus' ethical teachings in the Sermon on the Mount.

3. It placed Jesus' teachings into the context of earlier Jewish scripture.

4. It contained a powerful indictment of the scribes and Pharisees and depicted Jesus being rejected by Jews.

And most important of all,

5. It related for the first time that Mary was a virgin when she gave birth to Jesus.

6. It related Jesus' bestowal of the "whatever" power on his disciples.

The introduction to Matthew in my Bible states: "The position of the Gospel according to Matthew as the first of the four gospels in the New Testament reflects... the esteem in which it was held by the Church. No other was so frequently quoted in the non-canonical literature of earliest Christianity...The high estimation of this work remains."

No mystery there.

Would Jesus Have Done It?

Why would Jesus have granted his disciples this "whatever" power in the first place? Do you really believe that Jesus Christ, as reflected in the Gospels, with his brilliant intellect, his prescient powers of understanding humankind, his intuitive ability to see into people's hearts and minds, and above all his reputed power to foresee the future would have endowed members of our universally flawed human species with the godlike power to condemn fellow humans to Hell by retaining their "sins"?

God made us humans — everyone of us! — susceptible to the Seven Deadly Sins: pride, envy, gluttony, lust, anger, greed, and sloth as well as evil thoughts, unchastity, theft, murder, adultery, malice, deceit, licentiousness, blasphemy, arrogance, and folly. Greg Iles in his novel *Turning Angel*[27] described the human condition very well: "Sex is always there. People act civilized, they go through the motions of public life, but these secret attractions and affairs are always going on...That's why it was so shocking to the country when it was proved that Thomas Jefferson had children by his black slave. Suddenly he was no longer a granite figure on Mount Rushmore. He was just like us. Feet of clay. We tell ourselves that we know everyone's human, but then we act as if we expect something else." Would Jesus not have recognized that humans, all humans, have feet of clay? Of course he would have.

God made us humans arrogant, jealous, avaricious, hateful, vengeful, even criminal creatures. He made us racially, ethnically, geographically, socially, religiously, politically, academically, professionally, and sexually bigoted. He made us hunger for power of one kind or another from control over our children, our spouse, and our colleagues to wielding control over a major corporation or a colossal military force...even control over the White House in the person of the President. He made us inured to human suffering, famine, and disease and bedeviled by hypocrisy, apathy, and lack of spirituality. He made us capable of hacking into computers to steal money, to steal people's identities, and to implant rampaging computer viruses which randomly destroy priceless data, documents, and files and create computer memory chaos throughout the world in both commercial and home computers.

Above all, He made us love to hate. We hate the Yankees. We hate the Dallas Cowboys. We hate Republicans. We hate Democrats. We hate whites. We hate blacks. We hate gays and lesbians. We hate the religious right and the silent majority. We hate Moslems. We hate Catholics. We hate Baptists. We hate Jews. We hate Mormons. We hate rich people. (I know one man who even hated poor people!) We hate our next door neighbors. We hate this, we hate that. We are haters by nature. It is one of the defining characteristics of us members of the *Homo sapiens* species. We are all pronounced haters! Most will deny it, which is as expected, but everyone of us has something...no matter how small...that we hate, if only burnt toast.

I smile when I hear on the radio, read in the newspaper, or hear on television that particularly cruel actions were "inhuman". On the contrary, they were most certainly human. God made us a violent species with a history from time immemorial of fighting viciously tooth and nail over precious commodities, natural resources and, yes, women. He made us love war and contact sports. When a football player tackles an opponent, the tens of thousands of people in the stadium and the millions watching on TV joyfully join him vicariously, wrapping their arms around that sucker and viciously slamming him to the ground. God made us animalistically brutal and addicted to bloodshed, as the books we read and the plethora of violent bloody computer games, Hollywood movies, and television programs attest, especially those that show live savage boxing matches. At the end of a popular movie its hero sits astride the prone figure of his evil nemesis. With a look of fierce hatred the hero thrusts a knife into the man's throat. Millions of those who watch that scene, including millions of Christians, wrap their fingers around the hero's hand and help drive home the blade.

And to make matters worse, says Ehrman in *Misquoting Jesus*[28], despite our protestations to the contrary, God made us love being the self-indulgent creatures we are with our desires, longings, needs, wants, beliefs, perspectives, world views, opinions, likes, dislikes, and all the other things that make human beings deplorably human. If you think I'm exaggerating, you must be from another planet. *Homo sapiens* — as God intended — is a flawed species!

Good Christians reading this book will, of course, vigorously protest that not everyone fits my description of the human race. Gifted with unwavering faith in the fundamental goodness of humankind, they will contend that there are millions of "good" people who detest and oppose violence, bloodshed, war, bigotry of every kind, and so on. And I don't disagree. I am one of those millions. But opposing these things doesn't mean we are not besieged by them and forced to deal with them in this wretched world. You have to concede that being non-violent, opposed to war, etc. is a constant struggle against our innate human traits and the basic uncivilized nature of civilization. More telling, however, is the fact that we humans *love violence*! Consider the common reactions of young and old when two or more people attack each other with their fists on a playground, in the stands at an athletic competition, in a cafeteria, in a ticket line at a public event, in a classroom, in a workplace. Anywhere. People immediately circle around the belligerents, point and vie for a better view, to witness the anger, the blows, and the blood. The intense glow on the watchers' excited faces is all the evidence one needs to validate our basic violent nature.

Robert and Berdine Ardrey in their book, *African Genesis*, explained eloquently their theory of the origins of our violent, if normally restrained, nature. For instance, I myself most unChristianly would like to beat to death with a baseball bat men who sexually abuse children. And I'm not alone. The most common statement by the father of a sexually assaulted daughter is, "Give me five minutes alone with the bastard who raped her." In a heartbeat any of us can become violent. Look at the murder rate. Look at domestic violence. Look at road rage.

If you need further proof of our flawed nature, look at the awful selfish things people do that hurt others. I know it is a callous dereliction of my marital vows to imagine having sex with women other than my wife to whom I am devoted for life but, when I see a curvaceous female figure, my basic God-created human instincts kick in and, want them or not, my mind generates images of my joining that figure in bed. I have never been physically unfaithful to my wife nor would I, but I'm in the minority. According to surveys over many decades, about 50 percent of all American men — yes, 50 percent!...and about 25 percent of all American women commit adultery at one time or another in their lives.[29]

Every day those of us humans who strive to lead a "good" life must struggle end-lessly against our humanness to achieve that noble end. If that weren't the case, why do preachers of every religion harangue their congregations every week about overcoming temptations and fighting evil? Why do everyday people lie and de-ceive? Why do they resent others who are more beautiful, more successful, hap-pier, healthier, stronger, richer than they are?

That Jesus had the power to foresee events is clearly indicated in Mark 13:5, where he is reported to have said to his disciples, "When you hear of wars and reports of wars do not be alarmed; such things must happen...Nation will rise against nation and kingdom against kingdom. There will be earthquakes from place to place, and there will be famines." That Jesus, with his innate God-given insights into human behavior and motives and with his ability to see into the future, would have been so naively, wantonly careless as to entrust a "whatever" power to members of our irre-vocably flawed, emotionally driven human species is both unthinkable and absurd. As Jesus is reported in Matthew 12:33 to have said, "A good person brings forth good out of a store of goodness, but an evil person brings forth evil out of a store of evil." If Jesus truly believed this, would he have believed that all of the Chris-tian clergy who would forgive and not forgive sins would be only "good" persons? Would he believe that the "whatever" power would be used only for good? Not!

So, if Jesus never bestowed the "whatever" power on his disciples, why would the author of Matthew or someone else concoct the story that Jesus had done so? The answer is simple and obvious: POWER! Why power? Because the early followers of Jesus had none! No power at all. And they needed power to create an enduring church to proselytize Jesus' teachings in which they so devoutly believed.

Powerless Believers

Few in number, widespread, and without meaningful influence these early follow-ers of Jesus were a disparate, quarrelsome lot with as many different beliefs as there were communities. Most of the issues in question involved trivial but hotly debated differing interpretations of Jesus' teachings, but two were fundamental and pro-voked the greatest conflicts, bitterness, and even violence:

(a) Whether Jesus was a divinity — the actual Son of God — or just a plain old run-of-the-mill human like the rest of us, and

(b) Whether Jesus had ever truly existed, that is, whether he had been an actual flesh-and-blood human or was nothing more than the leading character in a popular myth.

Divine or Mortal

Oddly enough, according to the Gospels — and this will surprise that majority of Christians who are not well read in the New Testament — Jesus never claimed to be divine. He was never reported to even claim the title "Son of God". "Son of Man" was the only title he was said to use to refer to himself. He did indeed refer to God as his father, but he also referred to God as everyone's father, the father of all humankind. Indeed, his Lord's Prayer begins with, "Our Father", so Jesus didn't single himself out as the one and only son of God.

Many biblical scholars contend that the phrase "Son of Man" meant the "Divine Son of God". For example, Dr. William Lane Craig wrote in his book, *The Son Rises: Historical Evidence for the Resurrection of Jesus*[30], "The Son of Man was a divine figure in the Old Testament book of Daniel who would come at the end of the world to judge mankind and rule forever. Thus, [Jesus'] claim to be the Son of Man [was] in effect a claim to divinity."

What this quotation from Daniel (7:13-14) actually says is:

> I saw in the night visions, and, behold, there came with the clouds of the sky one **like a son of man**, and he came even to the an-cient of days, and they brought him near before him. There was given him dominion, and glory, and a kingdom, that all the peo-ples, nations, and languages should serve him: his dominion is an everlasting dominion, which shall not pass away, and his kingdom that which shall not be destroyed. [As I mention below, numerous ancient religions featured a nearly identical savior who came down from Heaven to establish his everlasting kingdom on Earth.]

Craig and like-minded scholars bent on selectively using the book of Daniel to prove Jesus was divine disregard, either purposely or out of ignorance, the fact that Jesus never cited Daniel as the source of his use of the phrase "son of man". They also disregard other Old Testament references to "son of man" (such as Job 25:6; Psalms 8:4, 144, and 146:3; and the Book of Isaiah 51:12). The phrase "son of man" was in fact a Semitic idiom originating in Ancient Mesopotamia (5th to the 4th century BCE — Before the Common Era), meaning *humanity* or *self*, not *divinity*.[30] It was simply a synonym for "human" and a substitute for the indefinite pronoun "one" or "someone"

> Genesis 13:16 makes clear that **son of man** was *every* man, *every* human. "And I will multiply your seed like the dirt of the Earth which no **son of man** can count."

> Book of Numbers 23:19: "God is not a man, that he should lie, nor a **son of man**, that he should repent."

> Job 25: "And the stars are not pure in (God's) sight; How much less man, who is a worm! The **son of man**, who is a worm!"

> Psalm 156: " Don't put your trust in princes, each a **son of man** in whom there is no help."

> **Son of Man** is a title frequently given to the prophet Ezekiel in the Old Testament, perhaps to emphasize his human weaknesses and mortality.

Christian theologians, as one might expect, see a foreshadowing of Jesus behind every rock and tree in the Old Testament, yet Johann Edelmann's article, "The Idea of Jesus", in the October 1967 issue of *The Harvard Theological Review* of the Cambridge University Press states, "It is stretching far beyond imagination to interpret sayings in the Old Testament as presaging Jesus." Craig's attempt to use Daniel to prove Jesus' divinity is a prime example of this stretching.

The language which Jesus and others of his time in Israel spoke was primarily Aramaic, which was also the original language of the book of Daniel. The salient point here is that Aramaic grammar lacks a definite article. That being the case, in Aramaic the phrase in question would simply have been "son of man" without the article "the". Its meaning would have been "one", "someone", or "anyone". For example:

> Luke 12:10 — "Everyone who speaks a word against a son of man [*someone*] will be forgiven."

Mark 2:25 — "The sabbath was made for man, not man for the sabbath. That is why a son of man [*any man*] is lord even of the sabbath."

If, as theologians and biblical scholars contend, the Gospels were originally written in Greek, it's easy to see how "son of man" became "**the** son of man," because the Greek language is flooded with the definite article "the". For example, when referring to someone, say, "my wife", in Greek it would be "the wife mine". "Mr. Charleston" would be phrased "**the** Mr. Charleston". Therefore when the Greek Gospels were translated into English, the Aramaic "son of man" automatically became "**the** son of man".

More to the point, if Jesus were indeed the Son of God, don't you think he would have said so to impress upon his disciples and others his special authority to speak for God and to establish the divine truth of his teachings? I do. The fact that he never did, as far as the New Testament warrants, is an unwieldy hurdle for Christian theologians and scholars to overcome, which their lame claims regarding Daniel attempt to do.

The chronologically earliest recorded intimation in the New Testament of Jesus' divinity was in Paul's Epistle to Titus (2:13) which said, "...as we await the blessed hope — the appearance of the glory of the great God and of our Savior Jesus Christ." So it was Paul and probably others, not Jesus, who reportedly claimed he was the Son of God.

The early believers fervently wanted their savior to be divine. If he weren't divine, if he were just another lowly mortal human, his teachings and proclamations, though still profound and wise, would have been of no greater repute than those of any number of other roaming prophets of the time. The gospels themselves say that many who heard Jesus — even members of his own family — did not believe in his divinity during his lifetime.[32] After the Christian Church had established itself, challenges to Jesus' divinity withered away over the centuries until his status as the "Divine Son of God" became unquestioned, a matter of irrefutable dogma. Indeed, to challenge his divinity became blasphemous. But to repeat, according to the Gospels, he never claimed to be the Divine Son of God.

Man or Myth

There is an awkward, and for Christians disturbing, dimension to the Bible story of Jesus. Kersey Graves in *The World's Sixteen Crucified Saviors*[33]: "Stories of incarnate Gods answering to and resembling the miraculous character of Jesus Christ have been prevalent in most if not all the principal religious heathen nations of antiquity. The accounts and narrations of some of these deific incarnations bear such a striking resemblance to that of the Christian Savior — not only in their general features but in some cases in the most minute details from the legend of the immaculate conception to that of the crucifixion and subsequent ascension into Heaven — that they [could easily] be mistaken for the other...Twenty Messiahs, Saviors, and Sons of God, according to history or tradition, have in past times descended from Heaven and taken upon themselves the form of men, clothing themselves with human flesh, and furnishing incontestable evidence of a divine origin by various miracles, marvelous works, and superlative virtues. [Each of these] twenty alternate Christs, like Jesus, laid the foundation for the salvation of the world and ascended back to Heaven."

Jesus' most notable counterparts were Krishna of India born 3,200 years before Christ,[34] Horus of Egypt 3,000 years before,[35] Buddha of India 600 years before,[36] and Mithras of Persia 200 years before.[37] Literalists were justifiably challenged by and worried about these ancient myths. To explain away the striking similarities between the life of Jesus and the lives of these and other Jesus prototypes, Literalists made the preposterous, even comical claim that Satan, knowing that Jesus was going to come in the flesh, had created these mythical Jesus-like deities in *advance* to deceive the Christian faithful and lead them astray.[38] Spare me!

Jesus' having been a living human was and is absolutely crucial to the credibility of the story upon which the Christian religion is based. If Jesus never existed in the flesh, then the haloed story of his virgin birth, persecution, crucifixion, death, and resurrection was all untrue, a wholesale though enchanting fairy tale. If that were the case, the hope of the early true believers to establish a permanent Christian Church was doomed.

What made this controversy particularly troublesome was that, while the early followers of Jesus who believed he had been a real person were spreading his "good news" and struggling to establish a Jesus religion, they came under relentless verbal, sometimes physical attack from three principal quarters: the ever increasing number of Gnostic Christians, who stridently believed Jesus was a mythical figure; the ubiquitous Pagans, who accused Christians, both Literalists and Gnostics, of modeling Jesus after the dying and resurrecting godman Osiris-Dionysus of The Mysteries; and the deeply-rooted Jewish communities, whose religion utterly rejected Jesus whether man or myth. Moreover, societies in the ancient world were conditioned by history and culture to believe that no gods were human.

Gnostic Christian Criticism

To better see Jesus as the Gnostic Christians saw him, replace "Jesus" in the sentences below with "Santa Claus". This is not to demean Jesus, but to make real how the Gnostic Christians viewed him as mythical.

Gnostics Christians:

- Taught that Jesus was a mythological figure who appeared in the imagination in different ways, according to the understanding of the individual.[39]

- Claimed that Jesus wasn't really a man, but the hero of an allegorical myth.[40]

- Believed in the spiritual, not bodily, resurrection of Jesus.[41]

- Believed that Jesus was a symbolic visionary figure, a doctrine known as "Docetism," which denied the reality of Christ's suffering and death.[42]

- Were free to interpret the Jesus "myth" as they liked.

- Saw emergent Christianity as an alternative version of the ancient Egyptian cult of Serapis, based upon a "holy" family made up of Osiris, his bride Isis, and their hawk-headed son Horus.[43]

Literalist intolerance was therefore a mounting threat to the Gnostics.[44] Ultimately Gnostics were expelled by the leaders of the risen Catholic Church and consigned to oblivion.[45]

Pagan Criticism

- Ammonius Saccas (175-240), born of Christian parents, the founder of Neoplatonism and the teacher of Origen, maintained that Christianity and Paganism differed on no essential points.[46]

- Pagan critics of Christianity complained that this new religion was nothing more than a pale reflection of their own ancient teachings.[47]

- The criticisms of Pagan philosopher and satirist Celsus, a famous outspoken critic of Christianity, stand out for their sharpness. Because the "just man unjustly accused" was such a familiar figure in the ancient world, Celsus ridiculed the Christians for trying to claim that Jesus was in any way unique. With wit and biting satire he suggested that, if they wanted to create a new religion, they would have been better to have based it around one of the many famous Pagan sages who also "died a hero's death".[48]

  He catalogued the number of figures to whom legend similarly attributed divine parentage and a miraculous birth.

He was disparaging of Christians who interpreted the Jesus myth as historical fact.

He regarded the notion that God could literally father a child on a mortal woman as plainly absurd.[49]

He stated that the Christian religion contained nothing but what Christians held in common with the heathen — nothing new.[50]

He criticized Christians for trying to pass off the Jesus story as a new revelation when it was actually an inferior imitation of Pagan myths.[51]

He and other Pagan theologians derided the idea that Jesus was a living person.[52]

He wrote that there was nothing new or impressive about the Christians' ethical teachings.[53]

To Celsus, the Christian claim that Jesus was the one and only Son of God was ridiculous. Celsus observed indignantly: "Good Lord! Is it not a silly sort of argument to reckon...by the same works that one man is a god while his rivals are mere 'sorcerers'?"[54]

Jewish Criticism

The Jewish and early Christian communities were on unfriendly terms from the very beginning. Reports of Jesus' harsh censure of Jewish religious leaders would have put his early followers automatically at odds with orthodox Judaism. The Christians' accusing Jews of causing Jesus' death only worsened the relationship between the two communities.

- Because most Jews rejected the notion that Jesus was the fulfillment of ancient prophecies concerning the Messiah, they rejected the Christian message.[55]

- "Jews in general would have been outraged at the mere idea that Jesus was divine. To orthodox Jews this idea was the ultimate sacrilege."[56]

- "As Jews and Christians came into greater conflict over Jesus' identity, Jewish texts took a polemical stance in order to counter Christian claims."[57]

- Jews in the 1st century referred to the followers of Christ as "Nazarenes," a name of reproach.[59] The Nazarenes (Nazorenes, Nazirites) were a select Jewish group which followed a spiritual lifestyle[60] at variance with orthodox Jewish customs.

Other Criticism

- A letter attributed to Polycarp (70-155), one of the so-called "fathers of the Christian Church", stated that "the great majority" of Christians [in Polycarp's day] didn't believe Jesus existed "in the flesh".[61]

- Robert Eisenman, professor of Middle East Religions and Archaeology and director of the Institute for the Study of Judeo-Christian Origins at California State University, says in *James, the Brother of Jesus*[62] that the Gospels largely present Jesus "in the framework of supernatural storytelling".

In light of all the ancient accusations that Jesus never lived, what is the archaeological, historical, scientific evidence that he actually lived in the flesh? Well, readers, fasten those seatbelts a bit tighter, because *there is no truly reliable evidence*!

There are no documents, contemporary records, or even casual reports from the time of Jesus that mention him as a physical human, says Ahmed Osman, noted scholar of Egyptian history, in *Christianity: An Ancient Egyptian Religion*[63]. Even Paul, the giant theologian of the Christian Faith, never spoke of a flesh-and-blood Jesus...only a spiritual one. Because later Jewish and Christian source materials were inherently and exceedingly biased either in favor of or against an historical Jesus, none of their reporting on the subject can be taken at face value. Indeed, all accounts of a living Jesus date from decades and even centuries *after* his "death" and are thus worthless in resolving this issue. Moreover, writes Michael White, who holds the Ronald Nelson Smith Chair in Classics and Christian Origins at the University of Texas in Austin, in his book *From Jesus to Christianity*, nothing written by Jesus himself has ever been found or mentioned, and he left on the landscape of Judea no direct archaeological evidence that he ever lived there.[64]

Here's a sampling of what other notable scholars have written denying Jesus' existence:

- Albert Schweitzer, Nobel Peace Prize recipient, in his *Quest of the Historical Jesus: A Critical Study of Its Progress from Reimarus to Wrede*[65]: "The Jesus of Nazareth who came forward publicly as the Messiah...never had any existence."

- Schweitzer is quoted in *The Pagan Christ: Recovering the Lost Light*[66], written by Tom Harpur, former professor of Greek and the New Testament at the

University of Toronto and internationally renowned writer on religious issues, as saying that after years of careful study he (Schweitzer) concluded there was no traditional Jesus of Nazareth as an historical person. He concluded that the Jesus figure of the theologians was the dramatized, ritualized, symbolic figure of our divine nature — grossly mistaken after centuries of ignorance for a man of flesh.

- The deceased comparative religions scholar Alvin Boyd Kuhn was cited in Harpur's *The Pagan Christ*[67] as writing: "It has always been an unfailing source of astonishment to the historical investigator of Christian beginnings that there is not one single word from the pen of any Pagan writer of the 1st century...which can in any fashion be referred to the marvelous story recounted by the Gospel writers. The very existence of Jesus seems unknown. What is even more curious is that the closer one gets to Jesus' alleged time, the greater and more general is the denial or ignorance of his existence, while the farther one draws away from it, the greater and more insistent are the 'proofs' of it...Of the Church Fathers, Irenaeus, a leading theologian of the day, seems never to have subscribed to the story of Jesus' death on the cross or his death at all at the early age of about thirty-three. It is most curious — given the repeated claim by conservatives that Jesus' life was accepted as historical by the early Church — that Irenaeus refers to a remarkable legend that flatly refutes the Gospel 'history'."

- Kuhn[68] concludes: "For Paul to write fifteen Epistles, basic treatises on the religion that Jesus founded, and find no reason to refer even once to anything Jesus said or did would be on the order of one's writing a thorough treatise on the American Revolution and never once mentioning George Washington!"

- Ahmed Osman[69]: "No contemporary Roman records exist that can bear witness, directly or indirectly, to the physical existence of Jesus. Even more surprising is the absence of any reference to Jesus in the writings of the Jewish authors living at that time in Jerusalem and Alexandria."

- Osman[70]: "If the Jesus of the gospels lived, suffered, and died during the period of Roman rule over Palestine, it is curious that his name does not appear in the writings of three distinguished contemporary authors — Philo Judaeus, Justus of Tiberias, and Flavius Josephus."

- Osman[71]: "In [Origen's] own writings, he referred to the account of John the Baptist's life and death to be found in Book 18 of *Antiquities of the Jews* [written by Josephus]. But nowhere in his works is there any reference whatever to Jesus, a curious omission by someone who believed in him."

- Osman[72]: "Despite [Philo's] close links with Christian thought, we find only one New Testament figure mentioned in Philo's work, Pontius Pilate, but nothing about Jesus."

- Bart Ehrman in *Lost Christianities*[73]: "At a later time (possibly the 4th century) Christians were puzzled that the important figures in their religion, especially Jesus and Paul, were completely unknown to the major political and intellectual leaders of [the figures'] day. [As far as anyone knows] neither of them was mentioned by any Roman author of the 1st century."

- Harry E. Barnes cited in *The Pagan Christ*[74]: "Very few periods in the history of the ancient world were so well documented as the period from Jesus' birth to his death when Emperors Caesar Augustus (27 BCE to 14 CE) and Tiberius (14 to 37 CE) reigned supreme. Yet one amazing fact must be faced: no contemporary non-Christian writer [is known to have ever written] of Jesus' existence."

- Barnes[75] lists the following among the eminent scholars and critics who have contended that Jesus was not historical: Bruno Bauer, Bolland, Emilio Bossi, Georg Brandes, Edward Carpenter, Ryner Couchoud, Arthur Drews, Emil Felden, Jensen, Albert Kaltoff, Lublinsk, Gerald Massey, G.R.S. Mead, John M. Robertson, W.B. Smith, J.C. Stendel, Van der Berg, Charles Virolleaud, and Whittaker.

- Harpur in *The Pagan Christ*[76]: After a thorough investigation of the relevant Jewish sources for 1st-century Judaism and history, Harold Leidner's *Fabrication of the Christ Myth* concludes: "There is not a particle of evidence that Jesus of Nazareth ever existed."

- Harpur[77]: "In his challenging work, *The Twilight of Christianity*, scholar [Harry E.] Barnes reviews the meager number of non-Gospel mentions of Jesus — a sum total of twenty-four lines from Pliny, Tacitus, Suetonius, and Josephus — and states that, given that these passages are virtually all forgeries and interpolations, they constitute poor evidence of what orthodox Christians insist on calling one of the best-attested events in history. Barnes points out that, even if this secular testimony were indisputably reliable and authentic, it would be faltering support for so great an edifice to rest upon. Add to all this the undeniable fact that there is, in the extant Jewish literature of the 1st century, not a single authentic reference to the founder of Christianity."

- Harpur[78]: "The earliest writings in the New Testament, which make up more than one quarter of its total content, are the letters of the Apostle

Paul. What is absolutely striking about them is their virtual silence on the whole subject of an historical Jesus of Nazareth...Paul never once mentions the man Jesus in the full historical sense. Yet...Paul is the earliest witness among all the Bible writers, the one nearest Jesus in actual time. His earliest letters antedate the appearance of Mark by at least a generation. Of course, a critic will argue that Paul does occasionally speak of Jesus by name. This is quite true. But today, most Bible theologians agree that, even when he does so, he is not talking about a man of flesh and blood, an historical person...Paul's Christ is nowhere called Jesus of Nazareth, nor is he born in Bethlehem. The Jesus Paul dilates upon repeatedly is in reality the spiritual entity in the core of each human's inner being. He is the spiritual Christ principle (the eternal Christos), not the man."

• Harpur: "As Benjamin Bacon of Yale Divinity School says in his book, *Jesus and Paul*[79], 'Paul is the first Bible writer in the 1st century, and he definitely knows no Christ except one he describes as 'not after the flesh'.''

• Osman[80]: "None of the appearances of Jesus reported in the Nag Hammadi gospels* represents an *historical physical appearance*; he always appears to his disciples as a *spiritual being*."

*The Nag Hammadi library discovered in Upper Egypt in 1945 is a collection of religious texts dating back to the 1st and 2nd centuries CE. They were written in Coptic (Egyptian language in Greek) and belonged to an Egyptian Gnostic-Christian community.

• Graham Stanton, a scholar who has written extensively on the Gospel of Matthew, in *Gospel Truth*[81]: "Paul fails to refer to a saying of Jesus at the very point where he might well have clinched his argument by doing so."

• Freke and Gandy[82]: "It is a completely remarkable fact...that Paul says nothing at all about the historical Jesus!...He makes it clear that he never met an historical Jesus. He writes: 'Neither did I receive the Gospel from man, nor was I taught it, but it came to me through a revelation of Jesus Christ.' Paul doesn't mention Jerusalem or Pilate either...In fact Paul does not link Jesus with any historical time and place, including Paul's recent past. Paul's Christ, like the Pagans' Osiris-Dionysus, is a timeless mythical figure. Paul says nothing about Nazareth and never calls Jesus a Nazarene...He tells us nothing about Jesus eating and drinking with tax collectors and sinners, his Sermon on the Mount, his parables, his arguments with Pharisees, or his clashes with Roman authorities. Paul doesn't even know the Lord's Prayer which, according to the gospels, Jesus gave to his disciples, saying, 'Pray then like this', for Paul writes, 'We don't even know how we ought to pray'. If Paul were actually following a recently deceased Messiah, it is astonishing that he did not feel it necessary to go and see the apostles who knew Jesus personally before starting off on his own teaching mission. Yet he says he did not gain his authority from anyone."

- Harpur[83]: When, in 1 Corinthians 15, Paul describes his experience of the risen Christ, he says that "last of all he was seen by me also". But the Greek word he uses for this...is *opthe*. It was the word regularly used by the Mystery religionists to describe a "visionary seeing". As Bacon of Yale Divinity School says, Paul expressly disavows even having any interest in a "Jesus after the flesh" and his letters bear this out because — and this is highly significant — they contain not a single reference to any of the great miracles, teachings, and other events related in the Gospel narratives as integral to Jesus' life and ministry. They are either unknown to Paul or are a matter of complete indifference to him. Stunning though it may be, Paul apparently knew nothing about or cared nothing for the Gospel story that had allegedly founded the very Faith he had so enthusiastically embraced. [I must point out that Paul did not "enthusiastically embrace" the Christian faith per se. His beliefs were so at odds with that of the leaders of the Literalist Christians, that they shunned him, leading in Acts to his subordination to Peter. See Diminution of Paul.]

- "Paul himself tells us in Galatians, 'I made known to you brethren, as touching the Gospel which was preached by me, that it was not after man (i.e., of human origin)'."[84]

- Freke and Gandy in *The Laughing Jesus*[85]: Dozens of Christian gospels in circulation [in the 1st and 2nd centuries and] found at Nag Hammadi clearly portray Jesus as a mythical figure.

- Freke and Gandy in *Jesus and the Lost Goddess*[86]: "When Paul reveals to us in his letters 'the secret' of Christianity, it has absolutely nothing to do with an historical Jesus. The secret he declares is the mystical revelation of 'Christ in you' — the one Consciousness of God in all of us. His Jesus is a mythic figure."

- Freke and Gandy in *The Jesus Mysteries*[87]: "The Romans...were renowned for keeping careful records of all their activities, especially legal proceedings...[But] there is no record, official or otherwise, of Jesus being tried by Pontius Pilate or executed. This was an extremely literate period in human history. The following is a list of Pagan writers who wrote at, or within a century of, the time that Jesus is said to have lived: Apollonius, Appain, Arrian, Dion Pruseus, Juvenal, Martial, Pausanias, Petronius, Pliny the Elder, Plutarch, Seneca, and Theon of Smyrna. The works of these writers would be enough to fill a library, but not one of them refers to Jesus."

- Freke and Gandy[88]: "Philo was an eminent Jewish author who lived at the same time that Jesus is supposed to have lived and wrote around fifty books that still survive. They deal with history, philosophy, and religion and tell us much about Pontius Pilate — yet make no mention at all of the coming of the Messiah Jesus."

- Freke and Gandy[89]: "Philo's contemporary, Justus of Tiberias, was a Jew who lived near Capernaum, where Jesus was often said to have stayed. Justus wrote a history that began with Moses and extended to his own times, but again made no mention of Jesus."

- Freke and Gandy[90]: "Amazingly, the Apostles, the letters of Paul, James, Peter, John, and Jude, and the Revelation of John do not concern themselves with an historical Jesus."

- Freke and Gandy[91]: "Like countless scholars who have made this quest before us, we have found that looking for an historical Jesus is futile. It is astonishing that we have no substantial evidence for the historical existence of a man who is said to have been the one and only incarnation of God throughout all of history. But the fact is we don't."

Freke and Gandy[92] conclude: "There are only two credible explanations for Jesus' conspicuous absence from Roman texts. Either there simply was no historical Jesus or Jesus seemed of so little importance to the official records-keepers and historians of his time that he was deemed unworthy of mention."

After considering all the evidence gathered in my research, I side with the latter explanation: that Jesus was indeed a living human being but was not memorable to historians in his time. Eisenman in *James, the Brother of Jesus*[93] agrees, stating categorically that, "The equation is simple: if James existed — which he undeniably did — then Jesus existed as well."

The question then is why Jesus was not memorable. The simple answer: he was a marginal and thus invisible Jew to those contemporaries who wrote about notable events in the early decades of the 1st century. An impoverished itinerant preacher who is said never to have ventured outside the regions around Palestine and generally avoided its major urban centers, he was an insignificant, unnoteworthy blip on the screen of the historians of his day. For example, he was not known to have been a member of any political organization, to have held any public office, to have written any philosophical treatise, or to have addressed any notable political body such as the Roman Senate, nor did he have any discernible influence or effect on Palestinian social, political, military, or economic circumstances. Jesus' reported baptism by John the Baptist, if it happened at all, would easily have passed unnoticed in the historical annals because Jesus would have been only one of hundreds, maybe thousands, John baptized. Jesus was, in short, a nobody.

Moreover, he reportedly associated mainly with the unimportant, the non-elite, the riffraff, even the despised and rejected of Palestinian society. Certainly he would have been ostracized by the Temple elite of his day. The political and religious leaders of his society would have labeled him a dangerous kook. They would have put him out of their memory the moment he died, never again to mention the ridiculous blasphemous claim by his followers that he was the Son of God, the Messiah. Why would the scribes maintaining Roman records of events in Palestine pay any notice to some laughable nut who people claimed was King of the Jews and who was crucified by the Romans? There were all kinds of crackpots, some probably insane, who were crucified during that period by Roman governors. Eisenman[14] notes that in Jesus' time "the terrifying political strife, disaffection, and day-to-day cruelties resulted in thousands of crucifixions [not just one]." Jesus would therefore not have stood out among those crucified.

But he could well have stood out if the Gospels (Mark 15:33-37; Matthew 27:45-50; Luke 23:44-46) are accurate in reporting that Pilate, in a contravention of Roman custom and procedure, allowed Jesus' body to be taken down, presumably dead, after only six hours on the cross. The fact that there is no mention in the scrupulously detailed Roman records of this apparent violation of Roman policy would suggest that it never happened. On the other hand, if Pilate did indeed authorize this contravention of Roman custom, he very well could have precluded any mention of it in the records to protect himself from disciplinary action by Rome. Who knows? There is no proof, as far as I know, that Pilate ever made such a concession…to anyone!

Still, if Jesus did indeed cure people of diseases, raise the dead, and perform other miracles all witnessed by any number of people, his name and fame would almost certainly have spread throughout Judea — a relatively small area — in which case he would have been a renowned and memorable figure for historians. The failure of historians to mention him strongly suggests, even proves, that he was neither renowned nor memorable, which would suggest he never performed the miracles attributed to him in the New Testament. I recommend to my devout Christian readers who are now comatose to breathe deeply, summon up their patience, and strive to be objective as they read on.

Catholic theologians and clergy are certainly aware of the controversy over Jesus' existence. Yet the Church, as far as I have been able to determine, has never publicly acknowledged the issue for two quite obvious reasons: (a) Church dogma is based on a living Jesus and (b) addressing the matter publicly would only draw attention to the controversy and raise questions that would inevitably undermine the Faithful's faith. As a result, your average Christians, who never read about the history of their religion, are ignorant of the controversy and oblivious to its potential to erode their religion's validity. As the saying goes, "ignorance is bliss". Therefore only a small fraction of the billion Catholics on Earth are aware that Jesus' existence in the flesh has ever been challenged. I was unaware of these challenges myself until I began my research. If you're interested in learning more about the debate over the historical Jesus, I recommend you do what I did. Read the books in my bibliography and go to your local library, book store, or the Internet, find your own sources, and read about it. Then make up your own mind. But do yourself a favor: read material on both sides of the debate, not just the one that supports your beliefs.

My reason for belaboring whether Jesus was real or mythical is to emphasize the dire dilemma in which early "Christians" found themselves, for they had no alternative but to insist he was a real person. Certainly only the minutest fraction of the first "Christians" ever met Jesus in person or heard him deliver his message. They knew of him only from the hearsay tales passed verbally from person to person, village to village, tales that were surely embellished as they made their way. (Hearsay means information derived from people who were not eyewitnesses and had no first-hand knowledge. Hearsay is as unreliable as the weather...as unreliable as the tendency of *all* humans to embellish, exaggerate, and even fabricate notable events.) And then, in the years that followed, they knew of him from having letters and other written materials about him read to them aloud because, as I have said, few people at that time or in the seventeen centuries to follow were literate. Just as early "Christians" gathered in homes, long before consecrated churches were constructed, to have epistles like Paul's read to them, so Christians today gather in churches to hear readings of extracts from the New Testament. Nothing has really changed. The Faithful today learn from and believe in these readings in exactly the same way that early "Christians" did...through weekly, fleeting, highly selective, disconnected readings of scripture at services. Indeed, in many cases they may be the same readings!

Just for fun, ask your Christian friends whether they believe Jesus was a flesh-and-blood human. Trust me. Their responses will be as indignant and surly as those of the early believers: "Of course Jesus was human. Are you nuts? It's inconceivable that He wasn't. Don't you realize Jesus was divine...the living, breathing Son of God on Earth. Good heavens! Read the Bible!"

Scholars and the "Real" Jesus

It is stunning how amazingly thin — even transparent — are the personas and backgrounds of the main characters in the Bible's famous story of Jesus. Eisenman writes in *James, the Brother of Jesus*,[95] "Of all the characters in the early stages of Christianity, Paul alone is known to us through reliable, first-hand autobiographical documents, that is, the letters attributed to him in the New Testament. They reveal his life, character, and thoughts in the most personal manner possible. All others, even Jesus and most of those generally called Apostles, we know only by second- or third-hand accounts, if we know them at all. We have Gospels or letters purportedly written about them or in their names, but these must be handled with the utmost care...Biblical scholars have not come to a consensus on which aspects of this legacy can properly be considered historical."

Whereas Acts is widely popularized as an historical recounting of actions by the Twelve Apostles, writes Eisenman, it tells us "next to nothing about Peter after he... leaves Palestine...nothing about his travels or experiences, not even what happens to him in Rome — if he ever gets there — and nothing about his death". Aside from Paul, John, and to some extent Philip, the other Apostles in Acts are simply shadowy, paper figures.[96] Nevertheless, people over the centuries have wondrously extrapolated inductively from the Christian scriptures the nature, personalities, ambitions, traits, strengths, weaknesses, and motivations of these individuals and the substance of their interrelationships, despite the fact there is, with the exception of James, the brother of Jesus, no fully reliable record of their existence outside of the New Testament. There have been many thousands of books and articles and scores of plays and movies by serious, highly talented, sincere scholars, theologians, playwrights, and screen writers analyzing the behavior and philosophies of these undocumented men and women, their spirituality, even sainthood, and more particularly their critical roles in the story of Jesus. These treatises relate, analyze, synthesize, and draw conclusions about the historical life of Jesus, his thoughts, his motivations, and his relationships with his closest followers...without solid proof that any of them, outside of Pontius Pilate, Paul, and James actually lived. It's mind-boggling.

The historical settings of these stories in the first four decades of the 1st century are, of course, authenticated by archaeology and documented history. For example, there was indeed a Pontius Pilate, the Roman prefect who governed the province of Judah from 26 to 36; there was indeed a Saul of Tarsus (Paul); and there was indeed a Jewish temple in Jerusalem, a city which was ruled, occupied, and eventually ruthlessly razed by the Romans. But that's as far as it goes. Beyond these few historical facts and others the story of Jesus becomes tenuous at best because all claims of Jesus' existence derive from hearsay accounts.

What I find most interesting — okay, annoying — is that, from what I've read, scholars who vigorously and eloquently proclaim that Jesus existed in the flesh seem to completely ignore the challenges to his existence by literate, educated Gnostics and Pagans *who lived both during the time he was supposed to have lived and during the time the Christian scriptures were written!* So it isn't merely today's "misinformed" scholars or "crackpot" critics who challenge Jesus' existence. *It was also his contemporaries!*

I can imagine a skeptic in Jesus' time challenging a believer to prove Jesus was human:

> Skeptic: If this Jesus of yours is human, I want to meet him, to see him with my own eyes!
> Believer: Well, he isn't here right now. He's away preaching.
> Skeptic: When will he be around here again?
> Believer: I don't know. He roams from one village to another.
> Skeptic: Have you seen him yourself?
> Believer: No, but a cousin of my neighbor said she's seen him.
> Skeptic: Where? When?
> Believer: She didn't say.

Surely the skeptics would have demanded proof of Jesus' existence. **The fact that the skeptics remained skeptical strongly suggests — I am tempted to say proves — that the Jesus believers were unable to offer proof of his existence. The critical question is: Why couldn't the believers during Jesus' three-year teaching stint prove to the non-believers that Jesus was a real, live, flesh-and-blood person when he was still alive?**

In the decades that followed, there being no hard evidence to present to their relentless Gnostic, Pagan, and Jewish critics that Jesus had ever actually lived, the Faithful — during the years between the writing of Mark and Matthew — were in an ever more precarious and vulnerable position. Admitting there was no evidence that the "Savior of Humankind" in whom they devoutly believed had ever existed was unthinkable, for it would have meant the demise of the budding, still unformed Church, whose very survival was increasingly in jeopardy.

Faced with this daunting predicament, would the author of Matthew really have invented the story of the "whatever" power and inserted it into that Gospel? Is the Pope Catholic? Like his Christian compatriots, the author of Matthew would have said or done anything to preserve his precious new religion and the sacred beliefs on which it rested. Inserting a few fictitious but surely well-intentioned words into the Gospel of Matthew paled to a wintry white in comparison to the unspeakable atrocities later Christians committed in defense of their beliefs and promotion of their Church.

And would the early "Christians" have believed this trumped up story of the "whatever" power? Of course they would. They were determined to keep their nascent religion alive, clutching at every straw to defend it against the contemptuous, defamatory verbal, written, and physical attacks of the Jews, Pagans, and Gnostic Christians. They would have accepted the story as credible without a second thought because they devoutly — I would say "desperately" — believed Jesus was the divine Son of God, their sole precious avenue to life everlasting in Heaven. That Jesus had endowed his disciples with this new dramatic "whatever" power would have been a godsend to them, like handing a canteen of cool water to a thirst-crazed wanderer in a desert.

Moreover, the insertion of the "whatever" power into the Gospel of Matthew had two all-important effects almost certainly intended by the author: it reinforced the claim that Jesus exercised the supreme authority of God, and it guaranteed that believers in Jesus would enjoy eternal life in Heaven. Both were essential for the Jesus religion to flourish and endure, as it indeed did.

To successfully market a product, today as well as two thousand years ago, it must offer benefits to the buyer that the competition doesn't. What's more, to attest to the product's high quality, its producer must be seen as reputable, a winner, a champion. Advertising endorsements, like a famous athlete's photo on a box of Wheaties or the Nike checkmark symbol on clothing, give a product accreditation, standing, and legitimacy. When the President of the United States makes a speech, the lectern traditionally displays the presidential seal, a confirmation of his position and its authority. The early Christians needed to attach supreme authority — like a logo — to Jesus' teachings, which the "whatever" statement in Matthew emphatically did. Who else but God's only Son could bestow such a gift? And what a gift it was!

The Turning Point

During the four centuries after Jesus' death the Christian Literalists, as I indicated, were continuously in bitter conflict with the Gnostic Christians. In Rome, in the late 2nd century, the Literalist Bishop Irenaeus composed his massive work *Against Heresies* to discredit his populous Gnostic rivals. In it he derided their allegorical interpretations of the Jesus story as "craftily constructed plausibilities" designed to "draw away the minds of the inexperienced and take them captive". Gnosticism, the work declared, was a conspiracy to deceive the Faithful by "drawing them away under a pretense of superior gnosis" [superior knowledge]. Freke and Gandy in *The Laughing Jesus*[97]: In response, Gnostics accused Literalists of setting up an "imitation church" by replacing the Gnostic understanding of the Jesus myth as a spiritual parable with something utterly banal, but beguilingly simple. Neither side could alter its hard-and-fast dogma without recanting the very beliefs that made them Literalists and Gnostics. It was a standoff. The most either could do was stay their course and pray for the best, and winner take all.

During this same period, Christians were subjected to persecutions of varying intensity and duration by their many enemies. Believing resolutely in the existence of a single all-powerful god, Christians defiantly refused to pay homage to any of the panoply of Pagan deities, including most particularly the exalted gods of the state. For that reason Jesus' followers naturally became pariahs in a society fearful of and dependent upon these gods. Observes Ehrman in *Lost Christianities*[98]: When disasters occurred such as famines, droughts, disease, earthquakes, political setbacks, or economic difficulties — all "obvious" signs the Pagan gods were angry — the Christians were blamed, which by the way conveniently shifted responsibility for these misfortunes away from the Pagan rulers and their Pagan citizenry.

Then the fates unaccountably smiled on the Christian Faithful. It happened wondrously enough during a single decade. Ehrman[99]: "Probably no ten-year period was more important for the fortunes of Christianity than 303-313...That decade saw a shift in Roman imperial policy away from increasingly massive proscription and persecution of Christians to the conversion of Emperor Constantine himself." Devout Christians will, of course, attribute his "conversion" to the intercession of the Holy Spirit. I, on the other hand, attribute it to a simple convergence of self-interests. Constantine needed the Christians to bolster his empirical power, and they needed him to stop their persecution. Harpur in *The Pagan Christ*[100] notes, however, that "Years after he was converted to Christianity, Constantine still worshiped the sun god Helios, as coins and other evidence reveal," clear evidence that his "conversion" had merely been a political ploy to strengthen his control over his empire.

But, say Freke and Gandy in *The Laughing Jesus*[101], the communities of Jesus followers continued to quarrel over doctrine, until in 325, for better or worse, Constantine perceived that, if he could unite and control this horde of squabbling undisciplined Christians — whose numbers by that time had grown into a "whatever"-powered, empire-wide movement that could no longer be ignored — the authoritarian nature of their Church might be just the ticket to shore up his weakened and troubled empire. To that end he convened the First Ecumenical Council of the Catholic Church at a place called Nicaea (possibly today's Iznik, Turkey, but no one knows for sure). At that assemblage he engineered the creation and peremptory adoption of a Christian credo — the Nicene Creed — which today, seventeen hundred years later, is still a bedrock of Catholic belief and a salient part of the Catholic Mass. More important to the future of the Church — and to history — he astoundingly but shrewdly proclaimed Christianity "the religion of the Empire". Freke and Gandy in *The Jesus Mysteries*[102]: To sweeten the pot, he provided vast continuing patronage to those bishops who supported the new Creed, while exiling those who did not. Thus in one amazing stroke Christianity vaulted miraculously — the Faithful again would say "by the power of the Holy Spirit" — over all of its long-time competitors to reign supreme. The tide had turned, and the Christian Church never looked back.

But why should the Church have been concerned with the past when the future was so alluringly bright. The emperor's desire to bring the bishops into the fabric of the state involved a dramatic reversal of their status. His enormous patronage gave them access to huge estates, vast wealth, titles of nobility, and social prestige. By the end of the 4th century, writes Freeman in *The Closing of the Western Mind*[103], the lifestyle of the bishops of Rome had become extravagant, dressing splendidly, riding in carriages, and outdoing kings in the lavishness of their tables.

That all of these events occurred in such a short period is both awesome and in hindsight deplorable, given what followed.

Christianity and the Power of the Church Take Root

Once Christianity became the religion of the Roman Empire, its membership began to swell by leaps and bounds because of the state's preferential treatment of Christians. If you wanted a peaceful and successful life, you became a Christian. Freke and Gandy in *The Jesus Mysteries*[104]: If you resisted, you risked being branded a Pagan dissident — an enemy of the Empire (namely the Emperor) and worse, an enemy of God, which could bring ostracism, excommunication, imprisonment, even death. By the end of the 4th century, writes *Ehrman*[105], fully half of the Roman empire were Christians, thanks in no small part I contend to Christianity's "whatever" power, which would certainly have had some effect on the emperor himself.

To better market itself to the masses, the Church, forgoing any elaborate, grueling apprenticeship and testing associated with certain other religions, simplified the criteria for membership. Anyone who confessed the Nicene Creed, accepted baptism, participated in worship, obeyed the Church hierarchy, and attested to "the one and only truth from the apostles" (as interpreted, of course, by the Church) was confirmed a Christian and therefore saved from Hell. As Ellerbe snidely writes in *The Dark Side of Christian History*[106], such criteria suggest that "to achieve salvation, an ignoramus need only believe without understanding and obey the authorities". And, with all due respect for the 21st-century Christian Faithful, nothing has really changed. These are the same criteria for becoming a Catholic today.

You may unconsciously have passed over the phrase "obeyed the Church hierarchy" in the preceding paragraph, but the Church was fanatically obsessive — and still is — about obedience, especially among the priesthood. It was no small thing. Indeed, it was everything. To the extent to which you obey someone like a traffic cop, your boss, or your priest, they control you. Without obedience there is no control. And without control there is no power.

As I have mentioned, what the early leaders of the Church needed above all to ensure its continued growth and survival was a plausible pretext with which not only to attract followers but to wield power over them and to enforce their continued loyalty and obedience. Preaching Jesus' message that the world would soon come to a fiery end would have won over many easily intimidated Pagans who were conditioned by their ancient cultures to believe in mystical predictions of catastrophic events. But what would really have lured people into the Christian fold was, first, fear of Hell, which the Church at every opportunity described in vivid, terrifying, and exhaustive detail and, second, the Church's promise of salvation from that very Hell. Sounds like the sales pitch of a traveling salesman selling lightning rods who warns persuasively of the horrific dangers of lightning.

For centuries upon centuries human society had functioned on patriarchal systems of subordination and obedience. There had always been leaders — the alpha male, the king, the queen, the pharaoh, the sultan, the emperor — who imposed their authority on their subjects arbitrarily and ruthlessly, answering to no one except perhaps their personal gods...or to no one at all if they claimed they were themselves gods. Allegiance and obedience were forever enforced by the threat and discharge of punishment. The people may not have liked it, but they saw nothing inherently wrong with it. It was the way of the world, the way things had always been done, and neither the common people nor their monarchical leaders expected anything different. For that reason there was no particular reason then or now to vilify the founders of Christianity that the Catholic Church structured itself in the same old hierarchy: one man on top with strict control and obedience filtering down through the system. And the means of control again was traditional: fear of punishment both here and in the hereafter.

Exercising its Jesus-granted "whatever" power, the Church became the source of all knowledge and understanding of the Bible and the Christian Faith. The Faithful were told what to believe, and their Church determined what that was. With the Church's ascension to unbridled empirical power in the 4th century the punishments for disbelief — heresy and blasphemy — became horrendous: floggings, torture, and public executions, among the most gruesome being burnings at the stake. Indeed, a guiding though unwritten tenet of the Church — even Christianity — has always been "where there is sin, there is punishment". All of these punishments, from the least to the most severe, incited fear among the Faithful who were at the total mercy of the clergy. As the centuries passed and the Church's power reached its apex as unchallenged ruler of kingdoms, it took only a word or two of warning from a priest — or a bishop in the case of the nobility — to keep most of the Faithful both spiritually and worldly in line.

Bearing in mind that few people in those times, as I have mentioned, could read or write and that the focus of the Church's recruitment efforts was aimed primarily, but not exclusively, at the illiterate population, the Church took every opportunity in every form of non-written communication — readings aloud at Mass, hymns, frescoes, paintings, murals, statues, symbols, you name it — to enflame fear of Hell, constantly reminding the Faithful, as it still does, that they were born sinners and what the inevitable inescapable penalties for sins were then and are today. Sin was and remains the staple of Christianity. Without sin and the vulture-like shadow of punishment lurking over its shoulder, Christianity as we know it would not exist.

Undoubtedly the words with the greatest controlling influence were and remain those attributed to Jesus and repeated at least once a year to Catholic congregations as part of the scripted readings of scripture: "Whatever you"...the priests..."bind on Earth shall be bound in Heaven, and whatever you loose on Earth shall be loosed in Heaven". I can't help but suspect that hearing those words read by a lector to a congregation gives priests a momentary relishing thrill to realize they have unlimited spiritual power over the congregation seated in front of them. I repeat, unlimited. It cannot but remind priests that they are the very sword of the Lord. During my life (I'm well over 60) I've heard the "whatever" passage countless times in readings of the New Testament at Mass. Its message is unmistakable: Obey the Church or it will send you to Hell...as the song goes, "not just for an hour, not just for a day, not for just a year, but always!" For the ranks of the Faithful this threat was not only credible but in many circumstances traumatizing.

The Church learned quickly that intimidation — a natural by-product of the "whatever" power — not only kept followers in line but encouraged them to donate money with which to build giant cathedrals and other notable Christian structures. These offerings also enabled many clergy, monks, and nuns to live comfortably, some, as history shows, in luxury. Thus the Church's use of fear as a tool of control became increasingly self-serving, indulgent, and addictive.

The Church magnified its power, authority, and control over the Faithful (and, of course, over the preservation of the Church as an institution) by requiring them to confess their sins in order to remove from their souls the blight of their constant misdeeds. Failure to confess was itself branded a sin. Confession had the desired effect of keeping guilt and fear ever visible in each human life. As Spong writes in *The Sins of Scripture*[107], "According to the way the Church has presented the Bible to the Faithful, to know oneself is to know one's own evil, to experience guilt, and finally to stand in need of punishment." The priest who heard one's confession, acting as the Church's self-proclaimed surrogate of Jesus or God, imposed "appropriate" penalties, as they do today. No other person on Earth possesses this same kind of spiritual power over others as a priest hearing a devout believer's confession.

Eventually the Church ritualized the act of confession through the establishment of the Sacrament of Penance, now renamed by the Church as the Sacrament of Reconciliation. Call it what you will, it's still admission of one's sins. For centuries the confession of one's sins had been public, a circumstance that could only have discouraged penitents from revealing sins that would embarrass themselves or others. Aware of this problem, the Church in 1565 introduced the enclosed, private confessional in which the priest sat more or less hidden, godlike, behind a thin curtain or screen only a foot or so from the penitent. During these sessions the penitents revealed, and do so today, in a near-whisper their innermost secrets, things they would tell no one else, even their spouses, family members, and dearest friends, even things they were loath to admit to themselves. The overall result was to make the penitent's experience during confession even more probing, stressful, and fearful...instilling in the penitent a heightened sense of the priest's power over the confessor.

Writes Faulkner in *Supreme Authority*[108], "Looming in the background [of the confessional] is Hell...[Confession] had for centuries been a sinister and intimidating ritual. One's eternity rested on it. If one were lucky enough to die on leaving the confessional box, one's soul would go straight to Heaven. If one died without confessing all of one's mortal sins, one went straight to Hell...The horrors of Hell were driven home to Catholics at every opportunity: the fire, the pain of loss, and the regret at opportunities missed...This was not a game of gotcha by cruel priests in certain backward localities. It was the universal teaching and practice of the Church." The intense secrecy of the confessional, says Ellerbe in *The Dark Side of Christian History*[109], played like a drum on the Faithful's guilt and fear — prerequisites for sustaining the Church's control.

And what about the retired elderly today who regularly attend Mass every morning? Every morning of every day year-round! Why do they do that? Because they're afraid, convinced by the Church that, when they die, which they know is in the offing, they will be convicted in the Final Judgment as sinners and be sent to Hell. They go to Mass every day to have their Get-Into-Heaven-Free card punched. Their daily attendance shows God how Christian they are: "Look, God. See what a good person, what a good Christian I am?" Each Mass, each figurative punch in their ticket, is a fervent prayer to Jesus to save them from the eternal fires of Hell.

Bishop Spong in *The Sins of Scripture*[110] addressed the role that fear plays in the human state: "From the moment in which human beings achieved the dramatic step into self-consciousness, the evolutionary struggle to survive became primary, carrying with it enormous emotional consequences. Self-conscious human beings knew the dangers of existence in a way no other creatures ever had. It was as if human life were hardwired to endure the traumas of an existence in which danger was always anticipated and unrelieved fear was a part of what it meant to be human." As Henry David Thoreau famously observed in *Walden*, "The mass of [humans] lead lives of quiet desperation." Thus, to be human has always meant to be conscious of and on guard against predators and other external enemies. Armed with the "whatever" power, the Church over the centuries, intentionally or otherwise, evolved into one of these predators, the likes of which would not be seen again until Marxists-Leninists overthrew the Russian monarchy in 1917.

Fear is the central mechanism and overriding message of Christian dogma. The common appellation "God-fearing Christian" speaks volumes about that dogma. As the popular novelist Daniel Silva astutely observed in *The Kill Artist*[111], "Fear is the only emotion that matters." Fear is the common link among all Christians of whatever denomination. Says Bishop Spong in Jesus for the *Non-Religious*[112]: "Fear of death terrifies the self-conscious human being perhaps more than anything else."

Christianity is all about FEAR. Fear of sin, fear of confession, fear of the Church, fear of God, fear of one's Final Judgment, and worst of all fear of being condemned forever to Hell. No surprise there, because the designers of Christianity took their lead from the Old Testament*, one of whose keystones is fear:

> Proverbs 8:10   Fear of God is the beginning of wisdom.
> Proverbs 14:17   Fear of God is the source of life.
> Sirach 30:16   Fear of God is the beginning of his love.

*I must add here an observation which the devout will despise, but the truth must out. Christians have a habit — deplorable in my opinion — of accepting as true whatever statements are made in the Old Testament. For example, Leviticus 17:18: "The Lord said to Moses, 'Speak to the Israelites and tell them, I, the Lord, am your God'." "Well," say the devout, "if it's in Leviticus, it must be true. After all, it's the Holy Bible!" Common sense will tell you that attestations that God spoke to anyone are by their very nature unprovable and therefore qualify as nothing more than hearsay legends and myths. Nevertheless, much of Catholic dogma is based on the Old Testament, which is why the Old Testament was incorporated into the Bible in the first place. Moreover, the Catholic Mass regularly quotes from Old Testament passages, passages that allegedly foreshadow Jesus life, lending these quotations an aura of unqualified truth. But there's no proof that these quotations are true. No proof at all. My own belief (which I cannot prove) is that most (90%) of the Old Testament is nothing more than legends, folklore, and myth. Strike me dead, if you want, but that is what I believe, nor have I ever found any "facts" to dispute that belief.

The Catholic Church and its spin-offs have so frightened their Faithful with the horror-filled imagery of Hell that virtually all Christians are afraid...scared to death, as it were...to die, worried that their sins will consign them to Satan's fiery lair. The Church has many of its followers so intimidated that even the *thought* of sinning is a sin! But it's no use; the Faithful still sin. All of us "sin". It's unavoidable. It's a human condition, but not because of Adam's legendary fall. It's the way God made us, which has nothing to do with a mythical Garden of Eden.

Today the threat of being burned at the stake has thankfully retreated into the horrific past. Outspoken defiance of the Christian Church now brings at most excommunication. But the message is essentially the same: adhere to the doctrine enunciated by the Church or take a hike and lose the Church's promise of salvation in the hereafter.

But isn't there a better non-intimidating way to *encourage* rather than *dictate* Christian behavior? Not according to the Church. From its inception the Church has deliberately, "with malice aforethought" as lawyers would say, employed fear as a means of exercising control over the Faithful. This continuing reinforcement, says Faulkner in *Supreme Authority*[113], "promotes passivity in the members", which is exactly its purpose. Control, like an electric generator, produces power in equal amounts: a little control gives a little power, lots of control — lots of power, absolute control — absolute power. Nothing is more absolute than the awesome fear of spending an eternity in the fires of Hell.

"At the Most Precious Blood parish in Dublin," said Reverend Thomas McCarthy to a Boston Globe reporter in 2005, "parishioners over age thirty say they remember when their church, which seats 1,700, was packed for all four Sunday Masses... There were fierce crowds coming back then. The message was clear: *Come to Mass or go to Hell.*"

And where did this absolute power propel the Church? Let's take a look.

Despotism

Tim Wallace-Murphy, psychologist and historian, in *Cracking the Symbol Code: Revealing the Secret Heretical Messages within Church and Renaissance Art*[114]: Despite being a religion based upon the teachings of "the Prince of Peace", the Catholic Church over the centuries has left in its wake a trail of repressive, institutionalized terror that reached its perfection in the Inquisition, centuries of war and brutality, and two thousand years of institutionalized anti-Semitism which created a sustained climate of bigotry and hatred that culminated in the Holocaust.

The works of scholars describe the Catholic Church's cruel unrestrained rise to ultimate power and the vast devastation which that rise caused:

> Freke and Gandy in *Jesus and the Lost Goddess*[115]: "With the full might of the Roman state behind them, Christian Literalists waged a barbaric war against Paganism and Christian Gnosticism, pulling down temples and libraries, burning books as well as dissidents, and plunging Western civilization into the Dark Ages," which lasted a thousand years, from the 5th through the 15th century.

> The famous Library of Alexandria in Egypt with its precious, massive, irreplaceable collection of scrolls on every known subject was burned, destroying literally centuries of accumulated knowledge and wisdom.

> Osman in *Christianity: An Ancient Egyptian Religion*[118]: All writings that did not agree with the Roman Church's dogma were regarded as heretical. All religious teachers who disagreed with the orthodox doctrines were punished. Throughout the Dark Ages only the Bible and the teachings of the Church of Rome were allowed as sources of knowledge and education.

> Ellerbe in *The Dark Side of Christian History*[119]: The Church's actions had a devastating impact on society. Activity in the fields of medicine, technology, science, education, history, art, and commerce all but collapsed. Most of what defines civilization disappeared.[120]

> "Orthodox Christians, believing that all aspects of the flesh should be reviled, discouraged washing as much as possible. Toilets and indoor plumbing disappeared. Disease became commonplace as sanitation and hygiene deteriorated."[121]

> "The vast network of roads that had enabled transportation and communication fell into neglect and would remain so until almost the 19th century."[122]

> "The losses in science were monumental, setting humanity back as much as two millennia in its scientific understanding."[123]

> "The rise of the Christian Church coincided with a severe economic collapse throughout the western world. The Church did little to encourage trade and stigmatized lending money at interest, even intervening to free a debtor from liabilities."[124]

The Church amassed immense wealth during these centuries. It made money "by collecting revenues from imperial rulers, by confiscating property as the result of court judgments, by selling the remission of sins (indulgences), by selling ecclesiastical offices, and sometimes simply taking land by force".[125] Church-held lands eventually constituted between one-quarter to one-third of western Europe.

As the sway of the Roman Empire steadily weakened, the Church, by skillful manipulation and intimidation, gradually supplanted Roman rule over the political and economic structure of Europe. Thus, when the Empire finally expired, it was replaced de facto by the Catholic Church, whose own power and presence had become firmly rooted all over Europe.

Wallace-Murphy in *Cracking the Symbol Code*[126]: "The new priesthood of the Christian religion erected a temporal power base of great wealth and enormous political influence...and claimed absolute authority over all who lived under its sway, be they peasants, priests, nobles, kings, or emperors."

"The Church became the principal lawmaker for the newly converted peoples of Europe. Their customary laws were given written form by the clergy, who were the scribes, codifiers, and final arbiters against whose decisions there was no appeal. Being the self-appointed and sole literate guardians of history, the priests wrote down the oral legends and myths of the various tribes, omitting all that was offensive to Christian teaching, retaining this, adding that, subtly changing people's ancient histories and creating the mold for a new, essentially Christian culture."[127] Soviet rulers, moved by similar motives, did the very same thing after they gained power in Russia in 1917.

"Education was restricted to the clergy to such an extent that the first Holy Roman Emperor, Charlemagne (742-814), could barely write his name."[127] Sharon Kay Penman wrote in her thoroughly researched historical novel, *When Christ and His Saints Slept*[128] that in the 12th century "many noblemen of high rank scorned reading as a clerk's skill".

"By restricting access to books, education, and understanding, the Church revealed its real objective — absolute power and control over kings, emperors, and princes; over territories, peoples, and individuals; over everyone in this world and their entrance to the next."[129]

"Augustine of Hippo [Saint Augustine] defined heresy as *the distortion of a revealed truth by a believer or an unbeliever.* The pivotal term, *a revealed truth, was defined by the Church hierarchy as what the Church itself had declared to be revealed truth.* This self-serving definition was used by Church leaders to establish a total monopoly on all access to the sacred. The Church's very need to survive caused it to refute anything it viewed as heretical with increasing venom and led to the rise of dogmatic statements of belief that papered over areas of dispute with dictatorial rigidity. The growing and ever more powerful Roman Church brooked no rivals, either within Christianity or in the Pagan world, and campaigned vigorously and effectively for the closure of temples and centers of worship of rival faiths, then hijacked these long-established sacred sites for its own use."[130]

A deplorable saga in the Church's history was the burning of so-called witches. "The Church's Witch Trials took place primarily in Europe from about 1450 to the middle of the 18th century. Accusations of malicious, harmful Satanic witchcraft were taken quite seriously. The victims of these charges were usually, but not exclusively, women. Older women and widows who lived alone were typical suspects. Scholars estimate the number of people tortured, imprisoned, and sometimes executed ranged between 100,000 to over one million. Most agree that at least 40,000 were executed, while some claim that count is no less than 100,000."[131]

Alfred North Whitehead, formerly the Chair of Philosophy at Harvard University, succinctly capsulized the Church's impact: "Christian theology has been the greatest disaster in the history of the human race."[132]

Discovering the full magnitude of the Catholic Church's evil history since its formation in the 1st century is like learning that your father, whom you have loved, respected, and looked up to your whole life, was years ago a serial killer who kidnapped, tortured, raped, and killed a dozen or more women or that your mother, whom you hold as dear as your father, was during her twenties a member of a violent, ruthless band of anti-government terrorists who blew up government buildings wantonly killing hundreds of employees as well as dozens of babies and children in day-care centers. But your parents, now older, enlightened, and contrite about their past evil doings, ask your forgiveness because their heinous deeds were long ago. Your parents say they are not the same persons who committed those crimes; it was another age, another era; things were different then; etc.

Yes, admit devout, dutifully forgiving Catholic Christians, the Church committed heinous crimes against humanity, but the Church, they would say, believed it was doing the right thing at the time. Intent was therefore its own expiation. Intent? Expiation? Hello! The Church's intent was to inflict punishments, vicious unspeakable punishments solely to enforce the Church's will over the "sinners"...the ultimate undisguised aim being to preserve the Church's standing as the ultimate, undeniable power on Earth.

But I will admit that the world was different then. Brutality was common. Misery was common. Disease and death were common. The Church, would say the apologists, simply patterned itself after the monarchical world in which kings and queens were unchallengeable and supreme in their power over the lives of their dutiful subjects. There was by custom a permanent and irresistible hierarchy of power and control flowing down from the monarchs through their realms' populations, demanding their obedience and monetary contributions to sustain the monarchies and punishing those who objected. The Church therefore was behaving only in a manner consistent with the times.

But ask yourself: Would the Jesus of the New Testament have approved of the Church's numberless despicable atrocities committed in his name over the centuries under the aegis of the "whatever" power?

If you are a faithful Christian, you believe that Jesus was the actual divine Son of God and performed miracles, cast out demons, cured the sick and the lame, and brought the dead back to life. You therefore must also believe that Jesus, if he had the God-given power to do all of these things, would surely have had the power to foresee the mournful trail of countless corpses over which the Church, armed with the "whatever power", would mercilessly trod in its manic quest for enduring supreme dominion. That Jesus had the power of foresight was evidenced in Mark 13:2 where he is reported to have predicted the destruction of the Temple in Jerusalem, and it was according to archaeologists destroyed. He also reportedly foresaw his own crucifixion. So the question remains: Would Jesus have granted the "whatever" power knowing the tumultuous pain, suffering, and devastation that would ensue...knowing the colossal evil the Church would inflict on humankind the world over? I think not. Moreover, humans being the flawed creatures they are, one needn't have been a farsighted prophet to foresee how grievously Jesus' "whatever" power would be misused.

The Christian Church came into being guided by Jesus' message of love, mercy, freedom, and equality but quickly morphed into a self-perpetuating, horrendously authoritarian monster that ruled a despotic empire. Verily the Church became the Fifth Horseman of the Apocalypse, coming to power by way of a tyrannical revolution, subjugating by force of arms and terror all competing religions, imposing its creed, however true, with threats, violence, and torture, and denying generations of countless human beings the right to think their own thoughts and find their personal route to spiritual salvation.

For that very reason there can be no doubt that Jesus never — I repeat *never* — granted a "whatever" power to his disciples! The self-serving contention in the Gospel of Matthew, *written a generation or two after Jesus' death*, that Jesus did so is a complete fabrication motivated obviously by the then Church leadership's desperate crusade for power...the wherewithal to triumph over its opponents and expand, unify, and above all control its membership.

> *I cannot quit this chapter on forgiveness without mentioning that the Catholic Church, exercising its "whatever" power, has for centuries in one notable case judiciously ignored Jesus' compelling edict to forgive one's enemies. To wit: The Church in the 17th century persecuted Galileo and Copernicus for their heretical theory that the Earth was not the center of the universe. Three centuries later, in 1993, the Church finally forgave Galileo. Copernicus has not been forgiven to this day.* [133]

CHAPTER 4

Messing with the Holy Bible

Many Christians who attend Bible classes can proudly recite by rote (meaning "without understanding or thought") memorable passages verbatim in both Testaments and the names of all their books in their proper order. But few of them critically comprehend how contradictory, unreliable, and mythical — yes, *mythical* — the Bible is. And when challenged to acknowledge its contradictions, their usual response is, "I have my beliefs. You have yours. Let's just leave it at that!" Indeed, explaining or defending the Bible can be intimidating because most people know so little about its origins, and any suggestion that the Bible is not the Word of God frightens them.

The intent of the Gospels was clearly stated in John 20:30. "These [words] are written that you may believe that Jesus is the Messiah, the Son of God." These texts therefore were not scholarly descriptions of his life by non-partisan historians with no particular axe to grind. On the contrary, the Gospels, written by devout believers, were intrinsically biased. They were meant to *persuade*, to *plant within the minds of their readers the seeds of belief in Jesus' divinity*, to *advertise*, if you will, *the advent of his Church on Earth*. Given their avowed purpose, one must necessarily view their accuracy, completeness, and objectivity with skepticism.

How about this for a conversation stopper? How many of you Christian Faithful know for a fact what the last of the Ten Commandments really is? Do you? No, it's not "You shall not covet your neighbor's wife". It's "Don't boil a young goat in the milk of its mother." Believe it or not, this prohibition in Exodus 34:26 is the *official* tenth commandment from the only set of stone tablets that the Old Testament claims were called "The Ten Commandments". You don't believe me? Check it out in your Bible.

> The first time Moses came down from Mount Sinai he merely recited a lengthy list of rules of moral behavior (Exodus 20:2-17). They were not engraved on stone tablets and were not called "the ten commandments".
>
> The second time Moses went up the mountain he came down with the first set of stone tablets on which God had written commandments. Again these were not identified as "the ten commandments" (Exodus 31:18). But Moses, angered by his people's

praying to a golden calf, petulantly destroyed the tablets (Exodus 32:19).

The third time Moses went up Mount Sinai, he came down with the second set of tablets on which God, a second time, had inscribed the "Ten Commandments". It was the tenth of these that proscribed boiling a young goat in its mother's milk (Exodus 34:14-26).

This third list differs obviously from the recitation in Exodus 20, but it is only this list, what we might call the "official" version, which the Old Testament calls the "Ten Commandments": "And he [God] wrote upon the tables the words of the covenant, the Ten Commandments" (Exodus 34:28).

Do you really think the Bible is the Word of God?

I never knew about the "goat" commandment until I undertook my research for this book. The reason I never knew about it is that the Church never publicized it. Yet, how could the Church publicize it without exposing the Commandments — and the Church — to ridicule?

(One Internet site suggests that this commandment sought to prevent Israelites from copying idolatrous pagan rituals. Sounds good to me.)

Are the Statements Attributed to Jesus in the New Testament Really His?

I must ask, as any reasonable person should, whether Jesus actually made the statements attributed to him in the New Testament. (Don't get all riled up, now. Relax and try to keep an open mind, at least until you finish reading the next few paragraphs. Then you can throw your tantrum.) The obvious and unquestionable truth is "No". It was not Jesus who said these things but rather the authors of the Gospels...authors who to a man never claimed to have met Jesus or heard his preaching in person. That modern copyists put Jesus' alleged statements in quotation marks is no help at all. In fact, the quotation marks are misleading, as they lend an undeserved aura of authenticity to the statements. The crucial question therefore is "How did these authors know Jesus made the statements they attributed to him in their gospels?"

Since none of the Gospel authors was an eyewitness, they had to have trusted someone else's record or recollection. Were there scribes with Jesus throughout his ministry recording his preachings word for word on clay tablets or parchments?

Were there people with remarkable memories who listened to him and later (hours? days? months? years?) repeated verbatim what he said so that scribes could make a record of it for posterity?

"Books — or actually scrolls of papyrus — were relatively rare [in Palestine in Jesus' time]," biblical scholar Craig L. Blomberg is quoted as saying in *The Case for Christ*.[1] [But not, I gather, rare among that thin stratum of Palestinian society that was educated and literate.] "Therefore education, learning, worship, teaching in religious communities — all this was done by word of mouth. Rabbis became famous for having the entire Old Testament committed to memory. So it would have been well within the capability of Jesus' disciples to have committed much more to memory than appears in all four gospels put together — and to have passed it along accurately."

Really? I don't think so. Jesus' disciples were decidedly not rabbis! Therefore, why would memorizing what Jesus said be "well within the disciples' capability"? Nor does the New Testament even hint at the disciples' ability to memorize anything. Furthermore, it goes without saying that not all rabbis in Jesus' time were capable of memorizing huge verbatim tracts of scripture. I'd venture to say only a few had this capability. Blomberg's statement is pure wishful self-serving thinking, striving to prove what cannot be proven — that the disciples, all eyewitnesses to Jesus teachings and final days, could recite later verbatim what Jesus had said to them. Nice try, Blomberg, but your claim simply won't stand.

Jesus, as I said, was a nobody, a poor traveling beggar-prophet with no possessions other than the clothes on his back, no different than other wandering prophets in Judah during his lifetime. He was so much a nobody that, as I related above, there's no historical record of his very existence. Now think about this. Jesus was so low-profile, so insignificant, that historians of his day knew nothing about him, yet writers decades and centuries later knew all about him. How was this possible? The answer is easy: his followers, who were few and far between when he died, repeated to others what they later recalled him saying. But their recountings were only as accurate as their memories. Furthermore, his followers and others with every good intention surely made up stories about him and his teachings, expanding on them, adding this or that and deleting this or that in each telling as they saw fit, and borrowing legends associated with earlier gods to ennoble the image of Jesus to make the greatest, most positive and most lasting impression on their listeners and to seed and nourish their belief in him. It's no surprise that the stories about Jesus mirror those of earlier gods; his followers simply transferred them wholesale. How else to explain the surprising similarities?

Moreover, according to the Gospels his ministry was remarkably brief, lasting only three years. His teachings thus became important and historic *only in retrospect*, indeed decades later. Why would anyone have kept verbatim records of what this "nobody" was saying as he said it? The Gospels tell us that even his closest disciples didn't fully understand who he was or what to make of him until near the end of his ministry. Indeed, if you believe the Gospels, they weren't really sure who he was until he appeared to them in the upper room after his resurrection.

The hard fact is there's no possible way — no way at all — to know whether the quoted statements in the four Gospels were actually his or someone putting words in his mouth. Remember that very few people in Jesus' time could read and write, so teachings were of necessity passed from one person to another verbally. At the same time, however, Jesus' time was ironically a highly literate period among the small fraction of that society one would classify as the intelligentsia. Historians one after another in that era, as I have noted, were recording events over the preceding centuries, so there was no shortage of talented writers who had a facility with words and could easily have interpolated the verbal and any written iterations of Jesus teachings to suit their own and others' beliefs and agendas. Again...there's no way of knowing to what degree these writers altered and "improved" the stories they heard about Jesus or, more important, whether those stories were in fact true to begin with.

As Michael White writes in *From Jesus to Christianity*[2], "The Gospels fall into the ancient literary category known as 'lives', such as were written of Alexander the Great and other famous people. It was quite common in such literature to embellish the story with fanciful or romantic details. Many times the sources were oral traditions, legends, and exaggerations that grew up to fit the fame or persona of the character in later times. It became common in the later 'lives' of Alexander the Great to attribute his birth to a miraculous conception, accompanied by a number of signs and omens, all of which were to demonstrate that this was to be a person with divine gifts and powers."

"A similar story," writes White, "later crept into some versions of the life of Augustus [the first Roman emperor]. Such hyperbole clearly comes from a time well after Augustus died, when his accomplishments had become legendary, and he had become an object of worship in the imperial cult."

"In like manner, the Gospels were written as 'lives' of Jesus as the founder of the Christian movement. They are thus products of later reflection on his life in light of the importance that later believers placed on him [my underlinings]. They are, in that sense, expressions of the faith of those early Christians who told and retold the story of Jesus in the later decades of the 1st century."[3] "The result was growing diversity [in the retellings] from region to region within Christianity. As time went on, diversity became more and more of an issue as some Christians, at least, realized they were not all telling the same stories."[4]

Are the Statements Attributed to Jesus
in the New Testament Unique?

Whether the Bible is or is not the Word of God, a salient question that researchers have posed — and answered — is whether Jesus' teachings were *unique*. The answer is an unqualified "No".

> The Golden Rule is clearly a borrowed gem, say Tim Leedom and Maria Murdy in *The Book Your Church Doesn't Want You to Read*[5]. Chinese, Greek, and Roman sages had preached and practiced it for centuries before the Sermon on the Mount was delivered.
>
> Freke and Gandy in *The Jesus Mysteries*[6]: "Jesus' instruction in Matthew to 'Treat others as you wish to be treated' was nothing new. It was a perennial and ubiquitous precept found in nearly all religious traditions. For example, among the sayings of the Pagan philosopher Sextus is, 'Such as you wish your neighbor to be to you, such also be to your neighbor'."
>
> The scholar Joseph Warshauer, quoted in Harpur's *The Pagan Christ*[7]: "Every one of Jesus' answers to Satan in the temptation in the wilderness comes from Deuteronomy (Old Testament). The principle of evil in the New Testament is fully paralleled in Zoroastrian (Persian) and Buddhist literature and the Egyptian scriptures."
>
> Thomas L. Thompson, teacher of biblical studies at the University of Copenhagen, in *The Messiah Myth: Near Eastern Roots of Jesus and David*[8]; "The central sayings attributed to Jesus in the Gospels were spoken by many figures of ancient literature. Many of these sayings were, in fact, well-known in Jesus' time and can be dated centuries earlier than the New Testament. Evidence for the prehistory of these sayings is so abundant and well attested that they can be traced through a continuous literary tradition over millennia."
>
> Harpur's *The Pagan Christ* quotes Madame H.P. Blavatsky in *Isis Unveiled*[9]: "In the four Gospels there is not a single narrative, sentence, or peculiar expression whose parallel can not be found in some older doctrine of philosophy."

Does the fact that Jesus' teachings were not unique mean they were untrue and have no value in our lives? Certainly not. Whether Sextus or Jesus said, "Love your neighbor as yourself," the message is the same and as true and as meaningful to living a "good" life. But, to repeat, that teaching like others was not unique to Jesus.

The Missing Years

According to the New Testament, Jesus' whereabouts from his early teens until he began his ministry at the age of thirty are unknown. The traditional view — the natural default position — of the Church is that Jesus resided in Israel during the "lost years" and that nothing was written about that period of his life because he did nothing noteworthy to report.[10] Wherever he was during those some seventeen years, he acquired during that period the profound, insightful philosophy he preached during his three-year ministry in Israel culminating in his crucifixion. How did he acquire this philosophy? Most of the Faithful will answer that it was by revelation from God and the Holy Spirit. I, on the other hand, contend that Jesus was a God-inspired common man with uncommon insights who, conforming to the practices of the Hebrew communities of his time, gained his knowledge in school — either in Israel or abroad.

The School Theory

When a Jewish boy in Jesus' time reached the age of 16 or 17, his parents were required by Judaic law to place him in a recognized school. Robert Feather in *The Secret Initiation of Jesus at Qumran*[11] makes a compelling case that Jesus' parents enrolled him as an apprentice in the Essene community at Qumran. Flavius Josephus, a noted historian of the time, wrote that it was the custom of the Qumran community to accept children at an age "when their spirit is still malleable enough to easily accept instruction".[12] Writes Feather: "That the Gospels and historical evidence tell us almost nothing of Jesus' formative years is not surprising if those years were spent at Qumran."[13]

In accordance with the Qumran Community Rule (the Essene Manual of Discipline) Jesus would have undergone ten years of study of the ancient texts and exclusive works of the Qumran Essenes, their philosophy, rituals, and strict rules of behavior.[14] "Each year of study, discussion, and interaction with the fundamentals of Israel's heritage culminated with a compulsory period of twenty-five days of total isolation in the desert wilderness of Judaea."[15]

After these years of study and preparation, he would have been tested on the Essene laws and beliefs. Following a year's probation, he would have been tested again. If he passed the second exam, he would have been placed on probation for yet another year. Only then, if he were nominated, would he have been voted into membership in the Essene Brotherhood and be sworn in with an oath of allegiance. It is significant that an apprentice could not complete his Essene training and education before the age of thirty, the age, according to the Gospels, when Jesus began his ministry.

If Jesus "graduated" from Qumran at the age of thirty, "he would have been immersed in the teachings of the Qumran Essenes, and their protocols would have been engraved on his conscious and subconscious minds"[16]. Thereafter, rather than remain at Qumran, he would by his own choice have become an "urban Essene", going with a small group of followers from village to village to preach the basic message of the Essenes and the Torah, enriched by his own sharp intellect.

A strong indication, writes Feather, that Jesus had been a member of the Qumran Essenes appears in Mark 1:21-27, where the Gospel describes Jesus' first public appearance in the synagogue at Capernaum: "The people were astounded at his doctrine; for he taught them as one that had authority, and not as the scribes." Says Feather, "I believe Mark 1:21-27 is one of the most telling passages in demonstrating Jesus' original membership in the Essene community." What is more, most of the geographic activities of Jesus are centered on Qumran: his supposed birthplace, baptism, ministry, and death.[17] Qumran is about fifteen miles from Jerusalem and Bethlehem.

Not all biblical scholars and Christian theologians accept Jesus' close association with the Qumran Essenes, but as Feather points out, "The more [that] emerging information from the Dead Sea Scrolls is examined and existing ancient texts are reevaluated, the more apparent it becomes that the hotbed of spiritual industry bubbling away at Qumran was a cauldron from which were cast many templates for early Christian ideas."[18] Indeed, Jesus' teachings resonate with Essene philosophy.

Writes Feather: "There are so many examples in which Jesus' own characteristics and teaching are parallel to and often congruent with those of the Essene community but are not reflected in the normative Jewish experience of his time that it becomes irresistible — if the accounts in the Christian Scriptures of Jesus' words and views are genuine and not those of later redactors — to assume he was once a member of the Qumran Essenes." Among the examples of the many connections between Jesus and the Essenes are the following:

> According to Mark 2:18-22, Matthew 9:14-17, and Luke 5:33-39, Jesus, a self-proclaimed devout Jew, did not observe the national feast days that were the letter of Jewish law and tradition, whereas the Qumran Essenes "followed a different calendar and would have observed these festivals on different days".

> In Matthew 5:22 Jesus is reported to have said, Whoever insults his brother shall be liable to the "council" (Greek, "*Sunédrio*"). He could not have been referring to the Jewish High Court, the Sanhedrin, because this type of offense — insults — did not fall within the purview of its jurisdiction. But within the Qumran-Essene

community insulting someone would have been heard by the community's "council".

In a letter to the Roman Emperor Trajan around 112, Pliny the Younger mentions Christians singing a hymn at dawn to Jesus. Singing a dawn hymn was a Qumran-Essene custom described in one of the scrolls, not a Jewish convention.[19]

Jesus' philosophy of "turning the other cheek" reported in Matthew 5:38-39 and Luke 6:29 was cited in the Essene Community Rule but was previously unknown in the Hebrew Scriptures and conflicts with the Jewish teaching of an "eye for an eye".[20]

Jesus preached, as did the Essenes, against divorce, a position alien to Jewish groups of his time.[21]

Like the Qumran Essenes, Jesus despised the Pharisees and Sadducees.[22]

As Feather notes, Jesus' message and teachings were mainstream monotheism, consistent with the devout traditions of the Qumran Essenes, who strove to return their religion to its essential roots.[23]

Would Jesus' being guided and nurtured by the Essenes weaken the import and validity of his teachings? Of course not. His teachings are inherently profound and valuable, no matter their origin. The resilient Faithful, however, insisting that Jesus was the divine Son of God and disregarding evidence to the contrary, will loudly chorus that Jesus received his philosophy directly from God, not from some "weird" Jewish sect in the desert.

The Training-Abroad Theory

There are numerous books by respected scholars who have visited India and Tibet detailing Jesus' supposedly documented travels there to study Eastern religions until he was thirty years old. I won't elaborate their testaments, which seem remarkably credible. If you're interested, here are three: probably the most famous is *The Lost Years of Jesus: The Life of Saint Issa*, translated by Nicolas Notovitch (versions have been published a number of times under different titles); *The Lost Years of Jesus: Documentary Evidence of Jesus' 17-Year Journey to the East* by Elizabeth Clare Prophet; and *The Mystical Life of Jesus* by psychic Sylvia Browne. Still other scholars contend Jesus spent time in Ireland and Europe. His putative travels abroad are becoming a field of widening research and publications.

Of course, none of the three alternative hypotheses — he remained at home, he apprenticed at Qumran, he traveled abroad — has yet to be proven.

The Veritable Word of God?

To true believers the Bible is the be-all and end-all of the Christian Faith...the foundation, the very bedrock of their religion. Without the Bible, without the four Gospels of the New Testament, they would have nothing on which to base their Faith. Within the Gospels' remarkably few pages rests the entire story, the sole repository, of Jesus' life and teachings. Christianity's utter dependence upon the New Testament, however, renders Christians' claims to its sacredness suspiciously self-serving, just like a poker player's bold assertion, after wagering all his chips, that he has the winning hand. How does he know he has the winning hand? Well, he *must* have the winning hand, he says, because if he doesn't he'll lose everything. But assertions don't win poker hands. It's only when all the cards are exposed on the table that a winner is determined. By the same token, just because the Faithful need the Bible to be the Word of God doesn't mean it is. So let me display my cards and let them speak for themselves.

Card 1: By Vote

It may shock a good many of my readers who are ignorant of the Bible's own history — as I was before I conducted my research — that the Bible was assembled by vote, guided naturally in the Church's partisan view by the will of the Holy Spirit. (The bishops would have said, "Since we voted for this text, it means the Holy Spirit wanted this text in the canon.") It's daunting to realize that, as Ehrman points out in *Lost Christianities*[24], "If some other form of Christianity had won the early struggles for dominance, the familiar doctrines of Christianity might never have become the standard belief of millions of people, including the belief that there is only one God, that he is the creator, and that Christ his son is both human and divine." The other contenders were the Marcionites (they spurned all things Jewish), Ebionite (they believed that Jesus had not preexisted, was not born of a virgin, and was not divine), and the Gnostics. In the end the votes were counted, and the New Testament, more or less as we know it today, was born.

Card 2: Non-Apostolic

In *The Case for Christ*[25], its author, Lee Strobel, interviewing biblical scholar Craig Blomberg, asked, "Is it really possible [for] an intelligent, critically thinking person [to] believe that the four gospels were written by the people whose names have been attached to them?" Blomberg, a devout Christian and recognized as an authority on the biographies of Jesus, replied, "The answer is yes."

But then he did an immediate and perplexing about-face. He said, "It's important to acknowledge that strictly speaking, the gospels are anonymous." What, you may ask as I did, does "strictly speaking" mean? According to the *Cambridge Dictionary of American Idioms* (Cambridge University Press, 2003), it means "complete accuracy" — *They're still married, strictly speaking, but they've been living apart for years.*

Ignoring his "strictly speaking" statement as if he hadn't made it, Blomberg went on to explain that it was the uniform tradition of the early Church — and evidently his — that the Apostle Matthew authored the first gospel, that John Mark, a companion of Peter, authored the second, and that Luke, known as Paul's "beloved physician", authored the third. "Uniform tradition" means "what early generations believed". It doesn't refer to what serious historians commonly refer to as *facts*, just *beliefs*. Moreover, "There are," said Blomberg, "no known competitors for these three gospels."

Is Blomberg really saying that these were the only candidates as authors of these gospels? That's patently absurd! If the authors, as he said, were strictly speaking anonymous, it means we *strictly speaking* don't know who they were. In that case the statement that there are "no known competitors" is nonsensical. [You can see why I get up tight when I read such drivel from respected biblical scholars!]

He went on to say, "John is the only gospel about which there is some question about authorship...The name of the author isn't in doubt — it's certainly John. The question is whether it was John the apostle or a different John." Naturally there is no proof either way.

Contesting Blomberg's views on the authors of the Gospels, the Church and most scholars assert that not one of the books in the New Testament was written by an eyewitness or a companion to an eyewitness to the events in Jesus' life.[26] According to *New Advent*[27], the titles of the four gospels were assigned to the texts no earlier than the first part of that 2nd century, which means the Gospels lack an apostolic imprimatur. More to the point, their respective authors are indeed wholly anonymous.

Why then, contrary to Blomberg's claim, were the authors of these works personified as Mark, Matthew, Luke, and John? Because in the 2nd century, the Literalists, in knock-down-drag-out competition with Gnostic Christians, were in dire need of apostolic authority to backstop their claims to be the one and only "orthodox" religion. They therefore unilaterally and arbitrarily attributed these books to the apostles Matthew and John and to Mark and Luke, the latter two, as I said, reputedly close companions of the apostles Peter and Paul respectively. Whether the Literalists knowingly lied about or earnestly believed in these attributions can never be known. Most biblical scholars today have abandoned these identifications for lack of reliable evidence.[28]

Clearly the primary criterion for selecting texts for inclusion in the New Testament was whether authorship could be attributed to an Apostle. There was, of course, no way in 1545, when the Council of Trent assembled the Bible as we know it today, to confirm such attribution, which was strictly a presumption based on (a) self-serving interpretation of a text and (b) tradition, that is, on what earlier Church leaders had believed. Simply because they believed in something did not, of course, make that something true.

Assigning authorship of a Gospel to one of the Apostles was critical, as it lent to the text necessary sacred authority. Texts whose Apostolic origin could not be reasonably established were easily and quickly dropped from consideration for inclusion in the canon. Thus the presumption of authority preceded the naming of the Gospels as Matthew, Mark, Luke, and John, and the naming in turn established the books' authority. Over time, the very inclusion of these books in the New Testament established by itself their unquestioned apostolic authority...and still does, as evidenced by the reverence the Church and the Faithful — and American courts of law which use the Bible for oath-taking — pay to the Gospels.

What is really irksome is that the Catholic Church for centuries and to date has known full well that the identities of the authors of the Gospels were at the very least debatable, if not anonymous, but has kept silent about it lest the Faith of the Faithful be weakened...and with it, of course, the Church's power over them. Today, hundreds of Catholic churches the world over feature stained-glass windows, paintings, tapestries, and sculptures depicting representations of the "authors" of the Gospels: Saint Matthew, Saint Mark, Saint Luke, and Saint John. And the Faithful who attend these churches and venerate the art works are none the wiser. They are led to believe, and do, that the authors of the Gospels were among Jesus' original apostles. That the Church has not made a clean breast of this indecent charade should shame every member of the Faithful. Indeed, that the Church allows and encourages the Faithful to pray to these anonymous individuals is ludicrous!

Card 3: Creation of a Self-Serving Canon

To wrest Christianity away from the Gnostic Christians and build a centralized religion based on a common dogma, the Literalist bishops needed to counteract the influence of a large number of "pernicious" Gnostic gospels in circulation at the time. Write Freke and Gandy in *The Jesus Mysteries*[29], by the 2nd century different Christian communities had adopted different texts as sacred. Ellerbe in *The Dark Side of Christian History*[30]: "As late as 450 [decades after the canon was established], Theodore of Cyrrhus wrote that there were at least two hundred different Christian gospels circulating in his own diocese." What Cyrrhus meant by "gospel" is anyone's guess. It could have been one short scroll containing a brief message or a batch of lengthy scrolls rendering something comparable to the Gospel of Matthew. In reaction, the budding Church's evolving congregation of bishops was moved to create a canon of "acceptable" scriptures as a definitive statement of Christianity. Naturally, they dismissed as spurious and heretical all "unacceptable" texts, i.e., writings that did not accord with the bishops' beliefs in common about Jesus...at that time. This rejection didn't mean the spurned texts were untrue; it merely meant they were in conflict with the bishops' agreed upon beliefs. Indeed, it is well to remember that *the bishops could not tell which of the probably hundreds of candidate texts were true any more than we can today.*

As the bishops examined and discussed each candidate book for inclusion, they would, of course, have taken into account the book's literary quality. But three other factors should/could/would have been uppermost in their decisions. Whether the bishops considered these factors is unknowable:

> (a) **The identity and pedigree of a book's author.** It being up to three hundred years since the Gospels were written, how could they have established the true author of each text? Answer: They couldn't! A book's authorship was pure conjecture and hearsay. All they could do was speculate and deliberate, reaching a consensus by vote. They could no more verify the identities of the authors than we can today.

> (b) **The truth of a book's contents.** How could they have established the truth of each candidate text? Again, they couldn't. Determining the "truth" was achieved again by conjecture, by hearsay, and ultimately by vote.

> (c) **Compatibility with the bishops' views about Jesus' birth, life, teachings, miracles, crucifixion, death, and resurrection.** The bishops' decision process was akin to a group of Red Sox executives reviewing submissions for an anthology on the team. They will accept only those stories that in the opinion of the executives give positive perceptions of the team's history. Stories that, while true or possibly true, degrade the team's reputation are rejected. Again, the bishops' decisions on which texts to include in the canon were tantamount to stacking a jury, selecting only those individuals who were sure to vote in favor of a particular verdict. The bishops' decisions were thus only as valid as the doctrine they professed...at that time!

As one might expect, the argument over which texts to include in the canon raged on for some time, from the end of the 2nd century until the 4th century.

Osman in *Christianity: An Ancient Egyptian Religion*[31]: Ever since the assemblage of the 27 books in the New Testament was approved in 397 by the Third Council of Carthage in North Africa, the Church has maintained that these texts represent the *original* and *only acceptable* Christian view. Well, the Church had to. To say otherwise would have been self-incriminating and self-defeating. Moreover, say Freke and Gandy in *Jesus and the Lost Goddess*[32], the triumph of the Literalists over the Christian Gnostics gave the distorted impression that the four Gospels were always the most popular Christian scriptures, but that, of course, wasn't true.

Many Gnostic works, such as the Acts of Thomas, were too popular to simply dismiss, so the Literalists purged them of their "heretical" content and adapted them to suit the then Literalist agenda. The Acts of the Apostles may well have been such an adaptation of originally Gnostic texts. At the end of the 2nd century Irenaeus and Tertullian, among the early Church's leaders, regarded Acts as holy scripture, yet just a generation earlier Justin Martyr had apparently not even heard of it. Freke and Gandy in *The Jesus Mysteries*[33] conclude that the Acts of the Apostles was written just in time to be a powerful but fanciful tool against Gnosticism, legitimatizing the bishops who, as a group, falsely laid claim to an unbroken lineage back to the original Apostles...a lineage that is still professed by the Catholic Church today.

Now I have no problem with writing something — a speech, a letter, an essay, a book — to foster support for a particular belief or to win an argument. Indeed, I've done that very thing in this book. But I certainly am not claiming that this book is the Word of God, although I immodestly pray He had a hand in it. Truth be told, the authors of the Gospels, like the authors of every work ever written, had their own personal axes to grind, as I do here. Whether those axes were honorable and well-intentioned can never be determined, since we can't interrogate the authors or examine their backgrounds. However, I find it hard to accept that, at the time they wrote the Gospels, they believed their thoughts and words were being guided unseen by the Holy Spirit. That claim, again inarguably self-serving, came much later from the Catholic Church. Conveniently it is a claim that can never be proven or disproven, which makes it, as Christians are fond of saying, "a matter of faith". Finally I fervently believe that everything that happens on Earth God allows to happen. To that extent God allowed the Bible to be assembled, but that doesn't mean the words in the Bible are His.

Card 4: Non-History

While fundamentalist Christians, of necessity, hold fast to the belief that the Bible is immutable history — as it must be if it's the Word of God — there is a near consensus among the world's serious-minded biblical scholars, theologians, and academicians that the Bible is most assuredly *not history per se*. Few Catholics appreciate that the Bible, rather than being an historical record, is a compilation of oft-told stories, some of which are true, and unverifiable legends all fitted nicely into a presumed historical and chronological context...what F.C. Burkitt, the author of the preface to Albert Schweitzer's *The Quest of the Historical Jesus*[34], described as "a simple series of disconnected anecdotes".

What distinguishes the Gospels in particular is their paucity of sound historical material. For example, the depiction of Jesus preaching and performing miracles and such around an allegedly peaceful Galilean countryside clashes outright with history, which indisputably describes that countryside as a "hotbed of revolutionary fervor and internecine strife".

Much of the material in the Gospels, writes Eisenman in *James, the Brother of Jesus*[35], "even allowing for hyperbole, patently borders on the fantastic". The Gospel of Matthew, he contends, more than the other Gospels, "has long been recognized as a collection of Messianic and other scriptural proof-texts taken out of context and woven into a gripping narrative of what purports to be the life of Jesus."[36] Then there's the Book of Acts which, he writes, contains "too much mythologizing, too much that is out-and-out fiction, too much fantasizing" to consider it an historical work.[37]

If you don't believe me, read the books in my bibliography or do your own research and read as many texts as you can find about the origins of the Bible. And, again, be sure to read sources on both sides of the argument.

Card 5: Miracles

If we limit our count of the miracles in the Gospels to things Jesus did himself, there are 23 different episodes. But there are considerable inconsistencies in the details. For example, the story of Jesus feeding the multitude with a small, finite number of loaves is actually told six times. Spong in *Jesus for the Non-Religious*[38]: "Is that a single miracle or six miracles? Mark and Matthew say this miraculous feeding episode happened twice in two different locations with a different number of people, a different number of loaves, and a different amount of leftovers. Luke and John say that a miraculous feeding of the multitude happened only once. John places the event in Jerusalem early in Jesus' ministry. Mark, Matthew, and Luke place the feeding episodes in Galilee."

> These variations on the story of the loaves show unmistakably how legends can easily evolve from a rumor into a legend into a full-blown tenet of belief. Incidentally, a similar ritual was part of ancient Egyptian beliefs.

The New Testament avers that Jesus performed "many miracles" beyond those described in the Gospels, but exactly how many and what these other miracles were is not revealed. Obviously the authors of the Gospels picked through the many stories — indeed, probably hundreds by the time the Gospels were written

— circulating about Jesus' miraculous exploits and selected those that were the most impressive and illustrative of his presumed powers, his mercifulness, and his divinity. And what were the selection criteria? Believability was obviously a factor, because any claim of a miracle rides a thin line between a reasonable proposition and a palpable falsehood. The masses in Jesus' time, being highly superstitious* and therefore gullible, would have been easily convinced that Jesus was born of a virgin because, as I have noted, many Gods then and in earlier ages were commonly believed to have been born of virgins. Indeed, as I explain below, in the minds of the gullible Faithful Jesus of necessity had to have been born of a virgin. If he wasn't, he couldn't be a god. The masses would also have readily believed that Jesus changed water into wine, a miracle attributed before him to many Pagan Gods. But the primary criterion was making the case for Jesus' power to save the masses from Hell.

> *For example, when Romans — all Pagans — at that time voted in elections of senators and other high officials on Rome's Field of Mars "the entrails [of sacred animals] were inspected, the skies were checked for suspicious flights of birds, the blessings of the gods were invoked, and all epileptics were asked to leave the field, for in those days an attack of epilepsy, or *morbus comitialis*, automatically rendered proceedings void."[39]

Yet, what were the stories of Jesus phenomenal acts that did not meet the assemblers' criteria and were therefore *not* selected? One can well imagine a Gospel author mulling over which of the innumerable miracle anecdotes circulating among the Christian communities to include.

> Ah, here's a good one from a member of the Faith in Jerusalem. He writes that his cousin in Galilee saw Jesus cure a crippled woman who was lying on a mat. "Rise," said Jesus. "Pick up your mat and go home." Oh, I like that. That's a keeper. And here's another one. A woman outside of Jerusalem says she witnessed Jesus raise a dog from the dead. But that's no good. Dog's don't have souls. Then my cousin in Antioch told me a number of his neighbors saw Jesus stop the sun in the sky. That's old stuff, an old wives' tale that's been said of a lot of mystics. But here's one that makes me laugh. My neighbor's mother-in-law said that people in her village claim Jesus baked bread without an oven. I'm sure bakers and housewives will be impressed, but it sounds too much like witchcraft. Not the message I want my text to convey.

People of every era, from ancient to modern, embellish legends, from the obscure to the ridiculous, until the tales are unrecognizable compared to the originals. Whether it be a horrible accident or a wonderful experience, its recounting takes on new contours and meanings each time it passes from one person's lips to the next.

Let me demonstrate how easy it would have been for true believers in Jesus time to invent accounts of his supposed miracles, based on rumors and such. The following three stories, each of which would fit nicely within any of the Gospels, are unrecognizable as forgeries compared with all of the other recountings of miracles in the New Testament.

And when Jesus arrived at the shore of the Sea of Galilee, he came upon a young woman with child lying on the sand, weeping and in pain. When she saw him, she cried, "Rabbi, rabbi. You who are with God and have the power of healing, help me. I am with child and in labor, yet the child has not moved." He had never seen the woman before, nor did she know him, yet she recognized him at once as God's chosen. He went to her and said, "Verily I say unto, you see and know the truth. Would that all people could see and believe." He bent over and laid his hands upon her swollen stomach. Immediately the child came forth, alive and healthy. The woman kissed Jesus' hand. "Thank you, Rabbi," she said. Jesus replied, "It was your faith that saved your child."

A fortnight after Jesus and the disciples had left Capernaum, they were resting beside the road when a man came running toward them shouting, "My child! My child! Have you seen my child? He has wandered off. The wolves will eat him." When he saw Jesus, he stopped in his tracks and cried, "Rabbi. It is you." He fell to his knees and said, "You are the holy prophet of whom many speak." Jesus stood and asked, "How is it you know me? We have never met." The man said, "The moment my son was missing I prayed to God that I would find you and you would help me find my son." Jesus took the man's hands in his own and said, "Fear not, my faithful friend. Your son is safe. As my Father guided you to me, so I guide you to your son. He lies sleeping beyond yonder hill. Go to him, and give thanks unto God."

As Jesus and his followers entered a village, they came upon a small crowd shouting at one another. "What is happening here?" he asked. At the sound of his voice everyone stopped arguing and turned toward him. The village elder stepped forward and, pointing at a man in the crowd, said, "This man stole a silver goblet from the house of this woman." Jesus looked at the accused and said, "Did you steal the goblet?" "No, no, I didn't," pleaded the man. "It was someone else." Speaking to the crowd, Jesus said, "Who accuses this man of stealing?" The elder pointed at another man and said, "He accused him" This man, feeling the power of God in Jesus, loudly denied making the accusation. "It wasn't I. It was him." He pointed at another man. That man, too, denied making the accusation. Jesus said, "Verily I ask you, which is worse? To steal or to bear false witness?" The crowd was silent. When no one answered Jesus, he said, "Whoever forgives another's transgression against him will be forgiven by God for his transgressions."

My point in making up these three tales — which took all of ten minutes! — and mentioning the unselected stories about Jesus is to emphasize that those selected for the Gospels were, as a group, no more valid — no more truthful — than the stories, as a group, not selected. The selected stories were merely of such a nature that they more fully met the Gospel authors' purposes than the unselected stories would have. One can only wonder what the unselected stories were...and how truthful were those selected.

Card 6: Contradictions

All of the books of the New Testament contradict each other in plentiful details. For example:

Who visited Jesus' birth?
> Matthew: Three Magi (Christian tradition also calls them
> > "wise men" and "kings")
> Luke: Three shepherds

Who carried the cross at Jesus' crucifixion?
> Mark, Matthew, Luke: Simon of Cyrene.
> John: Only Jesus himself carried the cross.

On which day of the month was Jesus crucified?
> Mark, Matthew, Luke: On the first day of Passover,
> > the 15th day of Nissan.
> John: On the day before Passover, the 14th day of Nissan.

Which of the two thieves on the cross believed in Jesus?
> Mark, Matthew: Neither of the thieves believed in Jesus.
> Luke: One thief did not believe, while the other did.
> John: The thieves are not mentioned.

How many days and how many nights was Jesus in the tomb?
> Mark, Matthew, Luke: Three days and two nights.
> John: Two days and two nights.

Who were the women who came to the tomb?
> Mark: Mary Magdalene, Mary the mother of James, and Salome.
> Matthew: Mary Magdalene and "the other Mary".
> Luke: Mary Magdalene, Mary the mother of
>   James, Joanna, and other women.
> John: Only Mary Magdalene.

What were angels (all males) doing at the tomb and where were they?
> Mark: One was sitting on the right side, inside the tomb.
> Matthew: One was sitting outside on the stone which
>   he had rolled away from the tomb.
> Luke: They were standing by the women, inside the tomb.
> John: There were no angels when Mary came to the tomb.
>   When she arrived at the tomb a second time, however,
>   she found two angels sitting inside the tomb.

After seeing the angels, whom does Mary meet first?
> Mark, Matthew, John: Jesus.
> Luke: The disciples.

To whom does Jesus make his first post-resurrection appearance?
> Mark, John: Only Mary Magdalene.
> Matthew: The two Marys.
> Luke: Cleopas and another.

How many times does Jesus appear after the resurrection?
> Mark: Three times.
> Matthew, Luke: Two times.
> John: Four times.[40]

What was the color of Jesus' cloak at his crucifixion?
> Mark: purple.
> Matthew: scarlet.

What were Jesus' last spoken words on the Cross?
> Mark, Matthew: "My God, my God, why hast thou forsaken me?"
> Luke: "Father, into thy hands I commend my spirit."
> John: "It is finished."

Who were the Apostles? Although much has been written over the centuries about them (see wikipedia.com "Twelve Apostles") — most of it based on legends — there's scant information on their backgrounds. There is not one single detail about the lives of Bartholomew, Matthew (possibly the tax collector in the Gospel of Matthew), James the son of Alphaeus, Simon the Cananaean, Thaddeus, and the other Judas not Iscariot.[41] Nor do the Gospels agree on the Apostles' "rankings" in the lists of names, which may or may not be significant. Judas replaces Thaddeus in both Luke and Acts.[42]

	Mark	Matthew	Luke	Acts	John
1	Simon named Peter	Simon called Peter	Peter	Peter	Three references to twelve disciples, but no names.
2	James son of Zebedee	Andrew Simon's brother	Andrew	James	
3	John brother of James	James son of Zebedee	James	John	
4	Andrew Simon's brother	John brother of James	John	Andrew	
5	Philip	Philip	Philip	Philip	
6	Bartholomew	Bartholomew	Bartholomew	Thomas	
7	Matthew	Thomas	Matthew	Bartholomew	
8	Thomas	Matthew	Thomas	Matthew	
9	James son of Alphaeus	James son of Alphaeus	James son of Alphaeus	James son of Alphaeus	
10	**Thaddeus**	**Thaddeus**	Simon the Cananaean	Simon the Cananaean	
11	Simon the Cananaean	Simon the Cananaean	**Judas**	**Judas**	
12	Judas Iscariot	Judas Iscariot	Judas Iscariot	Judas Iscariot	

According to the Gospels, Herod was king of Judea when Jesus was born. Luke 2:1-2 states that the Roman census, cited as the reason for Joseph's and the pregnant Mary's journey to Bethlehem, took place during the rule of Quirinius, the Roman Governor of Syria. Wallace-Murphy points out in *Cracking the Symbol Code*[453] that Roman records and histories show that Quirinius began his rule over Syria some ten years after the death of King Herod. Therefore the Gospel of Luke is obviously in error...or are God and the Holy Spirit simply confused? Numerous explanations have been proposed to reconcile this contradiction.

The title "Jesus of Nazareth" — used for centuries and everywhere today to refer to Jesus in books, movies, and sermons — is a misnomer. Early transcribers of the Gospels apparently mistook the Greek version of "Nazorean" to mean someone from "Nazareth." His true title was Jesus the Nazorean, indicating his membership in a sect that was an offshoot of the Essenes[44] — more ammunition for Feather's theory about Jesus' education at Qumran. Virtually all of the many books I have read concerning Jesus' life aver that the city of Nazareth came into being some time after Jesus' death. Indeed, in all of the Old Testament neither the word Nazareth nor Nazarene is mentioned.[45] There is, however, at least one dissenting view. According to Gerald Larue, emeritus professor of biblical history and archaeology at the University of Southern California and chairman of the Committee for the

Scientific Examination of Religion, "archaeological and historical research into the history of Nazareth indicates that, although it was inhabited as early as Neanderthal times (70,000-35,000 BCE), in Roman times it housed only a small Jewish community — a village so small and so insignificant that it was ignored in 1st-century CE geographical references."[46] Does Larue's finding mean Jesus was born in this tiny insignificant hamlet? Who knows? By the time the Gospels were written years after Jesus' reported crucifixion, that tiny habitation had grown into a distinct and probably well-known village called Nazareth, to which the Gospel authors apparently associated Jesus by virtue of their misinterpreting the word "Nazorean".

When congregations in church services hear little snippets of the Bible read to them, they are unable to perceive these contradictions, because only one version of a biblical episode is read at each service. Indeed, if a contradictory version were read immediately after the first reading, consternation would arise. To avoid this very problem, the Vatican has always been careful to schedule the reading of conflicting versions of an episode in different years. Notable examples are the differing accounts of the women who came to Jesus' tomb.

Card 7: Mistranslations

Not a single original has ever been found of any of the books that came to be included in the New Testament or indeed of any Christian text from antiquity. I hasten to admit that this circumstance by itself doesn't argue against the Bible's being the Word of God, but stay with me for a moment and I'll get to my point.

A fragment of the gospel of John, containing material from chapter 18, has been dated from the style of its script to between 100 and 150[47] — which is 65 to 115 years after Jesus' reported crucifixion. Some piecemeal manuscripts of the Gospels date from around the year 200, that is, 165 years after Jesus' death. The earliest existing copies of Paul's letters, all of which predate the Gospels, date from around 200, which is 150 years after he wrote the originals. The first complete compilations of *all* of the books in the New Testament date from no earlier than the 4th century, some three hundred years after the originals were written. Those Christians who cling to the Holy Bible like a life preserver in a storm will hate me for saying so, but there's no telling how faithful any of these copies are to their originals. Indeed, as I will shortly relate, they are in all likelihood not faithful at all.

During the centuries between the time the originals and oldest extant copies were penned, countless scribes of varying temperament, ability, and motive throughout the Christian world copied and regularly miscopied the scriptures, both inadvertently and intentionally. To be sure, reports Ehrman in *Misquoting Jesus*[48], the ancient manuscripts in our possession are copies made from countless copies of copies of the originals.

Considering the extremes to which humans and their organizations have always gone to protect their self-interests and justify their beliefs, imagine the "spin" that members of the Church during those three hundred years before the oldest known complete copy of the Bible was discovered would have put on the scriptures to defend and preserve the Church's supreme authority, which was based on its supreme authoritative dogma, which was based on its interpretations of the New Testament, which was based on the words, phrases, and language of the New Testament texts. If the leaders of the Roman Church over the centuries had no moral compunctions about killing the millions who opposed its doctrine and power, which was based on the Church's interpretations of the Holy Scriptures, how much more willing would they have been to delete, amend, and alter the language of those texts — the sole basis for Christianity — to bring their contents in line with the Church's "orthodox" beliefs at the time? The answer is obvious. They would have edited those texts in a Vatican minute!

When a publicly owned company begins to fail, its executives with the greatest stake in its survival become frantic. History has shown that many will do anything to save the company: publishing false financial statements and altering the books to hide their losses, letting employees go who have gotten wind of the trouble and having them sign non-disclosure agreements in return for hefty bribes, and lastly lying to stock holders and to the remaining unwitting employees about the company's increasingly dire straits. The stock holders are the key figures to keep in the dark, lest they dump their holdings and pitch the company into the black hole of bankruptcy. This is exactly the situation the Church faced in its formative years.

"It's not simply a matter of scholarly speculation," writes Erhman in *Lost Christianities*,[49] "to say that the words of the New Testament were changed in the process of copying. We *know* they were changed." He explains: "If we count up all of the ancient New Testament manuscripts that have been discovered, it is an impressive number overall: 5,400 Greek copies of all or part of the New Testament, ranging from tiny scraps to massive tomes" and "all of these 5,400 copies [have been] compared with one another. What is striking is that no two copies agree in all of their wording. There can be only one reason for this: the scribes who copied the texts changed them."

Defenders of the accuracy of the New Testament go to great lengths to prove it. For example, according to *New Advent*, the author of Matthew wrote his gospel in Aramaic but did not himself translate it into Greek. This, says the essay in *New Advent*, "supposes that between the original Aramaic and the Greek text there is, at least, a substantial conformity." Supposes? Substantial conformity? What sort of logic is this? None! How does the fact that the author of Matthew did not himself translate his gospel into Greek lead to the supposition that the translation into Greek by **someone else** conforms *substantially* to the original Aramaic text?

Please explain that to me. This is just one more irritating Christian obfuscation.

What *New Advent* really reveals is what is *not* known for certain about the Gospel of Matthew...which is everything:

Who precisely wrote it.
Precisely when.
Who precisely translated it from Aramaic into Greek.
When the translation precisely occurred.
Precisely how many copies of copies of the original Aramaic text intervened
    between the original and the one used for the original translation into Greek.
How precisely true the first Greek translation was to the Aramaic original.
Precisely how many copies of copies of the original Greek translation intervened
    before the earliest extant copy of that translation.

To these unknowns is added the truly overriding question: To what precise extent does the Gospel of Matthew we use today differ from its original Aramaic text? Scholars can blather all they want, make up all sorts of contorted, heartfelt reasoning and suppositions, but the answer to that question is unknowable. Precisely unknowable!

Christian biblical scholars simply push all of these unwelcome but imperative questions aside, devise seemingly reasonable interpretations to replace them, and move on, saying in effect, "Well, we do the best we can with what we have." But their best is far from good enough. Scholars who derive from these interpretations the "unerring" foundation of their Christian religion create a flimsy house of cards. They know it full well but are loath to admit it, for doing so would erode the foundation of Christian beliefs, which must be defended at all costs, lest their Church fall into ruin. Indeed, every single time I have researched some statement of Christian belief, whether it related to Jesus, to one of the Gospels, or to some doctrinal tenet, I found at bottom circular arguments, illogical syntax, highly conjectural sourcing, unprovable assertions, and inevitably a final resort to faith. Every time! In fact, I got so weary of challenging these statements that in most cases I simply gave up, lest this book become stultifyingly repetitive and boring.

The foundation of most Bibles used today is the King James translation, which, according to biblical scholars, was mostly transcribed from the "Great Bible", the first edition of the Bible in English authorized by King Henry VIII of England to be read aloud in church services. It had been translated straight from Greek texts. Because there were many instances where old Greek, Aramaic, and Semitic words and phrases had no counterparts in Jacobean English, certain errors were made, writes Gardner in *The Magdalene Legacy*.[50]

A humorous but telling example of the impact a simple copying mistake can have is related in *The Church That Forgot Christ*[51] by Jimmy Breslin, the Pulitzer prize-winning columnist with the *New York Times*. Breslin writes that [Saint] Jerome, translating a description of Moses in 405, mistranslated the word for "halo" as "horns". "Michelangelo, reading from Jerome's translation as if it were a recipe book, sculpted his magnificent statue of Moses with horns and not a halo." Oops! On the other hand, perhaps Michelangelo had a sense of humor and was giving the Church's or the Pope's tail a mischievous twist.

Card 8: Tamperings

Write Freke and Gandy in *The Jesus Mysteries*[52], the 2nd-century Roman philosopher Celsus, a self-proclaimed witness to the falsification of Christian writings, complained that Christians "altered the original texts of the gospels...with the intention of thus being able to destroy the arguments of their critics". The 3rd-century Christian philosopher Origen, acknowledged that Gospel manuscripts had been edited and interpolated to suit the needs of the changing theological climate.[53] Ellerbe says in *The Dark Side of Christian History*[54] that Celsus wrote of the revisionists, "Some of them, as if in a drunken state producing self-inflicted visions, remodel their Gospel from its first written form and reform it so that they can refute the objections brought against it."

There are many examples of tampering with, i.e., falsifying, the texts of the New Testament. Here are twelve notable ones:

Beloved Disciple

John 21:24 cites "the Beloved Disciple" as its author, based almost certainly on Irenaeus' improbable claim of a childhood memory that Saint John and the Beloved Disciple were one and the same. But according to the Christian texts discovered in 1945 at Nag Hammadi in Upper Egypt, Mary Magdalene was the Beloved Disciple. In *The Laughing Jesus*[55] Freke and Gandy write, "Crude alterations were made to the gospel to make John rather than Mary the supposed author." It has been suggested — there is, of course, no hard evidence — that Irenaeus, seeking to proselytize his beliefs among the Romans, changed the gender of the Beloved Disciple to patronize misogynist Romans who would have rejected a book written by a mere woman.

Virgin Birth

Mark, the first Gospel, makes no mention of Mary being a virgin when she gave birth to Jesus. Spong in Jesus for the *Non-Religious*[56]: "When the Gospel of Mark, at least a decade earlier than the Gospel of Matthew, had introduced the mother of

Jesus without naming her, it said she was the mother of four sons besides Jesus and at least two unnamed daughters (Mark 6:3). A mother of seven was certainly not a virgin in the mind of Mark's author."

The failure of Mark to characterize Mary as a virgin is in retrospect one of the most glaring and imponderable omissions in the New Testament, given the Church's later unwavering reverence for her. But then again, how could Mark's author claim a mother of seven children to be a virgin? Even 2nd-century Jewish writers pointed out this contradiction[57] to Christian leaders, but to no avail.[58] The leaders' minds were made up, and facts would not be allowed to interfere with Christianity's evolving dogma and developing institutional power.[59]

Surely, if the author of Mark had known about Jesus' virgin birth, he would have mentioned it, for it "proved" that Jesus was divine. Then did knowledge of Mary's virginity, like that of the "whatever" power, become strangely known thirty-some years *after* Jesus' death? Again it seems implausible that this remarkable information came to light only after the Gospel of Mark was written. My guess, whether you like it or not, is that, just as the author of Matthew or someone else invented the "whatever" power, the story of the virgin birth was likewise concocted. The story provided unassailable support both to Jesus' divinity and to his humanness, the two most divisive issues among the early Faithful. Bear in mind that many of the important gods in ancient times were alleged to have been born of virgins. If Jesus were divine, he, too, according to custom, would have to have been born of a virgin. It was that cultural necessity that would have justified the author of Matthew's including the concocted story of Jesus' virgin birth.

In this regard, Spong in *The Sins of Scripture*[60] writes that Mary's virginity did not become a part of Catholic tradition until Matthew 1:23 introduced the idea — "Behold, the virgin shall be with child and bear a son, and they shall name him Immanuel, which means 'God is with us'." Matthew's virgin-birth story was clearly plagiarized intact from Isaiah 7:14 — "Therefore the Lord himself will give you this sign: the virgin shall be with child, and bear a son, and shall name him Immanuel, which means 'God is with us'." Luke, the third Gospel, not to be outdone, expanded the tale of Mary's immaculate virginity into a full-fledged narrative (Luke 1:26), while the Gospel of John, for some unknown reason, curiously said nary a word about it. Perhaps its author didn't find mention of Jesus' birth or his mother's virginity relevant...or true!

Like most everything else in the Gospels, whether Mary conceived Jesus while still a virgin is impossible to determine. In any case, write Baigent, Leigh, and Lincoln in *The Messianic Legacy*[61], "During the middle of the 2nd century the concept of Mary's virginity evolved, becoming firmly established by 383, when [Saint] Jerome wrote *The Perpetual Virginity of Blessed Mary* for the newly devised Church of Rome."

Holy Trinity

The first known reference to the "Trinity", says *New Advent*[62], was around 180 in the work of Theophilus, the bishop of Antioch, 150 years after Jesus' death. Many Christians today, perhaps most, believe that 4th-century councils of the earliest Church Fathers did not formulate the doctrine of the Trinity, but rather articulated in the creeds the truths that the orthodox church had believed since the time of the apostles.[63] This theory may comfort its devotees, but there is no evidence whatever that such a belief existed prior to the 4th century. Indeed, the articulation of the Trinity doctrine was a clever expedience...an artifice...to resolve otherwise irresolvable theological conflicts among the Church Fathers over Jesus' divinity and his relationship with God. The idea of the Trinity was a hotly contested issue, writes Freeman in *The Closing of the Western Mind*,[64] because scriptural evidence was inconclusive. According to *New Advent*[65], "In Scripture there is as yet no single term by which the Three Divine Persons are denoted together." (I presume *New Advent* meant "denoted together in the New Testament", but I have no idea what "as yet" means here, and I'm not going to waste your time and mine trying to conceive an explanation.)

Perhaps the most contentious quotation of Jesus in the New Testament regarding his divinity is in John 10 — "The Father and I are one". The debate circles around the meaning of "one". One in spirit? One in abilities? One in purpose? One in power? The text from John is ambiguous and can be read in different ways. The Church, of course, reads it as one in spirit.

Emperor Constantine tried to settle the divisive matter of the Trinity in 325 at the Council of Nicaea, which under his influence and control formulated and promulgated the Nicene Creed, which encompassed the Trinity. But the issue would not go away. In the end there was, understandably, so much ferment within the early Church concerning the Trinity doctrine that the Roman Emperor had finally to enforce belief in it by edict,[66] sidestepping the lack of biblical evidence. To provide that evidence, however, two phrases, cunningly inserted into the New Testament, served to vindicate the movement within the Church to adopt the Holy Trinity as official Church doctrine.

One of the two insertions was the infamous so-called *Comma Johanneum* — the John Clause — a deliberate textual manipulation or, more candidly, a fabrication around the 5th century. Highlighted here for emphasis, the John Clause was inserted into 1 John 5:7 as follows: "For there are three that bear record *in Heaven, the Father, the Word, and the Holy Ghost: and these three are one.* And there are three that bear witness on Earth, the Spirit, and the water, and the blood: and these three agree in one." Without the *Comma Johanneum*, 1 John 5:7 reads simply: "For there are three that bear record: the Spirit, the water, and the blood, and the three are of one *accord*". Note that the latter phrase — the three are of one accord — conveys only that they were *in agreement*, not that the three were literally one. I don't know what the original Greek was for "are of one accord". My dictionary's definition of *accord* is "all in agreement; with no one dissenting". There's a distinct and unqualified difference between "are one" and "agree". The author of John may have inserted the John Clause in an attempt to eliminate any confusion and to provide Gospel truth to the existence of the Trinity.

The John Clause is notably absent from all of the recovered ancient versions of the New Testament translated from Greek, e.g., Syriac, Coptic, Ethiopic, Arabic, the Old Latin, and the Vulgate in its early forms. The earliest appearance on record of the wayward clause was in Spain in 380 in an essay titled *Liber Apologeticus* (roughly Book of Defense). From there the John Clause, clearly owing to its obvious significance to the dispute over the Trinity doctrine, made its way into the writings of the Latin Fathers and into the Old Latin and Vulgate versions of the New Testament circa 5th and 8th centuries respectively. Most translations of 1 John published from 1522 until the latter part of the 19th century contain the Clause. It does not appear, however, in more recent copies of the Epistle,[67] the Church apparently having been forced to recognize the Clause as the fabrication it was. Says the *Christian Courier**, it was not until 1927 that the Vatican finally acknowledged officially that the *Comma Johanneum* was "open to dispute", a nifty deceptive way of avoiding admitting it was a falsehood. The updated *Nova Vulgata* edition of the Vulgate Bible, published in 1979 as a result of the Second Vatican Council in 1962, does not include the Clause.[68] There is today general agreement among biblical scholars that the Comma Johanneum was a blatant forgery and has no place in the New Testament.

*Christian Courier is an independent Christian newspaper published by Reformed Faith Witness, a non-profit ministry (www.christiancourier.ca).

As for the other insertion, it has never been disputed, at least as far as I have been able to determine from my research. (If it has, I humbly stand corrected.) The phrase in question, again highlighted here, occurs in Matthew 28:18, where Jesus is reported to have instructed the Apostles to "make disciples of all nations, baptizing them **in the name of the Father, and of the Son, and of the holy Spirit**". I am moved to question whether Jesus ever spoke the highlighted phrase, which sounds like a doctrinaire blessing commonly rendered by priests after the Trinity had been accepted as holy doctrine.

Secondly, the phrase precisely and remarkably defines the meaning of the Holy Trinity as defined in the 4th century by the Church. Lastly, the phrase "in the name of the Father, and of the Son, and of the holy Spirit" is not attributed to Jesus anywhere else in the Gospels: not in Mark, not in Luke, not in John. I therefore contend that the phrase's absence in these scriptures is powerful evidence that someone along the way made it up. [I have been unable to establish whether the phrase appeared in the oldest copies of Matthew.]

New Advent goes on to state that the Trinity dogma was made known to the Church by divine revelation. Says *New Advent*, "It is manifest that a dogma so mysterious presupposes a Divine revelation." Come again? Mysterious? Presupposes? So it was God or the Holy Spirit, not humans, who conceived the Trinity doctrine. How convenient! How outrageous! This stratagem, used again and again over the centuries by the Church, was a shrewd but conspicuous ploy to circumvent the absence of direct unequivocal scriptural evidence to support a controversial doctrine. Coming by way of revelation, no defense of the doctrine was therefore necessary or possible. It was immediately ordained as the infallible Word of God, silencing any challenge. So when the Church could not logically prove a particular dogma either by interpretation of the New Testament or by theological argument, it resorted to *revelation*, which brooked no dissent. What nonsense!

To lend validation, however flimsy, to the Trinity doctrine, *New Advent*[69] proffers that the term *Trinity* "may have been in use before 180" but *New Advent*, in keeping with the mystery of the *Trinity*, cites no examples. As I said, devising the Trinity doctrine in the 4th century was a clever expedience...an artifice...to resolve irresolvable theological conflicts of the time. Those conflicts still remain irresolvable today, making belief in the Trinity wholly a matter of faith, not reason.

Gospel of John

The introduction to John states that the Gospel contains "some inconsistencies"... an altogether evasive understatement. The introduction states, for example, that "there are two endings of Jesus' discourse in the upper room — 14:31 and 18:1". Two endings? Good grief! Most scholars, it says, conclude that "the inconsistencies were probably produced by subsequent editing in which *homogeneous* materials were added to a shorter original". But where did these homogeneous materials come from? My Bible doesn't say, presumably because the sources are unknown. But if that's true, then the citation of these materials is unreliable. Were the *homogeneous* materials found on scraps of ancient papyrus copies of the Gospel of John? Were they mentioned in the text of some ancient scriptural scroll? Were they revelations from on high? No answers are provided. Be that as it may, I conclude that the use of the word *homogeneous* — which my dictionary defines as "the same in structure, quality, etc.; similar or identical" — was a clever way of camouflaging falsifications, better known as lies, which the introduction veils as "inconsistencies". But that's my own personal unverifiable opinion of the same ilk as the introduction's statement.

In addition, the introduction to the Gospel of John in my Bible states that its

"Chapter 21 seems to have been added after the Gospel was complete." Added? By whom? When? The introduction provides no explanation, leaving the reader hanging. What's going on here? How does one justify "adding" to Holy Scripture? I'd like to add a homogeneous phrase or two to the Gospel of Mark from the theme song of the movie *The Sound of Music*; it would add some sparkle and tenderness to the text. Why not? The precedent has been well established. Am I being overly cynical and sarcastic? You bet!

Old Is Better

A notable example of revisions to the New Testament, writes Ehrman in *Misquoting Jesus*[70], is the Jesus' parable about new and old wineskins. In Luke 5:38 Jesus says "The old is better." This statement was apparently troubling to some scribes or churchmen who likely interpreted it to mean that Judaism, the old religion, was superior to Christianity, the new religion. So they simply deleted it from the copies they were scripting, ensuring that Jesus, at least in those copies, said nothing about the old being better than the new.

Mark's Long Ending

As noted above, scholars know that whole sections of the gospels were added to the originals. For example, writes Gardner in *The Magdalene Legacy*[71], Mark originally did not contain any text beyond Chapter 16 verse 8 where Mary Magdalene and two other women depart from Jesus' empty tomb. Sometime after 397 twelve new verses, the so-called "long ending", were appended in a distinctively different literary style, relating that the risen Jesus appeared to his disciples. It's remarkable that the publishers of the New Testament in one of my Bibles made no attempt to conceal this addition, for a capitalized, bold font title "THE LONG ENDING" appears before Chapter 16 verse 9. My other Bible makes no such identification. This so-called "long ending," report Freke and Gandy in *The Jesus Mysteries*[72], is not found in any early manuscripts of Mark and yet now appears in nearly all New Testaments and is part of the scripted readings of scripture during Mass. What the heck is going on? I presume God and the Holy Spirit approved of these additions. Moreover, when the "long ending" is read by a lector at Mass, does the celebrant inform the congregation about the text's mysterious addition to the Gospel of Mark? What do you think?

Jesus' Ascension in Luke

An early copy of Luke 24:51-52 recounts Jesus' departing: "And it happened that while he was blessing [his disciples], he was removed from them; and they returned into Jerusalem with great joy." In some subsequent copies there is an addition to the text — "and he was taken up into Heaven" — to stress the physicality of Jesus during his ascension, rather than the bland "he was removed". The revision obviously was intended to provide scriptural proof that Jesus physically ascended into Heaven, another then contemporary subject of controversy.[73]

Paul's Pastorals

Of the thirteen letters attributed to Paul in the New Testament, the "pastorals" are widely dismissed by scholars as forgeries, write Freke and Gandy in *The Laughing Jesus*[74]. These letters were so named because they were ostensibly to provide "pastoral" rules for guiding the organization of the Church. But Paul could have had no interest in such matters because, when he wrote his letters, there was no church of bishops and deacons to organize. Indeed, he never established a priesthood in the churches he founded. One explanation offered by scholars is that the authors of the pastorals sought scriptural justification for a particular organizational structure of the Church they were forming.

Forgeries

Scholars, says Ehrman in *Misquoting Jesus*, believe that a number of New Testament books are plain and simple forgeries by people who claimed to be someone else in order to get a hearing for their views. Among these are "almost certainly 2 Peter, probably 1 and 2 Timothy and Titus, quite likely 2 Thessalonians, Colossians, and Ephesians, and possibly 1 Peter and Jude"[75]. Despite their questionable authorship, these texts were accepted, respected, granted authority, and included in the sacred Scripture. Why? Because their contents squared with the beliefs of the bishops who assembled the Bible. Why else?

Diminution of Paul

Harpur writes in *The Pagan Christ*[76] that scholars have concluded that in the last quarter of the 2nd century the Acts of the Apostles was substantially edited to enhance Peter's stature at Paul's expense. This editing was evident by comparing the earliest extant copy of Acts with a later Greek text. Scholars deduce that the editings sought to diminish Paul's importance because (a) he had made it clear that his encounter with Christ had been purely spiritual, not physical and (b) he had never established a priesthood in the churches he founded, something the Literalists deemed necessary to ensure the subjection of its clergy and Faithful to the Church's authority. Moreover, the bishops did not want the masses doing what Paul had so strongly urged: working out their own salvation. The Church wanted passive obedience, not karmic self-responsibility. The bishops therefore turned to Peter, who allegedly had organized his church in Jerusalem along the authoritarian lines the bishops favored and wished to promote.

Gnostic Christians — the Literalist Christians called them "misguided" — regarded the Acts of the Apostles as a crude anti-Gnostic forgery whose purpose was to claim Peter as the founder of the Literalist Church. "Literalists," say Freke and Gandy in *The Laughing Jesus[77]*, "needed an apostle of their own with the clout to rival the Gnostic Christians' great apostle Paul." Using the fact that Paul himself said he had never met Jesus, Acts...forgery or not...deftly converted him into a Literalist subordinate to Peter.

Anti-Semitism

The most heinous and insidious manipulation of the New Testament was and remains its systematic condemnation of Jews.

Jesus' alleged statement from the cross, "Forgive them, Father, for they know not what they do", is found only in Luke (23:34). This prayer has been interpreted as a reference either to the Roman soldiers who were carrying out the crucifixion or more commonly to the Jewish crowd, i.e., Jesus was asking God to forgive the Jewish people and their leaders for crucifying him. Scholars have long been divided, writes Ehrman in *Misquoting Jesus[78]*, on whether the prayer was in the original version of Luke. It's easy to see why there was a division of opinion.

According to a footnote in my Bible, Jesus' statement above from the cross "does not occur in the oldest papyrus manuscript of Luke and in other early Greek manuscripts and ancient versions of wide geographical distribution". I must ask, if this statement attributed to Jesus does not appear in the oldest manuscript of Luke, why was it included in later versions? The obvious answer is to vilify Jews. Yet clearly the statement is a forgery. Supporting this conclusion is the fact that the other three Gospels don't mention this prayer from the cross. Luke was written some 60 years after Jesus' death, during which period both Mark and Matthew were written. The author of Luke or someone else simply made up the "forgive them" line to heighten the culpability of the Jerusalem Jews for Jesus' crucifixion.

Spong notes that, whenever the phrase "the Jews" is used in the Gospel of John, it carries a pejorative undertone. For example, John 8:44 quotes Jesus as saying to the Jews, "You belong to your father the devil, and you willingly carry out your father's desires." Do you really believe that the loving, kind, merciful Jesus could have spoken such villainous words? I don't. They sound to me like an early Christian bishop's virulent curse voiced before his congregation to rile them up against the hated Jews. Indeed, I suggest that these words were concocted by the author of John or someone else.

Another example is John 20:19, which says that after Jesus' crucifixion the disciples locked the doors of their room "for fear of the Jews". The Gospels built a daunting case that not surprisingly completely exonerated Pontius Pilate of Jesus' death while fixing blame squarely on the Jews. Identified below are the passages in each Gospel that describe Jesus' trial before Pilate, the salient event upon which Christian anti-Semitism is based, and that absolve Pilate and by association the Romans of any guilt. Each Gospel hammered home the message that the Jews were culpable.

Number of Times the Crowd Shouts "Crucify him!"

Mark	15:13, 14	2
Matthew	27:22, 23	2
Luke	23:21, 23	3
John	19:6, 15	4

Jewish Accusations Against Jesus

Mark	15:3	The chief priests accused him of many things.
Mark	15:4	See how many things they [the Jews] accuse you of?
Matt.	27:13	Do you not hear how many things they [the Jews] are testifying against you?
Luke	23:2	We [the Jews] found this man misleading our people; he opposes the payment of taxes to Caesar and maintains that he is the Messiah, a king.
Luke	23:5	He is inciting the people [the Jews] with his teaching.
Luke	23:10	The chief priests and scribes stood by accusing him harshly.
Luke	23:14	You [chief priests, rulers, and the people]...accused him of inciting the people to revolt.
John	19:7	According to [our Jewish] law he ought to die, because he made himself the Son of God.
John	19:12	[The Jews cried out] If you [Pilate] release him, you are not a friend of Caesar. Everyone who makes himself a king opposes Caesar.

Pilate Exonerates Himself

Mark	15:14	What evil has he done?
Matt.	27:23	What evil has he done?
Matt.	27:24	I am innocent of this man's blood.
Luke	23:4	I find this man not guilty.
Luke	23:14	I have not found this man guilty.
Luke	23:22	What evil has this man done? I found him guilty of no capital crime.
John	18:38	I find no guilt in him.
John	19:4	I find no guilt in him.
John	19:6	I find no guilt in him.

Pilate Hands Jesus over to the Jews

Matt.	27:24	Look to it yourselves [the crowd/the Jews].
Mark	15:15	Pilate handed him over [to the crowd/the Jews] to be crucified.
Luke	23:25	Pilate handed Jesus over to them [the crowd/the Jews] to deal with as they wished.
John	18:31	Take him yourselves [the crowd/the Jews] and judge him according to your law.
John	19:6	Take him yourselves [the crowd/the Jews] and crucify him.
John	19:16	Pilate handed him over to them [the crowd/the Jews] to be crucified.

The Historic Admission of Jewish Culpability

Matt.	27:25	And the whole people [the crowd/the Jews] said, "His blood be upon us and upon our children."

The last quotation is the most curious of all and the most questionable. Why would people in the crowd, the Jews, say this? It clearly is a case of cursing themselves. Why would they do that? If they were, as the New Testament alleges, demanding Jesus' crucifixion, they certainly didn't believe that Jesus was divine, the Son of God, the Messiah. That being the case, why would they think that their crucifying Jesus merited cursing themselves? Eisenman agrees in *James, the Brother of Jesus*[79]: "Who could conceive of a crowd en masse uttering such an absurd statement. The answer is simple. No crowd ever did." Indeed, the quotation is downright implausible and a pure, glaring, outrageous anti-Semitic fabrication. That it remains in the sanctified holy writ of the Catholic Church is an abomination.

These manipulations are consistent with the anti-Semitic tone evident throughout the Gospels. "The clear message portrayed in the gospels," writes Spong[80], "is that Jews are negative, sinister, anti-Christian characters who were responsible for the death of Jesus." Do you really believe God and the Holy Spirit had a hand in writing the Gospel of John?

Erhman in *Lost Christianities*[81]: Reflecting their intense anti-Semitic indoctrination, Christians in the 2nd and 3rd centuries in self-righteous hindsight claimed that the destruction of Jerusalem and the slaughter of its inhabitants in the year 70 by Roman armies were God's vengeance upon the Jews for killing Christ.

During the early centuries, the descriptions in the Gospels of Jesus' trial reflect not only an increasing early-Christian enmity toward Jews but a persistent and increasing need to attack them, possibly to ingratiate the Christians with Roman gentiles, who became the primary target of Christian recruiting. In no time at all, condemning Jews for Jesus' death and every other evil became one of the keystones of Catholic doctrine...and a blight on the human conscience.

"European Jews," writes Ellerbe in *The Dark Side of Christian History*[82], "were often the first victims of a crusade. But the Church's persecution of Jews continued long after the crusades. Jews became the scapegoats for many problems that the Church could not fix. When the bubonic plague struck in the 14th century, the Church explained that Jews were to blame and prompted attacks upon them. A whole folklore developed claiming that Jews kidnapped and ate Christian children in Jewish rituals of cannibalism, and that Jews stole and profaned the blessed Christian sacraments... Pogroms, the raiding and destroying of Jewish synagogues and ghettos, became a common demonstration of Christian righteousness throughout Christendom."

Falsely blaming all Jews worldwide and from ages past for Jesus' death was one of the most nefarious allegations in history, for it resulted in the persecution, brutalization, torture, and death of literally tens of millions of Jews over the centuries — innocent men, women, children, and babies. An example of this common bigotry and its evil effects was manifest in an incident in Poland related by Spong[83]:

> Well before Pope John Paul II became the Vicar of Christ, he attended performances in Kalwaria, Poland of the annual Easter passion play where his grandfather and great-grandfather had volunteered as guides. People from all over Poland flocked to the shrine to take part in the drama of the Savior's crucifixion . The actor playing Christ stumbled and bled as he pulled the cross up to Golgotha. Crowds were worked to a frenzy as Jesus died, the victim of the Jews, "the Christ killers!" Afterwards, as peasants streamed out of the monastery, their passions stirred by religion and vodka, they attacked Jews whose distinctive Hassidic appearance made them easy to identify.

Most of the Faithful aren't aware of it, but there is uncontestable evidence that the Vatican appealed to Hitler — in vain, as you might expect — to spare German Jews who had converted to the Catholic Faith, writes John Cornwell, award-winning journalist, author, and director of the Science and Human Dimension Project at Jesus College, Cambridge, in his book, *Hitler's Pope: The Secret History of Pius XII*.[84] That the Pope did not see fit to appeal for the lives of all German Jews was unforgivable and showed that the Church even in the late 1930s and early 1940s not only still held the Jews accountable for Jesus' death but continued to harbor and promulgate a deep animosity toward them.

Even today, at Easter time, Catholics at Masses around the world, role-playing the "crowd", i.e., the Jews, at the annual re-enactment of Jesus' trial before Pilate, chorus those infamous vicious words, "Crucify him! Crucify him!" Clearly the Vatican intends for this role-playing to indelibly reinforce in the parishioners' minds each year the familiar charge against the Jews. Why else do it? And a lame rationale that it isn't "Jews" the congregations role play but the "crowd" at Jesus' trial won't sell. According to the Gospels, Jerusalem at that time of year was crowded with Jews who came to celebrate Passover. Jerusalem, moreover, was a Jewish city. If the Catholic Church seriously regrets and wishes to atone for its evil treatment of Jews in ages past, it would do well to exclude from this annual dramatization of Jesus' crucifixion the congregation's crying out "Crucify him! Crucify him!"

The Church has publicly but temperately apologized for its past predations against Jews. Fifty years — fifty years! — after the monstrous German atrocities against Jews in the Thirty's and throughout the Second World War, the Vatican, grudgingly I would say, it never having done so in the past two thousand years, expressed its regrets to the Jewish people around the world. In 1986, Pope John Paul II made an historic visit, the first ever by any Pope, to the central synagogue in Rome. In 1998 he expressed remorse for the cowardice <u>of some Christians</u> during World War II. On the first Sunday in Lent in 2000, notes Spong in *The Sins of Scripture*[85], the Pope issued a widely publicized apology to those people who had been hurt by the "sons and daughters" of the church. His was an interesting choice of words. You see, it was not the Catholic Church but its "sons and daughters" who were culpable. In 2001 he issued a sweeping apology for the sins of action and omission by Roman Catholics against Orthodox Christians and for missionary abuses against indigenous peoples of the South Pacific.[86]

Why did the Vatican defer for fifty years? The answer is obvious. Even the faintest apology bespoke the Church's 2,000-year-old bigotry. Popular novelist Daniel Silva in *The Confessor*[87] aptly describes the Church's dilemma over its history of anti-Semitism. "What they [the Jews and their friends in the media] do not understand...is that the Church, as the embodiment of Christ on Earth, cannot be *wrong*. The Church is truth itself." Therefore the Church can never admit culpability for the plight and fate of the Jews throughout history including the Nazi Holocaust without admitting the Church's infernal hypocrisy to the entire world.

"I apologize for wrecking your car. I was driving too fast and missed a turn. I'm sorry." How does this apology compare to "The Church is sorry it caused the cruel deaths of tens of millions of innocent people over the centuries"? The driver of the car can pay for the damages. The Church can <u>never</u> pay for the lives of the dead, which are priceless. "But," would say the Church and its most Christian Faithful, "it's time to forgive and forget. That was then; now is now. We have to put the past behind us." Why? Why sweep all of the Church's crimes and horrors under the rug of consciousness conveniently out of sight and out of mind? Because to believe Holy Mother Church could be complicit in these outrages against humanity is too shameful?

The Church's culpability flows from one generation to the next, because the Church again and again, century after century, endorsed these outrages, even through the Second World War. Therefore it will never be time for me and a great many others to forgive and forget until the Catholic Church admits to the world that it was the *Church itself*, not just its *sons and daughters*, who committed these crimes. It will never be time to forgive and forget until the Church desists from its Easter re-enactment of Jesus' trial and its blatant message of anti-Semitic hate. It will never be time to forgive and forget until the Church publishes a history of its crimes against humanity, especially the Jews, and apologizes to the people of the entire world. In a court of law this is called *allocution*, when the accused, after pleading guilty and before sentencing, stands before the judge and describes his or her criminal actions. It is only then, in the eyes of the court, that the guilty parties fully acknowledge responsibility for their crimes.

Archbishop Rembert Weakland of Milwaukee came close to doing exactly that before the Congregation Shalom in Fox Point, Wisconsin, in November 1999. "We Catholics [a pseudonym for the *Catholic Church*?] through the centuries acted in a fashion contrary to God's law toward our Jewish brothers and sisters. Such actions harmed the Jewish community through the ages in both physical and psychological ways. I acknowledge that we Catholics — by preaching a doctrine that the Jewish people were unfaithful, hypocritical and God-killers — reduced the human dignity of our Jewish brothers and sisters and created attitudes that made reprisals against them seem like acts of conformity to God's will. By doing so, I confess that we Catholics contributed to the attitudes that made the Holocaust possible."[88] It is high time the Vatican, speaking for the Catholic Church as an organization, made a comparable confession to the world. Do I believe the Vatican will ever publicly allocute the evils the Church has committed? Of course not.

To sum up the foregoing:

The evidence for forgery and wholesale tinkering with the Bible is overwhelming. Words and phrases, even entire sections of the New Testament were added, deleted, and changed over the centuries. It is not my intent, nor is there room in this book, nor do I want to bore you, to present an exhaustive list of all the "known" inconsistencies and perversions of the biblical texts. The "unknowns" are surely vast but regrettably unknowable. To find out for yourself the extent of the "known" falsifications, if you dare, read the books in my bibliography and whatever else you can find on the history of the Bible.

Diehard Christians, of course, paying no heed to that scurrilous *man behind the cur-*

tain, will contend that the story of Jesus, though its recountings in the New Testament admittedly vary, are contradictory, and have, yes, been falsified in part, is still essentially true...the veritable Word of God. I and any number of biblical scholars, to the contrary, contend that the Gospels are an ungodlike mish-mash of unprovable stories, legends, myths, folktales, and postulations. A public phone book is more reliable and truthful than the Gospels because one can at least verify that the listed phone numbers belong to the listed people and organizations. Nothing in the stories of Jesus in the Gospels can be verified. Nothing! If the Gospels are the Word of God, then God must have intended them to be confusing, misleading, and unreliable. But why on Earth (literally) would He do that? To what end? Why would He intentionally blur the message of Jesus, His messenger. And don't tell me He wanted to confuse us in order to "test our faith". That's one of those nonsensical phrases Christian theologians pull out of their magical hats whenever they attribute something to God that is self-contradictory or unexplainable.

I am bothered by the fact that, with one exception, the authors of the research materials I cite for this book repeatedly quote from the New Testament to support their findings without warning of the possible unreliability of those quotes. Of all the many books and other materials I have read, Robert Feather was the only author who I noticed gave such a warning quoted earlier: "...if the accounts in the Christian Scriptures of Jesus' words and views are genuine and not those of later redactors".

Devout Christians who read this book and who would readily gamble their lives on the God's honest truth of the Bible are by now close to losing their tempers and hunting me down to punish me as an heretical blasphemer, maybe burn me at the stake. But to them I say, "Pray be patient. Read on. All will become clear." Of course they may fire me up anyway just for unmasking the Bible's exaggerations and deceptive, misleading language.

Lastly, I concur with Bishop Spong's view[80]: "It is clear that the traditional claim that the Bible is in any literal way the 'Word of God' is problematic at best and absurd at worst." Indeed, I challenge you to prove that the Gospels are the Word of God. You can't, of course. The belief that they are the Word of God is purely a *matter of faith*!

Which is an apt lead-in to the next chapter.

CHAPTER 5

"We prefer to believe what we prefer to be true."
Sir Francis Bacon (1561-1626)

It's a Matter of Faith

Freke and Gandy write in *Jesus and the Lost Goddess*[1] that today's fundamentalist Christian conviction that the Bible is literally the Word of God and cannot therefore be questioned "goes back to the beginnings of the Roman Church at the end of the 2nd century, when Tertullian included *thirst for knowledge* among his list of vices, to be replaced by the virtue of blind faith in scripture". Charles Freeman in *The Closing of the Western Mind*[2] further illuminated the death of reason. With the elaboration of Christian doctrine, he wrote, acquiescing to the Church's teachings was seen as a virtue in itself. Reason took a back seat to faith. The principles of empirical observation and logic were overruled in the conviction that all knowledge came from God, that is, from the Church, God's alter ego on Earth. In particular the writings of Augustine, accepted by the Church as virtual God-inspired gospel, concluded that the human mind, burdened with Adam's original sin, could not think for itself. The abject subjection of reason to faith and authority did much to undermine the classical tradition of rational thought harking back to the Greek philosopher giants. For centuries thereafter any form of independent scientific or philosophical thinking was suppressed.[3] This repression of free thought endured throughout the appropriately named thousand-year Dark Ages.

As I have said, all but a few Catholics are ignorant of Church history and theology. Some adults — a very small percentage — may attend a Bible class now and then, but these sessions are merely conduits for reindoctrinating the Faithful. These inoculations, like getting a tetanus booster shot, preclude the Faithful from having to "think". All they have to do, all the Faithful have ever had to do, is *believe*. To have *faith*.

I dare say the most ludicrous and outrageous statement I have read in my research is attributed in *The Case for Christ*[4] to British theologian Michael Green. "The appearances of Jesus [following his crucifixion] are as well authenticated as anything in antiquity...There can be no rational doubt that they occurred." There being (a) no credible, reliable evidence that Jesus ever existed, (b) only hearsay accounts by devout believers in his divinity of the events that occurred after his alleged crucifixion, and (c) no written official Roman record of the crucifixion, "rational doubt" is indeed the phrase that best describes his appearances. Green's statement clearly was born not from facts or reason but from his unqualified devotion to the veracity of the New Testament. The common phrase "blinded by one's faith" well applies here.

The next time you read the Bible or follow a scriptural reading in church, mentally insert "according to the author" at the end of each sentence. You'll find that your *faith* in the reliability of the Bible will be quickly tested. This experiment will reinforce the fact that the events "reported" are unreliable because they lack proof. I eschew the word "recorded" because it implies the events "reported" actually happened...when there's no conclusive evidence whatever that they did. The Faithful are habituated to using the phrase "The Bible says" as proof of some point or argument. But in truth it isn't the Bible that "says", it's the *authors* of the Bible, which is a completely different thing.

Let's make up a story published hypothetically in the *New York Times* of a Chicago man who his close friends claim was born of a virgin, walked across Lake Michigan atop the water, cured by the touch of his hand the Illinois governor's wife of terminal cancer, changed water into wine at the marriage of the governor's daughter, brought back to life in a mortuary a close friend of the governor, and exorcised demons from a number of crazed people walking the sidewalks of Chicago's State Street. Would serious people believe it? Of course not! Then why do Christians believe in the identical 2,000-year-old tale of a prophet-preacher named Jesus? Because they WANT to believe it! We prefer to believe what we prefer to be true. The Faithful want and need to believe that the Scriptures are true, because they are afraid of dying and desperately hope there is life after death.

Devout Christians are so thoroughly steeped in Christian beliefs that just saying "Jesus Christ" is heartening and spiritual like repeating a holy mantra. For the same reason, televangelists like to proclaim "JESus CHRIST!" and "GAWD!" dramatically in a thundering voice to their spellbound audiences. Doing so enthralls listeners, literally and thankfully drawing them closer spiritually to God, to the evangelist, and to one another, even through the invisible ether of telecommunications. It's no wonder these evangelical television programs — I've watched them, and they can be grand, even thrilling entertainment — rake in millions of dollars in viewer donations. My sincerest hope is that people who watch these programs and attend evangelical meetings will read this book and studiously rethink their unshakable belief that the Bible is the Word of God.

Christians, both Catholic and Protestant, believe what their church leaderships tell them to believe. How do they know that what their leaderships tell them is the truth? It's a matter of faith. When you get right down to it, Christians don't put their trust in their Faith because it's true; they put their trust in it because they have nothing with which to replace it. If Jesus was not divine, then Christianity, as I have said, is nothing but a house of blank cards, most any one of which, like his divinity, if removed, would cause the entire house to collapse, in which case the Faithful would be spiritually marooned, living lives without purpose or reason. Essentially lost souls!

When people are challenged by the discovery of some chink in the armor of their dogmatic beliefs, they react in a universal conditioned reflex, covering that tiny fissure with the time-worn band-aid-like phrase, "It's a matter faith". Frankly, I'm sick of hearing people say in any context, "It's a matter of faith". Synonymous sayings are "have faith," "take it on faith," "your faith will guide you," and so on. What the heck does the word "faith" mean? People bandy the word about as if they and everyone else understood its meaning. It's as if just saying "It's a matter of faith" settles by itself whatever question is under discussion.

> "Will the Green Bay Packers win the Super Bowl this year?"
> "Of course they will."
> "How do you know?"
> "It's a matter of faith!"

> "Will the stock market rise?"
> "Of course it will."
> "How do you know?"
> "I have faith!"

On and on it goes, recycling over and over again in people's conversations and thoughts. Yet few outside of perhaps philosophers, theologians, and stodgy tight-lipped grammarians ever examine what "faith" really means. So let me, the self-professed font of all knowledge, tell you. It means "hope" and nothing more. I repeat, nothing more! When evidence is inconclusive, "faith" and "belief" take over as a last resort.

> Doubter: "There is no reliable evidence that Jesus ever existed."
> Believer: "I don't care. I believe he did. It's a matter of faith!
>   And that's all that counts."

What an empty meaningless statement! What the respondent is really saying is, "I hope he existed because, if he didn't, I'm lost and so is everyone else!"

One of the most absurd spectacles is athletes on *both* of the opposing teams in a competition pointing their fingers toward the sky when they score, say, a touch-down, a goal, or a home run. This gesture means either of two things: "Thank you, God, for giving me the athletic prowess which enabled me to score" or more likely "Thank you, God, for siding with my team," as if God had directly intervened. The implication in the latter case is that God favored the athlete's team over its opponents. That's absurd. More absurd is the notion that God deserted the losing side, the vanquished. God surely loves all of his creations equally. I repeat, equally. (I can't prove it, of course! But it seems logical to me.) Why would an athlete believe that God would favor the athlete's team winning rather than the opponents? Because the victorious athlete, the victorious army, the victorious whoever want to win! And when they do, they gratefully attribute their victory to God. Humans have been doing that for centuries. To the true believer, ignoring His involvement is a serious sin.

There's no substance to either "faith" or "belief" and certainly none whatever to "hope". "Faith" is a meaningless word because, being an assertion, it by definition requires no proof. In other words, Faith is believing in something that can't be proven. "Assertion" means "to state positively with great confidence but with no objective proof". Without proof, without evidence, assertions are hollower and more futile than a mournful cry in the wilderness. For that reason they occur whenever evidence runs out, like the air in a tire, causing the "proofs" of one's arguments and contentions to go flat, founder, and disappear, leaving one only to claim, profess, and assume. Consider, for example, the following bit of illuminating dogma excerpted from *The Catechism of the Catholic Church*[5]:

> "If God the Father almighty, the Creator of the ordered and good world, cares for all his creatures, why does evil exist? To this question, as pressing as it is unavoidable and as painful as it is <u>mysterious, no quick answer</u> will suffice. <u>Only Christian faith as a whole constitutes the answer to this question.</u>" [my underlinings]

As you can see, when there is "no quick answer" — no defensible proof — to some aspect of Catholic dogma, the Church is quick to label it a "mystery," in which case the Church's only conceivable recourse is to *faith*. "Only *faith* is the answer," says the Church. But, of course, it's no answer at all. It simply evades the question, a tactic that Catholic theologians have employed for centuries — and still do — when the "logic" of their dogma leads to a dead end. And there are countless dead ends in Catholic dogma.

I can hear your outraged cries: "Blasphemer!" "Heretic!" "Demon!" Yeah, yeah, I know you'd like to get your hands around my neck and choke me to death. That is, is it not, the tried and true Christian tradition established over the past two thousand years? Persecute the godless non-believer! The faithless one! Torture him! Kill him! It is partly because of that very tradition that I have written this book under the pen name Philip Charleston. I don't want any wacko fundamentalists to assault me, my family, my house, or my car or flood my post box or email in-box with death threats and other nasty messages. The other reason, equally practical, is that publicizing my authorship would place me and my employer in an awkward professional position.

Belief can never be relied upon as *truth*, whether it's belief in the Tooth Fairy or the Divinity of Jesus. In the world of science expounding a theory simply because "you believe it to be true" won't get you very far. In fact, it will almost certainly subject you to intense and justifiable derision. What scientists and others whose professions rely on truth look for and demand is "proof" (objectively defensible evidence) not "belief". Will a defense attorney persuade a jury of her client's innocence by merely asserting, "I believe my client is innocent". Of course not. The jury needs to hear and see evidence of the defendant's innocence before rendering a verdict. When a group of architects designs a skyscraper, do they use a particular steel because they simply *believe* it will support the upper stories or because reliable scientific tests have confirmed the steel's strength? The latter, of course. When analysts write reports for CEOs, government officials, high-ranking military brass, and other weighty decision makers, they would be well advised to strike out the words "we believe" and "it is our belief" and replace them where appropriate with phrases like "the following evidence indicates" and "according to". Rational decision makers don't care what analysts *believe*. They want to see the evidence. Assertions without evidence are worthless.

But in the world of religion, which marches to the thundering beat of a wholly different drummer, it is "faith" and "belief," not "evidence," that are the premier guides and final arbiters. A "religious belief," however well reasoned and appealing, is fundamentally nothing more than a "religious myth" because it can't be proven. In the last analysis, as I say, *faith* is nothing more than *hope*. That's why *faith* is routinely called *blind*. The very expression "a leap of faith" connotes a jumping over the void of evidence. The inability to prove a religious *belief* is every religion's Achilles Heel because interpretation of evidence for any "belief" is entirely imaginative and subjective. But that has never deterred Christian theologians and believers. Their dogma is founded upon layer upon layer of nothing more substantial than assertions in which they have devout but necessary *faith*. As Reverend Terrance A. Sweeney stated in the forward to Margaret Starbird's *The Woman with the Alabaster Jar*, "Truth is not defined by political power, nor by religious conviction."

Jesus' descending into the realm of the dead, i.e., Hell, is a good example of dogma based purely on *faith* and *conviction*. There are four and only four statements in the four Gospels — one each — relating that in the aftermath of his crucifixion Jesus "rose from the dead":

Mark	16:6	He has been raised.
Matthew	28:6	He has been raised.
Luke	24:6	He has been raised.
John	20:9	For they did not yet understand the scriptures that he had to rise from the dead.

The Catechism[6] explains: "The frequent New Testament affirmations that Jesus was 'raised from the dead' **presuppose** that the crucified one sojourned in the realm of the dead prior to his resurrection" [my emphasis]. Let's be clear about this. The Catechism therefore confirms that there is no *proof* that Jesus was raised from the dead. Nor for that matter is there proof he descended into Hell. It's <u>all</u> a matter of faith: faith in the veracity of the original texts, faith in the accuracy of the copies of copies of copies of the original texts, faith in the particular words of the Gospels as translated from earlier Greek versions, and faith in the Church's interpretation of those translations. And, of course, that interpretation will always confirm the Church's dogma.

As is the custom among theologians of any religion, "proof" as a matter of practice is found in the findings — the conclusions and interpretations — of earlier texts, just as lawyers in court cite judges' decisions in earlier court cases as precedents to support the lawyers' contentions. To see what I'm talking about, take a peek into www.newadvent.com, the online Catholic encyclopedia. Click on any letter in the reference alphabet and on any subject under that letter. For example, click on "o," then on "Original Sin". You'll find that the discussion of Original Sin, like every other discussion on that website, is littered with source citations such as:

> The "Excerpta Theodori" by Marius Mercator; cf. Smith, "A Dictionary of Christian Biography," IV, 942.

> FMercator, "Liber Subnotationem," preface.

> St. Augustine, "Contra duas epist. Pelag.," IV, iv, 6.

> Denz., n. 175 (145).

> Council of Trent, Session. V, can. ii; Denz., n. 789 (671).

> And so on.

Just because the cited scholars, ancient theologians, ancient convocations, ancient traditions, and ancient believers all agreed upon something doesn't mean that the "something" agreed upon is true. A clear example was the ancient belief, endorsed for centuries as categorically true by the Church, that our solar system revolved around the Earth. But citations merely *reassert*, they don't *prove*. I can cite a hundred writings that claim God spoke to Joan of Arc, the Maid of Orleans, but they don't *prove* He did; they're merely assertions, affirmations, and presuppositions. Likewise the Church's justifications for its intricate dogma that explains every facet of the Catholic Faith are based entirely on assertions, not proofs. Assertions, like "hearsay," are, as I said earlier, as unreliable as the weather.

As the devout will proudly claim, Christianity is replete with "proofs" of its truth: magnificent cathedrals, mesmerizing windows of stained glass, beautiful sculptures, captivating paintings, enthralling music, and eloquent books. Without the inspiration of the *truth* of the story of Jesus and his teachings, claim the devout, these works of art would never have been created. That these works were *inspired* by the story of Jesus, yes; that they *prove* the truth of that story, no. These works are all meaningless window dressing. Do the wondrous pyramids in Egypt prove the truth of the ancient Egyptian religion? Does the breathtakingly beautiful Parthenon in Athens prove that its goddess Athena existed? Does the majesty of the temples dedicated to the gods of Rome prove their existence? Nonsense. They are no more proof than a gifted artist's rendering of his or her personal image of Jesus.

Imagined statue of Jesus by unknown sculptor[7]

The most famous artist's rendering of Jesus is Warren Sallman's 1941 painting, *Head of Jesus*. It has appeared in many different media to illustrate the pages of the Bible, Sunday school literature, calendars, posters, church bulletins, lamps, buttons, and even bumper stickers. The *Head of Christ* has been reproduced over 500 million times, making it one of the most popular art works of all time. David Morgan, an art historian who teaches at Valparaiso University, published a book on the impact this painting has had upon an entire generation of Christians around the world. As one woman put it, the picture appealed to her simply because it showed "just what Jesus looked like". Many millions of devout Christians do take this as an accurate representation.[8]

What I find particularly fascinating is the common practice of putting an ancient painting of eminent figures from the Christian past on the cover of modern books about them. The pictures help the readers to imagine what the individuals looked like, when in fact the paintings are pure fantasy.

What the art works of any religion do is make real the unreal. Humans have been doing this for millennia — sculpting, carving, drawing, stitching representations of their gods both to pray to them and to reinforce belief in them. Do the strains of Handel's Messiah touch our hearts? Indeed, they do, but so do the strains of Puccini's opera La Bohème. Does the Messiah prove the story of Jesus is true? Does

La Bohème prove its characters actually lived? Of course not.

For the past 70 years movies — like The Greatest Story Ever Told, Quo Vadis, Ben Hur, Jesus, The Robe, Jesus of Nazareth, The Ten Commandments, The Passion of Jesus Christ, Jesus the Complete Story, Jesus and His Times, The Miracle Maker, Jesus the Word Became Flesh, The Jesus Film, Mary Mother of Jesus, The Life and Passion of Jesus, The Nativity: The Life of Jesus Christ, Jesus: The Complete Story, The Jesus Film, Jesus of Nazareth and, of course, Mel Gibson's bloody The Passion of the Christ — have brought the events of the Jesus story believably to life, imprinting on them an aura of impeccable historical reality: the virgin birth of Jesus, the three attending Magi, the Star of Bethlehem, Jesus' sermons, his miracles, his disciples, the Blessed Virgin, Pontius Pilate, Jesus' trial, his crucifixion, his resurrection, and so on. Just like ancient works of art, movies in theaters and on television implant in the minds of viewers vivid, and thus memorable and persuasive images...living images...that stay with people and confirm and reaffirm their heartfelt faith in the Jesus story every time they view these works of Christian art. These works in fact make the viewers veritable "eyewitnesses" to the events in that story.

But do such works prove the story of Jesus. Of course not.

What about Hell?

Hell, like a towering monolith, casts its formidable shadow across the full range of Catholic dogma. Fifty-nine percent of 35,000 Americans in a survey conducted in 2007 said they believe there is a Hell where people who have led bad lives and die without being sorry are eternally punished.[9] Belief in Hell is mandated by Christianity. *It's a matter of faith.* Indeed, if you call yourself a Christian but don't believe in Hell, you're in the wrong pew, the wrong church, and the wrong religion.

The *Encyclopedic Dictionary* in my Bible says, "In the New Testament teachings, Hell is the place and state of eternal punishment to which are condemned all who die with unrepented mortal sin on their souls. Here the damned suffer primarily the pain of loss by being deprived of the sight of God face to face; and secondly, the pain of sense, a positive physical punishment which we call fire. [As you can well imagine, it's the secondary pain on which Christians understandably fixate.] The degree to which each soul suffers is not necessarily equal but is determined by the measure of the individual's sinfulness." That sums it up pretty well. If you sin, you deserve punishment. That punishment, by fire in proportion to your sins, is inflicted in Hell, where you can't see the face of God and are tortuously separated from Him.

Is the concept of Hell as depicted in the Bible unique? Not at all. Belief in an underworld where humans go after death to be judged and punished has been a mythical feature of religions for millennia. Take the Romans. They believed that, when you died, your life was reviewed by three underworld judges. If the judges decided your behavior in life had offended the gods, you were punished until your "debt to society" was paid. Take the ancient Egyptians. Osman writes in *Christianity*[10] that they believed the god Osiris resided in the underworld as the punishing judge of the dead.

According to the four Gospels, Jesus never used the word "hell". Instead he is said to have used the word "gehénna" — the equivalent of the Christian Hell — eleven times:

> Mark — three times (9:43, 9:45, 9:47)
> Matthew — seven times (5:21, 5:29, 5:30, 10:28, 18:9, 23:15, 24:32)
> Luke — once (12:5)
> John — not at all.

It turns out that the Jewish word "Gehenna" in Jesus' time meant the "Valley of Hinnom's son" and referred to a garbage dump in a valley not far from Jerusalem. The bodies of executed criminals, individuals denied a proper burial, the carcasses of animals, and every other kind of filth were dumped there. Fires were kept burning, unquenchably, at the dump to consume the refuse and keep down the stench, which could be smelled downwind for miles. The use of the word Gehenna was an allegorical phrase likening the fate of sinners to that of garbage.[11]

The Catechism claims that the proof of Hell is found in the New Testament, which contains the following specific references to it. The Catechism cites other New Testament phrases as well, but the relevance of those citations to the existence of Hell is in my opinion strained and unconvincing.

Matthew

3:12	His [Jesus'] winnowing fan is in his hand, and he will thoroughly clean out his threshing floor, and will gather his wheat into the barn; but *the chaff he will burn up with unquenchable fire.*
5:29-30	It is better for you to lose one of your members than to have *your whole body thrown into Gehenna*...It is better for you to lose one of *your members than to have your whole body thrown into Gehenna.* [repeated once]
10:28	Be afraid of the one who can *destroy both soul and body in Gehenna.*
13:42	They will *throw them into the fiery furnace*, where there will be *wailing and grinding of teeth.*
13:50	And *throw them into the fiery furnace* where there will be *wailing and grinding of teeth.*
18:8	It is better for thee to enter life maimed or lame, than...to be cast into *the everlasting fire.*

25:41	Then he will say to those on his left, "Depart from me, you accursed, into *the internal fire* prepared for the devil and his angels."
25:46	And these will go off to *eternal punishment*, but the righteous to *eternal life*.

Luke

8:31	And they entreated him not to command them to *depart into the abyss*.
16:22	When the poor man died, he was carried away by angels to the bosom of Abraham. The rich man also died and was buried, and from the netherworld, where he was in torment, he raised his eyes and saw Abraham far off and Lazarus at his side. And he cried out, "Father Abraham, have pity on me. Send Lazarus to dip the tip of his finger in water and cool my tongue, for I am suffering torment in these flames."
16:28	For I have five brothers, that he may testify to them, lest they too come into *this* place of torments.

2 Thessalonians

1:7-9	For it is surely just on God's part to repay with afflictions who are afflicting you, and to grant rest along with us to you who are undergoing afflictions, at the revelation of the Lord Jesus from Heaven with his mighty angels, *in blazing fire, inflicting punishment* on those who do not acknowledge God and on those who do not obey the gospel of our Lord Jesus.
Jude 7	Just as Sodom and Gomorrah, and the neighboring cities which like them committed sins of immorality and practiced unnatural vice, have been made an example, undergoing *the punishment of eternal fire*.

2 Peter

2:4	For God did not spare the angels when they sinned, but *dragged them down by infernal ropes to Tartarus* [in Greek mythology the god of Hell], and delivered them to be *tortured* and kept in custody for judgment.
2:17	These men are springs without water and mists driven by storms; *the blackness of darkness* is reserved for them.

Revelation

1:18	I [Jesus] hold the keys to death and *the netherworld*.
14:10	Anyone who worships the beast [Satan] or its image, or accepts its mark on forehead or hand, will also drink the wine of God's fury, poured full strength into the cup of his wrath, and *will be tormented in burning sulfur* before the holy angels and before the Lamb.
20:15	Anyone whose name was not found written in the book of life was thrown into *the pool of fire*.

Revelation

Since the New Testament as well as the Church say there's a Gehenna or Hell, then that settles it for Christians. Hell exists.

Or does it? The authors of the texts in the New Testament certainly *believed* it existed, but that, as I have said, doesn't mean it did.

The age-old Christian belief in Hell follows from basically four premises:

> Premise #1: The Gospels are the actual Word of God.

> Premise #2: According to the Gospels, we are all sinners.

> Premise #3: According to the Gospels, sinners are detested and punished by God after death.

> Premise #4: According to the Gospels, sinners, after death, go to a place called Hell for their punishment.

Let's examine each of these premises and see how much water they hold.

Premise #1: The Gospels are the actual Word of God.

> Not! As I explained in the previous chapter, the Gospels are a mish-mash of unprovable stories and assertions hardly warranting God's authorship. For devout Christians to claim they are the actual Word of God is self-serving, unprovable, and *solely a matter of faith.*

Premise #2: According to the Gospels, we are all sinners.

> As Alexander Pope so profoundly observed, to be human is to err, that is, in the context of Catholic dogma, "to sin". Erring/sinning (being prideful, envious, gluttonous, lustful, angry, greedy, slothful, arrogant, jealous, avaricious, hateful, vengeful, spiteful, unchaste, malicious, deceitful, licentious, adulterous, lying, cheating, harboring evil thoughts, stealing, hurting others, or murdering someone) is what <u>all</u> humans do in widely varying degrees. As Wilbur Smith observed in his novel, *Heaven and Hell*[12], we humans "always are prey to evil ideas that cloak themselves in a seductive righteous-

ness". We err because we are the flawed humans God made us. He certainly didn't make us saints — at least not all of us. Both the Old and New Testaments misconstrue the truth when they label these "errors" acts of disobedience to God and an insult to God. That's ridiculous. How can they be disobedient and insulting to God when they are the direct result of the way He made us? If He had not intended for us to err/sin, He would not have made us prone to err/sin. We err/sin because He designed us to err/sin. How are we then culpable? We're not! We're doing precisely what He intended our human frailty to cause us to do. Are we therefore "sinners"? Never!

As anyone who has observed human behavior will testify, "People rarely use the brains God gave them." Three examples — there are thousands:

> Motorcyclists speed down highways without wearing a helmet or other protective clothing. As the saying goes, *It's not if you're motorcycle is going to be involved in an accident, it's when!* Obviously these cyclists, unlike the rest of us, know exactly when, where, and how they're going to die. Or do they?

> Then there are people, both young, middle-aged, and old, who are heavy smokers. Now that's really stupid, since everyone by now knows full well the dangers involved and the price that some day they will most likely have to pay in the form of a prolonged, horrifically painful withering away until they're dead. The truth is they like to smoke, so they simply shut down their brains rather than consider the awful consequences.

> Lastly, how about high-salaried, high-living lawyers who haven't made out wills to protect their families. And I thought lawyers were smart people.

Everyone of us does stupid things, especially while driving an automotive vehicle, myself included. I figure I make at least one really stupid decision a month while driving, mostly when I'm in a hurry or tired, any of which decisions could kill me or someone else or send all of us to a hospital. Yes, there's no arguing about it: people don't always use their brains. But does that make them sinners? Not at all. It makes them human, as God made them.

Premise #3: According to the Gospels, sinners are detested and punished by God in the afterlife.

Ancient humans attributed the most serious setbacks in life to "angry" gods. The sound of thunder was sure evidence of a god's anger. A lightning bolt was the finger of an angry god. If a clan could find no food, it was because the clan or some member had angered a god and the whole clan was being punished. If a child died, it was a punishment imposed on the parents for something they did that made the gods angry. Century after century humans put the blame for their suffering on their gods or, in Christian times, on the One God or alternatively on Satan, the god of evil. For example, Jimmy Breslin in *The Church That Forgot Christ*[13] relates that Cardinal Paul Cullen said the great famine in Ireland in 1845 was "a calamity with which God wished to purify the Irish people". How else to explain these misfortunes? How else indeed?

It's easy to see how natural calamities prompted ancient peoples to attribute the causes of any misfortunes to gods. Fear of gods thus became a driving force in the way people in every ancient civilization ordered their lives, leading universally to animal and even human sacrifices to appease deities, atone for "sins", and forestall punishments.

The Old and New Testaments therefore did not invent fear of God or the concept of divine retribution. Those two ideas had been around for millennia. So it was no great leap, indeed, it was a very small step, for early Christians to transfer their fear of their many earlier gods to Jesus' single god and to his everlasting punishment. Moreover, there being then only ONE god, not hundreds, the power of Jesus' god became greater than that of all the others put together. The greater the power, the greater the punishment, the greater the fear.

But was it true that lightning bolts, miscarriages, crop failures, hurricanes, and disease were evidence of God's anger? Of course not. We know today they are the result of natural causes. Still a devout Christian, especially one of the fundamentalist crowd, would argue that God instigated these natural calamities to inflict hardships on sinners as punishment for their wrongdoings. True, a devout Christian could make that argument, but there is no proof that God inflicts hardships on us as a means of punishment. Still, say the devout, it's possible.

This possibility raises two decisive questions:

Does God get angry and vengeful? Anger and vengeance are human emotions. As much as the authors of the Old and New Testaments strove to humanize God, following the traditions and beliefs of ancient civilizations, especially the Greeks, it's a non-starter. Freke and Gandy write in *The Jesus Mysteries*[14] that the early Christians and authors of the Gospels carried on the Hebrew tradition of humanizing god, provoking the Roman Pagan philosopher and satirist Celsus to write: "The Christians' absurd doctrines even contain reference to God walking about in the garden [of Eden] he created for man. And they speak of him being angry, jealous, moved to repentance, sorry, sleepy — in short, being in every respect more a man than a God."

Christians are easily led to believe God exhibits human emotions because, according to Genesis, He created humans "in His own image". Humans are therefore driven to the implausible logic that, if they have emotions, so does God.

To claim that God has human traits, however, is to minimize Him, to make Him human, to make Him fallible, like the gods of the ancient Greeks. In Mark 8:27, Jesus reportedly chastises his listeners for doing that very thing: "You are thinking not as God does, but as human beings do." If God can exhibit anger and vengeance, what other human traits does He have. Does God relish strawberry sundaes? Does an enticing female figure arouse His lust? Does He enjoy watching a major-league sport like European football or American baseball? Can He be jealous? Envious? Prideful? When you think about it, it's absurd. God's essence is beyond understanding.

To suggest that God has human traits is an aberration, a clutching at straws to defend an indefensible dogma which claims to understand God and to know His thoughts. The only possible way today's Christian theologians — like their ancient predecessors — can understand God and know His thoughts is to humanize Him. Make Him like us. Mirror-image Him to make Him recognizable and understandable. Bring Him down to our infinitesimally primitive level. We are envious of others, so God, too, must be envious. We are prideful, so God, too, must be prideful. We get angry, so God, too, must get angry. We are vengeful, so God, too, must be vengeful. We punish those who make us angry, so

God, too, must punish those who anger Him. Such self-imaging is absurd because God, the all-powerful, omniscient, omnipresent Creator of the Universe, is *not human*. He does not have human characteristics. He is *God*!

Does God punish us? If God lacks human traits, He lacks cause or impetus to punish us. He created us and, being all-knowing, He knows beforehand how, when, and why we will *stumble* (sin) during our sojourns on Earth. Indeed, in Matthew 6:5 Jesus reportedly acknowledged God's power of precognition: "Your Father knows what you need before you ask Him." Since God, according to Matthew, knows in advance what our downfalls will be, why in Heaven's name would He be angry and vengeful and punish us for doing what the failings He inculcated in us predictably cause us to do?

The fact is, as I mentioned earlier, humans, not God, created the concept of punishment for sins...a concept elaborated by the "all-seeing" Augustine into a shining pillar of Catholic dogma. His line of reasoning ran as follows:

Humans suffer (aches, sickness, accidents, miscarriages, torture, etc.).
Why do they suffer? Because they angered God in some way.
Why did they anger God? Because they acted in ways He did not intend.

I ask you, how could Augustine possibly know what God intended? He could read God's mind? Absurd! Moreover, as I have said earlier, if we are not what God intended, why didn't He correct His "mistake"? The answer is simple: God doesn't make mistakes, so we are indeed what He intended.

Augustine's reasoning and its conclusion are simple: doing things that offend God is evil; evil deserves God's punishment; God metes out this punishment. After all, in the eyes of the Church and all faithful Christians, don't "sinners" <u>deserve</u> God's punishment?

In the Christian view of the world, punishment follows evil. Stories, movies, television shows where the bad guys and gals get it at the end have strong appeal to Christians. These tales reaffirm and vindicate Christian belief in God's punishment of sinners.

Augustine cited the plight of babies as "proof" that God punishes us. *New Advent*[15] reports that, according to Augustine, the maladies that some infants suffer — born blind, deaf, ailing, deformed, or retarded — are clear evidence of punishment imposed by God on the infants' parents for some sin they committed. Asserts Augustine, *"God would not allow suffering where there was no prior fault."* How did Augustine know this? He must have been reading God's mind again. In fact, Augustine's assertion is a mammoth assumption, nothing more...and a patently false one in my view.

Does God punish people who ride motorcycles without putting on a helmet? Does God punish shoplifters? Does God punish two teenagers who get carried away while necking and end up having sex? Does God punish the husband or wife who, after several stiff alcoholic drinks, has sex with a stranger in a hotel room? The Church surely would...with relish! Does God punish a stressed-out driver who in a rage shoots the driver of another car? I can't believe God would. He would understand that people, especially the young and the downhearted, do foolish, rash things driven by their raging hormones or the endless stress and frustration of life — the very stress and frustration that God willed to be part of life on Earth. Do they deserve then to be condemned to Hell? The Church says so. I don't. Nor do I believe God would, because He would understand, with monumentally greater insight into human behavior than we minimally simplistic humans could with our ridiculously rudimentary pea brains, why these "sinners" did what they did.

In the Forward to this book I related my asking a knowledgeable priest that niggling question: "Why would an all-loving, all-merciful, limitlessly omniscient God create souls and place them on Earth, knowing in advance as He must, that certain of those souls would commit unpardonable sins and be condemned to the torturous fires of Hell for all eternity?" His response was, "It's one of the great mysteries." The reason he called it a "mystery" is that the Catholic Church has no reasonable explanation for this timeless enigma. The priest's response to my question was that time-honored standby "Don't bother me with unanswerable questions. Just believe! Be quiet! And pay no attention to that annoying *man behind the curtain!*"

In other words, "Have faith!"

Premise #4: Sinners, after death, go to a place called Hell for punishment.

If one believes, as the Church alleges, that God punishes sinners after death, then logically there must be a place where that punishment occurs. So where the hell is this place called Hell? All of the many sources I researched, while in unanimous agreement that Hell by design totally separates the sinner from God and Heaven, offer no evidence as to its location. Indeed, neither the Bible nor New Advent's online encyclopedia nor any other religious text I could find offers an answer to this question...and for obvious reasons.

The essay on Hell in *New Advent* is no help at all:

> "As to [Hell's] locality all kinds of conjectures have been made...The Bible seems to indicate that Hell is within the Earth, for it describes Hell as an abyss into which the wicked descend...[Hell] is said to be as remote as possible from [God's] dwelling, far from Heaven above and its light, and consequently hidden away in the dark abysses of the Earth... Theologians generally accept the opinion that Hell is really within the Earth. But the Church has decided nothing on this subject; hence we may say Hell is a definite place; but where it is, we do not know".

No kidding!

The science of geology, however, has scotched the notion that Hell is deep within the Earth. Unassailable scientific evidence indicates that at the center of the Earth lies "a solid inner core of pure iron the size of the Moon, an outer liquid core rich in iron the size of Mars, and an irregular boundary between the liquid core and the bottom of the rocky mantle".[16] The Faithful will, of course, argue that Hell could still be in a cavern or some other structure within the Earth's iron core. If you agree with that argument, be my guest.

Elsewhere the *New Advent* essay[17] makes an outlandish declaration: "The Bible proves the existence of Hell." The Bible, of course, does nothing of the kind. Nevertheless, New Advent goes on to claim that the existence of Hell can be demonstrated "by the light of mere reason". New Advent's reasoning goes like this:

God must avenge the violation of the moral order in such a way as to preserve a balance between the gravity of sin and the severity of its punishment.

First of all, what makes the Church think God is an avenger? It's that tendency again among all people of whatever god-believing religion to humanize Him. But avenging oneself or others is a human trait. God is not human. God is God! The Church avers that God is all-loving and all-merciful. Therefore there can't be a vengeful bone in his "body".

Secondly, if, as I maintain, God doesn't punish us for our "sins," the notion of a balance between gravity of sin and severity of punishment is illogical and senseless. The only reason the Church claims the necessity for such a balance is because the Church needs (a) to claim that God, *through the Church*, punishes sinners and (b) punishments vary according to the severity of the sin, the severity being determined, of course, by the Church by dint of its "God-given authority" on Earth, an authority to which any adversity will be severely punished...by God!

It is evident that God does not always punish sinners on Earth.

The truth is there's no evidence that He punishes anyone *anywhere*! If people injure themselves by falling off ladders, is it purely accidental or are they being punished by God for their sins? If a woman suffers a miscarriage, is she being punished by God? Is someone who wakes up in the morning suffering a blinding headache from guzzling too much alcohol the night before being punished by God? Members of the Women's Christian Temperance Union would certainly contend so, but where's the proof? If a husband beats his wife, is she being punished by God or is her beating just one of the hardships that life on Earth inflicts on all of us by God's design? Since there's no way to tell, the "evidence" is in the eye of the beholder...which is no proof at all.

If all people were convinced that the sinner need fear no kind of punishment after death, moral and social order would be seriously menaced.

Rephrased for clarity, this convoluted sentence means, as I read it, that if people fear punishment for their sins, moral and social order won't be seriously menaced. Yet, what is the evidence over the past two thousand years, despite widespread fear of punishment after death, that moral and social order in the world have not been seriously menaced? Take a look at history. Look at the world today. Have "moral and social order" ever <u>not</u> been menaced? Case closed!

God cannot permit the disruption of moral and social order.

Why can't He? To assert that He can't is to restrict His powers and again to read His mind. Moreover, as I just said, the moral and social order of Earth's civilizations have always been disrupted.

If God did not exact retribution on sinners, He would be indifferent to good and evil.

Who says He isn't? The Church, of course. If God were indifferent to good and evil, the entire foundation of Christian doctrine would evaporate in a nanosecond, so it doesn't take a rocket or any other kind of scientist to understand why the Church makes this phony claim.

If God were indifferent to good and evil, we could not account for His justice and holiness.

We can't account for His justice and holiness in any case. Doing so means reading His mind. It is outrageously presumptuous, indeed silly, of the Church to presume it knows what God thinks and wants.

Punishment of evil is the natural counterpart of the reward of virtue.

Really? Sounds like another perverted theological assertion to me. What if "punishment" — by which I mean life's inevitable struggle, pain, and uncertainty — is nothing more than what God meant life to be? It could very well be the "virtue" of life. I for one believe it is.

If all wicked people were annihilated indiscriminately, there would be no due proportion between demerit and punishment.

Proportion? This statement is ridiculous. From where did the Church acquire this notion of proportionality? Out of thin air! Moreover, if God, as I contend, doesn't punish, then the concept of proportionality doesn't apply. What else can I say?

If there were no punishment for sins, there would be no deterrent to sinning.

Who says there's a deterrent? If "sinning" (making mistakes) is a natural component of life, then there's no reason for God's punishment of "sinners". If there's no reason for punishment, its deterrent effect on "sinning" (making mistakes) is non-existent.

So much for proving the existence of Hell by "mere reason". These premises — uniformly assertions without proof — are so full of holes they wouldn't hold a drop of water, not even Holy water.

Critics of my conclusions who believe the Bible is the Word of God will argue that the Bible tells a quite different story. Of course it does! But that story is fatally flawed. The bottom line here is that God does not punish "sinners," i.e., those humans who make mistakes. As I explained in Chapter 2, we are not sinners. Do we make mistakes, hurt people, conduct ourselves in less than honorable ways? Of course we do. We are flawed humans as God made us, and He made us prone to err...prone to "sin". So if we're not sinners, and the errors we make are the result of being human, why would God punish us? The answer is obvious: He wouldn't.

Allow me to digress for a moment to point out that research, according to a 2006 article in *USA Today*[18], has determined that we humans do not become fully concerned about the consequences of our actions until we reach the age of 26. This is one, if not the primary, reason the actuarially determined cost of automobile insurance drops precipitously when drivers reach 26, at which time they become more responsible, less impulsive, and accordingly have fewer accidents. It's probably a primary reason why the base criminal impulses of convicts sent to prison for stealing automobiles, breaking into homes, and other minor crimes ebb when they enter their Thirties. My point — again! — is that we err/sin because our human instincts and other mental traits condition us to err/sin. Do you really believe God punishes car thieves?

If God doesn't punish us, then there's no need for a Hell, which is by any definition a pure myth, a very human-created aberration.

What About Satan?

Pagels in *The Origin of Satan*[19] writes: "In the Hebrew Bible, as in mainstream Judaism to this day, Satan never appears as Western Christendom has come to know him, as the leader of an evil empire, an army of hostile spirits who make war on God and humankind alike. As he first appears in the Hebrew Bible, Satan is not necessarily even evil, much less opposed to God. On the contrary, he appears in the book of Numbers and in Job as one of God's obedient servants — a messenger or angel. In biblical sources the Hebrew term *'the satan'* describes an adversarial role. It is not the name of a particular character. Although Hebrew storytellers as early as the 6th century before Christ occasionally introduced a supernatural character whom they called *the satan*, what they meant was any one of the angels sent by God for the specific purpose of blocking or obstructing human activity."

From this Judaic belief...I repeat "belief"...evolved the Christian Church's tradition of viewing Satan, the Devil, as a fallen angel. *The Catechism*[20] says, "The Church teaches that Satan was at first a good angel, made by God." That the Church "teaches" something automatically makes it "true" for the Faithful, even though no evidence is offered. Because no evidence is offered, the story qualifies as nothing more than a *legend*. So, as the *legend* goes, Satan, growing at odds with God for some unknown reason (another Christian mystery!) was evicted by God from Heaven and fell to Earth where he has since reigned supreme. Sounds like a fairy tale, doesn't it? Something the authors of the novel about the fantasy land named *Narnia* might have dreamed up.

The Catechism,[21] in almost comical fashion, states, "It is a great mystery that providence should permit diabolical activity," meaning it's a mystery that God permits first the existence of Satan on Earth and second Satan's evil activities here. It's comical because, like I said, when an element of Catholic dogma is unexplainable, the Church is quick to label it a "mystery". In fact, there's no *mystery* about Satan at all, because Satan is as much a fiction as the evil queen in *Narnia*.

Ellerbe in *The Dark Side of Christian History*[22] writes: "Why does an almighty loving God, who creates everything, create human suffering? The most common answer was that there must be a conflicting force, power, or god creating the evil; there must be a Devil, a Satan." This answer explained the unexplainable, and no one cared whether the answer was true because it thankfully resolved the question. A "dualistic" theology thus arose which understood life to be a struggle between good and evil, a "war" between God and Satan. But the concept, she says, of a Devil is exclusive to monotheism; evil is easier to understand and does not pose the need for a Devil when there are many deities.

In his book *Religion and the Decline of Magic*[23], Keith Thomas writes of early, pre-monotheistic Judaism: "It was only the triumph of monotheism which made it necessary to explain why there should be evil in the world if God were good. Satan thus helped to sustain the notion of an all-perfect divinity." Accordingly, writes Pagels in *The Origin of Satan*[24], a father of the Church, Justin Martyr, like most other 2nd-century Christians, attributed human afflictions not to God's will but to the malevolence of Satan. The thinking was that, if God were perfect Good, He would never cause His human creations to suffer. Therefore, as Ellerbe writes, there had to be some other deity causing all the trouble. Hence the existence of God was used to "prove" the existence of Satan. Such circular reasoning gives me a headache.

Satan therefore became an increasingly important and personified figure in the Christian Faith, and stories about his origin proliferated.[25] Satan, the stories went, was not an animal or monster but one of God's angels, thus a being of superior intelligence and status — a superhuman alien enemy.[26] He became a convenient stalking horse to absolve Christians of guilt, as they and the Church were and still are understandably committed to blaming Satan — not God — for their weaknesses. In that regard, a famous quip of Flip Wilson, the late comedian who was fond of role-playing a woman complete with wig and outlandish dress, was "the Devil made me do it!" People laughed heartily at the joke because it resonated with them, as most of them were conditioned to blame the Devil for making them sin. Ignoring the fact that Wilson was ridiculing the practice of blaming the Devil for our weaknesses, belief in Satan's existence and his role in sin has not waned. Satan, Christians are taught by their Churches, leads people to sin. Shifting the blame to Satan eases their consciences, shielding them, they hope, from God's wrath.

"The Trent Catechism*," Ellerbe explains[27], "echoed the importance of belief in the devil. Belief in the devil's power became an essential counterpart to belief in God." In other words, the Church needed a Satan. Belief in Satan became and still is a vital Christian tool with which to frighten the Faithful into obedience.

> *The Catholic Church's first and highly revered catechism produced at the Council of Trent in 1545.[28]

The entity of Satan was created by humans to explain misfortune. I repeat, Satan, the Devil, is a human-made creation, not God-made. When bad things happened — headaches, accidents, illness, loss of vision or hearing, starvation, attacks by bestial predators, defeats by hostile invaders, and so on — our long-ago forbears searched for explanations for these adversities. When you slugged a deer in the head with a rock, the animal fell. Cause and effect. When you slipped on wet leaves and hit your head on a log, your head hurt. Cause and effect. Every event had a cause, every cause an effect. But when the cause could not be discerned, say, of a woeful drought, humans looked beyond what they could see and fathom to find some hidden "evil" entity, some causal factor, wielding its wicked power over them. That entity could not have been God, because God protected His beloved humans. Voila! Satan was born. It was only a hop, step, and a jump from Satan to Hell, where Satan surely lived and reigned. Well, he had to reside somewhere!

Please forgive my bluntness, but it's ridiculous to claim that God was powerless to defeat Satan in their purported battle for control over the souls on Earth. Is it truly conceivable that the God who created the vast universe, numberless galaxies, Earth, humans, brains, corpuscles, atoms, and the like would let a "fallen angel" wreak havoc here? Is it conceivable God was powerless against the evil spirit called "Satan"...a very spirit God created? Of course not. It's absurd to believe it. With a blink of God's "eye" this mythical Satan would disappear, leaving behind not a wisp of his mythical blistering brimstone and reeking smoke. God warring with Satan? Ludicrous!

How's this for a conundrum: According to Catholic doctrine, Satan rules the world and leads us Earth-bound souls into sin. God punishes us for our Satan-inspired sins by condemning us to Hell. Satan, who resides in Hell, is therefore God's punishing agent. It's a two-sided whipsawing team effort: Satan leads souls to sin, God sentences the sinners to Hell, Satan in Hell punishes them. At the same time, however, God is supposedly warring with Satan, a powerful, fallen, formerly elitist angel, for dominion over the human souls on Earth. Isn't that a wholesale contradiction? Either God is an ally and collaborator of Satan or an enemy. He can't very well be both, though Catholic dogma, turning its back on that *man behind the curtain*, would have it that way. I'm not going to try to unravel this mythical enigma for you, because it's an insoluble Gordian Knot founded entirely on unprovable assertions and fanciful legends.

What About Purgatory?

The name Purgatory comes from the Latin purgatorius meaning cleansing, which in Church "tradition" (meaning "old beliefs") by reference to certain texts of Scripture means a cleansing by fire. Purgatory, according to the *Encyclopedic Dictionary* in my Bible, is that place or state of punishment where the souls of those who have died still stained by sin "suffer until admitted to Heaven". This suffering purifies the sinners, making them eligible to pass through the Golden Gates.

Where did the concept of Purgatory come from? The Catechism states, "The Church formulated her doctrine of...purgatory especially at the Councils of Florence (1431-1445) and Trent (1545-1563)." *New Advent*[29] elaborates: "The Catholic Church, instructed by the Holy Ghost [by revelation again!], has from the Sacred Scriptures and the ancient tradition of the Fathers taught in Councils and very recently in an Ecumenical synod that there is a purgatory." This is another example of how the Church habitually invokes the participation and approval of the Holy Ghost to validate its dogma, however tenuous that dogma might be. Missing in all of this explanation is that rare commodity called "evidence". What we have in place of "evidence" is *faith, tradition, scripture, councils, synod,* and *instruction by the Holy Ghost.*

Truth be told, Catholic bishops and theologians simply made up the idea of Purgatory from whole cloth. It's all a matter of subjective, highly imaginative interpretation driven by unsupportable dogma. One article of faith is based upon another, one council's findings are based upon those of an earlier council, one tradition is founded upon an earlier tradition, one belief upon an earlier belief. On and on the process goes, spinning delicate, intricate webs of dogma allegedly inspired by revelations from the Holy Spirit

The Florence and Trent thinking about Purgatory went like this: God through Satan punishes Earthly sinners. Those humans who commit mortal sins suffer in Hell for all eternity. But then how is someone punished who commits non-mortal sins or who fails to do penance for venial sins, sins that do not warrant eternal punishment in Hell but would still preclude one's entry into Heaven? The Florence and Trent theologians pondered this puzzle. If these sinners didn't merit Hell, there must be some other place where they go to be punished...to be cleansed of their sins. There just had to be a place for this punishment because, according to Catholic doctrine, you can't enter Heaven with any sins whatever on your soul however menial they might be. This "other" place therefore must lie somewhere between Heaven and Hell. Voila! Purgatory was born.

But there's more. The early theologians, putting their weighty heads together while pensively stroking their snowy beards, perceived that, while sinners condemned to Hell should remain there for eternity, those sent to Purgatory should not, their sins not warranting eternal punishment. They determined, no doubt by further revelation from the Holy Spirit, that the duration of a sinner's stay in Purgatory could be shortened remotely, as it were, by the prayers of humans still alive on Earth. Of course, there's no evidence, hard or soft, either of Purgatory or that prayers free sinners from Purgatory. It's one shaky belief hinging on another, on another, and so on.

What About Limbo?

Having sorted out these imponderables, the Church's great thinkers, both in its early years and in the centuries that followed, wondered what happened to babies who died before being baptized. It was a daunting, highly controversial question. If babies were not baptized, upon death their souls would still carry the burden of Adam's Original Sin, or so the theologians devoutly believed, in which case these unbaptized infants could not enter Heaven. Augustine, a hardliner on punishment to be sure, was decidedly emphatic about it. According to *New Advent*[30], he proclaimed, "If you wish to be a Catholic, do not believe, nor say, nor teach, that infants who die before baptism can obtain the remission of Original Sin....Whoever says that even infants are vivified in Christ when they depart this life without the participation of his Sacrament [baptism] both opposes the Apostolic preaching and condemns the whole Church, which hastens to baptize infants, because it unhesitatingly believes that otherwise they cannot possibly be vivified in Christ."

If unbaptized babies' souls could not enter Heaven because their souls, it was believed, were still tainted by Adam's Original Sin, where did they go upon the death of their human bodies? Not Hell. Not Purgatory. Somewhere else that was neither in Hell nor in Purgatory but also not in Heaven. Somewhere else. So for want of a better name they called it "limbo" meaning neither here nor there. As far as I have been able to determine, the Church has never speculated publicly where Limbo might be. It's location, like that of Hell and Purgatory, is unknown. But it has to be somewhere!

Did the souls of babies suffer in this in-between state, wherever it was? Yes, the theologians concluded, but certainly not physical punishment; it was purely emotional — the pain of separation from God, not knowing Him, not enjoying His beatific vision. That's a relief, because I certainly wouldn't want innocent little babes to suffer the torment of fire.

The doctrine of Limbo rests, like most of Catholic dogma, squarely on the existence of Original Sin. Since, as I explained in Chapter 1, there is no Original Sin, the issue of whether unbaptized babies can enter Heaven is irrelevant, nullifying the already silly doctrine of Limbo.

The logic of my conclusion places the Church in that old proverbial spot between a rock and a hard place. The Church cannot publicly disavow the existence of Limbo, because doing so would belie the Church's supposed God-given (self-proclaimed) infallibility on questions of morals and faith. Moreover, the Church can't recant the existence of Limbo without recanting Purgatory and Hell; they are all peas in the same pod. The only way the Church can deal with this dilemma is to ignore it, which it most certainly will...together with that obnoxious *man behind the curtain*.

My Bible's *Encyclopedic Dictionary* attempts to minimize Limbo's punishment of innocents who, even burdened by Adam's sin, never committed a sin of their own. "Our trust in God's goodness and love leads us to believe that no sincere [I presume "sincere" means "God-loving"] person will be abandoned by God. Limbo is understood in this context." I believe, though I'm far from certain, that this statement means God won't abandon the babes in Limbo *forever*, just for a while — which means Limbo is **not** understood in this or any other context, because if God were ever to punish anyone — which I profess He would never do anyway — it certainly wouldn't be the souls of innocent unbaptized babies. And it doesn't make any difference whether these souls remain in Limbo temporarily (say, a few minutes , an hour, a day, a week, a month, a year, a century, a millennium) or permanently.

To sum up Limbo:

> Since the Garden of Eden never existed, there is no such thing as Original Sin. Therefore the souls of babies, baptized or unbaptized, do not carry the stain of sin...any sin!.

Therefore the sole premise on which Limbo's existence rests is both false and implausible. Furthermore, not only does God not punish souls who have never committed a sin, He doesn't punish *any* souls.

My conclusion, which stands to reason and common sense, is that Limbo, like Hell and Purgatory, is a total myth, notwithstanding the ardent creative efforts of the Church's theologians throughout the centuries to devise, in vain I contend, a flimsy rationale for the existence of these purely hypothetical places which they themselves dreamed up.

To put the icing on the cake of this ridiculous dogma, my *Encyclopedic Dictionary* states, "It should be recognized that Limbo is not a teaching of the Church of the highest degree of certitude. It is a *common teaching*, but not part of the *deposit of faith*." [my italics]

THE TEACHING OF CATHOLIC DOGMA
LEVELS OF CERTAINTY IN DESCENDING ORDER

Infallible Teaching Authority of the Church

Sole Authority of the Church

Proximate to Faith

Pertaining to Faith

Common Teaching

Probable

More Probable

Well-Founded Pious

Tolerated Opinion — the least degree of certainty

According to the Catholic Faith and Reason website[31], "the Deposit of Faith is the body of saving truth entrusted by Christ to the Apostles and handed on by them to be preserved and proclaimed."

My *Encyclopedic Dictionary* goes on to say that the dogma of Limbo is "a theological teaching which became popular in the early centuries of the Church and has endured through the centuries...This theory does not provide an absolutely satisfactory answer." Do tell! [my underlining]

It's all rubbish, of course. Mysteries resting upon mysteries preserved in Catholic thinking by nothing more than doctrinaire faith and belief...nothing more! Again, one idea, one belief, one tenet leads inexorably to the next and to the next right off into outer space, where belief in Limbo, Purgatory, and Hell belongs. I make no apology to robotic believers who swallow everything the Church says without challenging it. The entire line of reasoning, if you can call it that, for the existence of Hell, Purgatory, and Limbo rests on the single premise that all of us humans are born sinners who deserve punishment and who remain punishable sinners throughout our lives and into the afterlife. As I explained (proved) in Chapter 1, that premise is inarguably untrue. We are <u>not</u> sinners. We make mistakes, some grievous, but God made us prone to make mistakes...to sin.

There is no Hell, no Purgatory, no Limbo. These places are pure fictions created by the Church to fulfill and justify its mythical theology which is designed to strike fear in the hearts of the Faithful, placing them ever more securely under the power and control of the Church, the only avenue through which, so says the Church, sins can be forgiven. What a tangled web they weave! Hell, Purgatory, and Limbo exist only in the minds of the Christian clergy and Faithful...not in the real world from where <u>everyone</u> — "sinners" and "non-sinners" alike, the bad, the good, and the ugly — is welcomed by God without exception back to Heaven from whence we came. If God is, as I and the Faithful believe, all-loving and all-merciful, He would never make the distinctions the Catholic Church makes.

What about Saints?

According to the Vatican website www.catholic.org, there are over 10,000 named Saints and Blesseds from history, Roman Martyology, and Orthodox sources, but there is no definitive head count. During the first twelve centuries of the Church's existence, men and women of exemplary faith, such as the Apostles, were simply "acclaimed" as saints publicly. Thus the (anonymous!) authors of the Gospels achieved sainthood without undergoing a thorough investigation of their lives to establish their irrefutable fitness for sainthood. Since the Church didn't know who these authors were, they couldn't very well investigate their fitness. It was therefore assumed, given their authorships, that they were the chosen of God. In apparent recognition of the obvious shortcomings of this practice, Pope Gregory IX in the 13th century formally codified the process of canonization.[32]

Belief in saints, like belief in any tenet of Catholic dogma, as the Catholic clergy and Faithful will hasten to acknowledge, is strictly *a matter of faith*. Indeed, as the priest years ago who instructed me prior to my confirmation said, you don't have to believe in saints to be a member of the Catholic Church. And I assuredly don't. Why? Let me explain.

What is a saint? If you'll pardon my use of a sports analogy, saints are certified Catholics who merit, by their illustrious lives, election to what I would call the Catholic Hall of Fame in Heaven where they assume reverential positions. Before you tear this page out of this book in resentful anger, let me explain that I'm not demeaning in the slightest way the hallowed character of the Church's saints. As far as I know, they were all indeed saintly people who led exemplary lives. I should be so good. No, my complaint is fundamental, because canonization, according to Church dogma, allots those individuals canonized as saints *elevated standing in Heaven* through the Church's "whatever" power: "Whatever you bind on Earth is bound in Heaven." So if the Church, exercising its "whatever" power, determines that the souls of certain deceased, because of their virtuous lives, are to be granted exalted positions in Heaven, so be it.

But, as I contend in Chapter 3, Jesus never bestowed the "whatever" power on his disciples. Indeed, for the Church to claim it has the power to determine a soul's status in Heaven is outrageously arrogant and, as always, self-serving and clearly usurps the power of God. The pope, the cardinals, the bishops, and the priests are not God whether they act individually or in concert. The very idea of the Church prescribing what goes on in Heaven is farcical.

But the Church, comprised from head to toe of members of our flawed human species, goes even further, endorsing and promoting the *veneration* of saints. Veneration is enacted through prayer and by bowing or making the sign of the cross before a saint's icon, relic, or statue and even kissing these objects. Moreover, most of today's Faithful (I have no data on which to venture an estimate of the percentage, but I dare say it must be large) believe — and the Church claims — that the saints in Heaven will intercede with God on behalf of the Faithful in response to the latter's fervent prayers.[33] Talk about praying to false idols! How is canonizing people after their dead, bowing before and kissing their paintings and statues, and praying to them any different from ancient people carving figures out of stone, proclaiming them gods, and praying to them? Please explain the difference to me...without, pray tell, using the words "faith" or "belief" or their kindred expressions.

To answer this very accusation about praying to false idols, Catholic Online[34] states that Catholics do not pray "to" saints but "with" them. Really? I doubt many Catholics would agree. I'll wager that when Catholics around the world kneel before a statue or painting of a saint to pray, they are aiming their prayers not at Jesus or God but directly at the saint in Heaven, hoping the latter will intercede for them with God. Even the Hail Mary, the most holy of Catholic prayers (next to the Lord's Prayer), calls for the intercession of Jesus' mother: "Pray for us sinners now and at the hour of our death". This is not a "joint" prayer with Mary to God as in "Pray *with me* for us sinners now and at the hour of our death". It's a plea for Mary's personal, private, unilateral intercession with God. It's a prayer from the supplicant to God *through* Mary. Mary, like the Church's saints, is the go-between. The notion that saint and supplicant are praying together is an implausible defense against the charge that praying to saints is akin to praying to false idols.

In further defense against the charge of idolatry, *New Advent* declares, "The Church does not pretend to make gods." Actually the Church does that very thing, as the following *New Advent* statement attests: "They [the saints] reign with God in the heavenly fatherland as His chosen friends and faithful servants." Saints reign with God? "Reign" means "to rule as king or queen, wield royal authority, hold sway, prevail, predominate". If that's not making saints gods, what is it? And incidentally, how does the Church know that these individuals are God's "chosen friends"? Because the Church says so? Isn't choosing His friends strictly God's prerogative? It's more of that silly business of reading God's mind and pretending that the "whatever" power extends to Heaven.

What is even more troublesome is that the Church doesn't canonize non-Catholics who would otherwise merit sainthood on the basis of the Church's own criteria for canonization. This fact calls into question by itself the legitimacy of the Catholic Church's canonization dogma. There are today some six billion humans on Earth. Does the Church mean to claim that out of that six billion only those virtuous individuals who are of the Catholic Faith deserve sainthood...deserve God's favor...deserve an honored revered position in Heaven? Absurd. Surely there are thousands, maybe tens of thousands of people in the world whose exemplary hallowed lives would more than satisfy the Church's criteria for sainthood, including miracles attributed to these individuals. But again, I'm reasonably certain there's some theological caveat planted deep within the layered edifice of Catholic doctrine that makes allowance for this glaring inconsistency.

CHAPTER 6

The Death of Catholic Dogma

The discovery in the late 19th century by Charles Darwin...and by the generally unheralded Alfred Russel Wallace...of evolution by natural selection challenged the veracity of the Genesis story about both Adam, the alleged first human, and his sinful Fall, which the Church fathers had, since the Council of Carthage in 418, codified as the Original Sin. To repeat, Original Sin, as defined and taught by the Church, makes humans permanent sinners, instilling in them an inherent life-long evil-prone nature that merits continual punishment, and then forgiveness by the Church, God's self-declared surrogate on Earth. Not surprisingly the Church at the time disdainfully ignored Darwin's "abominable" theory, which completely contradicted the central tenet, the cornerstone, of Catholic dogma.

The current Pope, Benedict XVI, as the former Cardinal Joseph Ratzinger, former president of the Church's International Theological Commission, and former head of the Congregation for the Doctrine of the Faith, wrote about this growing threat to Church dogma in his 1986 pre-papal book, *In the Beginning*[1]: "There is an almost ineluctable fear that the whole landscape of Scripture and of the faith will be overrun by a kind of reason [stemming primarily from the Darwin's theory of evolution] that will no longer be able to take any of Christian dogma seriously." "Human beings," he wrote, "see themselves imperiled as never before."[2]

He meant, of course, that it was the Roman Catholic Church that saw itself imperiled. Clear evidence of this growing imperilment was a survey of one thousand adult Catholics conducted in February 2008 by the Catholic Church's research arm in the U.S.[3] which showed that only 43 percent look to the Church's teachings, the pope, and the bishops "in deciding what is morally acceptable" (see Annex A for further survey results).

Wikipedia[4], the non-denominational online encyclopedia, observes that "the position of the Catholic Church on the theory of evolution has changed over the last two centuries from a long period of no official mention [simply ignoring the issue], to a statement of [anxious] neutrality in the 1950s, to a more explicit [but grudging] acceptance in recent years." Given the ever-more inescapable evidence supporting Darwinian evolution of *Homo sapiens*, the Church had no alternative but to accept the theory, but *only* as a theory, not something proven.

In his book, *In the Beginning*[5], Ratzinger sought, as a face-saving Church-saving tactic, to distance the Church from evolution theory by making a clear distinction between our separate physical and spiritual origins, which he described as two complementary, not contradictory, realms of knowledge...two quite different realities that are not mutually exclusive. "The story [the allegorical tale in Genesis] of the dust of the Earth and the breath of God...does not in fact explain how human persons come to be but rather what they are [spiritually]."

Genesis, wrote Ratzinger, explains humans' inmost [spiritual] origin and casts light on [their essence as God's] projects. And, vice versa, the theory of evolution seeks to understand and describe biological developments. But in so doing it cannot explain where the 'project' of human persons comes from, nor their inner origin, nor their [spiritual] nature.

Ratzinger's (the Pope's) portrayal of Genesis represents a radically different interpretation of the Garden of Eden and the events that allegedly occurred there. Church dogma has from the very beginning interpreted Adam, the first man, and Eve, the first woman, as living, breathing, physical human beings, not spiritual entities. The Pope clearly is trying to distance the Church's "new" dogma of our *spiritual* evolution from the "old" dogma of our *physical* evolution.

Ratzinger's use of the word "seeks" in the phrase "seeks to understand and describe" is significant. He purposely didn't say "the theory of evolution understands and describes" because, according to an article by John L. Allen Jr., in *National Catholic Reporter*,[6] "the Pope has questioned the evidence for *macro-evolution*, meaning the transition from one species to another on the basis of random mutation and natural selection." Macro-evolution is the central component of Darwin's theory of evolution. Ratzinger made his stand on evolution unmistakably clear in *In the Beginning*[7]: humans were not created by accident or chance as the theory of evolution propounds. "Human beings are not a mistake [of Nature] but something willed by God." Ratzinger therefore dismissed out of hand the possibility — I would call it a fact — that God *willed* the gradual macro-evolution of man.

Then, searching for a way out of the Church's unspoken dilemma, Ratzinger, the future Pope, the final voice of Catholic doctrine, made the most astounding statement: "What does Original Sin mean? Nothing seems to us today to be stranger or, indeed, more absurd than to insist upon Original Sin."[8] Stranger??? More absurd??? Augustine, the revered expounder of the holy doctrine of Original Sin, must surely be raging in his grave (or wherever he is!) at this unmitigated refutation of ancient and holy Church doctrine by the new pontiff, the new bishop of Rome, the very head of Holy Mother Church on Earth.

But in retrospect the Pope's stark denunciation of Original Sin was not at all surprising and could well have been foreseen as inevitable, because the Church's devotion to and belief in Original Sin have become ever more untenable as proof of evolution by gradual descent has mounted over the years. The final proof — the nail in Original Sin's coffin — came years ago with the discovery that the mitochondrial DNA in each cell of the human body is inherited only from the mother, that mitochondrial DNA does not combine with other DNA, and that random mutations in mitochondrial DNA occur at a regular rate, enabling scientists to trace a direct, dependable genetic line between species and to construct reliable evolutionary trees.[9]

What is most astonishing is that the Pope's recanting of the doctrine of Original Sin blatantly refutes the Church's iron-bound Catechism. Pope John Paul II (term 1978-2005) declared that the Catechism was unquestionably authoritative, "a sure norm for teaching the faith and thus a valid and legitimate instrument for ecclesial communion".[10] Says the Catechism[11]: "The Church, which has the mind of Christ, knows very well that <u>we cannot tamper with the revelation of Original Sin without undermining the mystery of Christ</u>" [my underlining]. Indeed, as I have said, Original Sin is the lynchpin in the monolithic structure of Catholic doctrine.

You may be wondering, if Pope Benedict is in the process of reconstructing the Church's dogmatic pyramid, why I didn't mention this staggering event at the start of this book. The reason is quite simple. I wanted you to fully understand what that dogma was with which Benedict was tampering.

The Pope's debunking of Original Sin is all the more shocking because in his book, *In the Beginning*[12], he said, "If theologians or even the Church can shift [doctrinal] boundaries...such an operation often ends up by putting the Faith itself in doubt, by raising the question of the honesty of those who are interpreting it and of whether anything at all there is enduring." Yet that is precisely what he has done: he has raised serious doubts about Church dogma...perilous doubts that will come to validate another statement he made: "Quite a number of people have the abiding impression that the Church's Faith is like a jellyfish: no one can get a grip on it, and it has no firm center. A sickly Christianity [would] no longer [be] true to itself and consequently [could not] radiate encouragement and enthusiasm. It [would be] an organization that keeps on talking, although it has nothing else to say, because twisted words are not convincing and are only concerned to hide their emptiness." Emptiness, indeed! I think the Pope and his colleagues are in deep trouble.

"Original sin," proclaims the official Catechism of the Catholic Church, "is an essential truth of the Faith." An essential truth! Then how in Heaven's name can the Pope call Original Sin absurd? What's going on? I'll tell you what's going. It is nothing less than the start of a complete reinvention of Catholic dogma to cope with the reality, attested by the proof of evolution by gradual descent, that the creation story in Genesis is a purely symbolic myth, with all the vast implications its demise entails.

Recanting of Original Sin will of necessity require rewriting much of Catholic doctrine, triggering a domino-effect wave of changes throughout the body of Catholic beliefs. The very notion of the Church redesigning its dogma is staggering. Therefore the Pope is clearly playing with fire, but he and the Church have no realistic, practical alternative. Since the 5th century, Catholics of all ages have been taught and have accepted as infallible, unchallengeable gospel that Original Sin is real, that it can be purged from our souls <u>only through the Holy Sacrament of Baptism</u>. How will the billion duly-indoctrinated, duly baptized Catholics on Earth react when they learn that the Vatican has switched horses in the middle of the belief stream and proclaimed that Original Sin is not only "absurd" but is no longer part of the so-called "deposit of faith"? And what of the holy rite of baptism? If its principal function is not to purge ourselves of Original Sin, what is it?

Without any question, the hundreds of millions of copies of the Catholic Catechism need to be replaced with a new edition. I look forward to reading the revised version to see how the Church tries to wiggle its way out of this monstrous dogmatic quagmire.

The Pope in his book began the reinvention of Church dogma by articulating a brand new explanation of how we humans become lifelong sinners, a precondition for the Church's exclusive role as forgiver of sins. Pay close attention, because this is the new doctrine. "At the very moment that a person begins human existence, which is a good, he or she is confronted by a sin-damaged world. Sin [in the person of Satan?] pursues the human being, and he or she capitulates to it."[13] So there it is, folks. It's the sinful Satan-controlled world that makes us sinners, not that old obsolete, Garden-of-Eden Original Sin. What's next? Jesus wasn't crucified after all? He didn't ascend bodily into Heaven? I especially await the "new" explanation of how the Ever Virgin Mary, the mother of Jesus, was preserved, according to the Catechism[14], "from all stain of Original Sin" when there was no Original Sin.

Then the Pope added this all-important thought: "But from this it is also clear that human beings alone cannot save themselves."[15] Guess to whom he's referring. To the Church, of course. Even with the Pope's extinction of Original Sin, it's still the Church and only the Church that can save us.

CHAPTER 7

So where does all of this leave us?

I have exposed as whimsically false the Christian beliefs in the Garden of Eden, Adam and Eve, and Adam's "fall from grace". That being the case, I have exposed as baseless the purging of Original Sin through baptism, that sin allegedly attached to our souls as a consequence of Adam's disobedience to God. Since the Garden of Eden never existed, neither did Adam nor Original Sin. Baptism therefore serves no real purpose other than to formalize one's joining the human race and a church of Christ. If you enjoy traditional ceremonies like birthdays and graduations, be my guest, but don't pretend that baptism removes Original Sin. It doesn't, because there is no Original Sin. Baptism is no more meaningful from the standpoint of purging sins than jumping into a swimming pool.

I have explained in Chapter 3 — proven, I contend — why Jesus never bestowed on his disciples what I call the "whatever" power: "Whatever you bind on earth shall be bound in heaven, and whatever you loose on earth shall be loosed in heaven". According to this bestowal, whatever the Church's decisions might be — good or evil, beneficent or malevolent — they are automatically endorsed by God in Heaven. Absolutely not! Dogmatic believers will assert that it is understood that Church decisions made with ill intent don't fall under the aegis of the "whatever" power, just as insincere confessions forgiven by a priest are not forgiven by God. Really? Prove it! And don't tell me it's plain common sense. There's nothing commonsensical about Catholic dogma. And by the way, if Jesus meant to exclude "ill-intentioned" bindings, why didn't he say so? Instead he reportedly used the word "whatever", which my dictionary defines as "of no matter what type, degree, quality, etc." But a discussion of ill intent is irrelevant, because Jesus never bestowed a "whatever" power.

I also refuted the belief that God commanded Adam to "be fruitful and multiply". Since Adam never existed, neither did God's command. Therefore the Church's ancient edict to Catholic husbands and wives to breed families rabbit-like is void and meaningless. Thank goodness!

Speaking of God, do you really believe that using His name in vain offends Him, the Creator of the unknowable Universe? Do you think He really cares if we use His name in anger? The Church and its vindictive punishing priests certainly do, but does God? If God "smiles", as I believe He does (I can't, of course, prove it!) in His own indecipherable way at His human children's flounderings here on Earth, then he must surely "chuckle" when I in pain from hitting my thumb with a hammer or in frustration over some daunting event in my life exclaim, "God damn it!" Does my outburst insult His "pride"? Does it "anger" him? Does it offend and demean God's infinite might and glory? Don't be absurd. Only a dogma-infested believer would attribute human emotional traits to the immortal God of the Universe.

Following the lead of established biblical scholars, I have pointed out that the Bible is not history. It is, moreover, replete with anachronisms, contradictions, and outright falsifications. That being the case, the Bible is completely unreliable. Completely! Especially when it comes to statements attributed to Jesus.

The New Testament reports that Jesus stated and restated his belief that the world would soon end. Two thousand years later we're still here, which raises the question of whether he, the self-declared messenger of God, somehow got the message wrong Or did the word "soon" mean in geologic time? Or did he in fact never say anything about the world ending? Devout believers who hold the Bible to be the Word of God do all kinds of mental gymnastics to reconcile this discontinuity... which I dare say is irreconcilable.

You can pick and choose as you wish which stories and statements in the biblical texts to believe, but don't pretend they are all true. None of it can be proven. And without proof the texts are nothing more than rumors and hearsay. Indeed, the Bible, for the most part, is no more reliable than the fairy tale of Cinderella. Yes, the Bible contains profound truths about humans, their motives, hates, and fears, but so do Grimm's fairy tales and Aesop's fables.

If my contempt offends you, be offended. If the truth hurts, bear it. And it *is* a tough truth for the Faithful to swallow, primarily because they don't want to believe that the New Testament is nothing more than a digest of craftily connected fictional anecdotes about an actual living prophet named Jesus. The myths about this prophet grew exponentially, borrowed largely from the lives of earlier gods, and spread throughout the lands, driven by the very same mindset that holds the Faithful captives of their Faith today: the overriding compulsion and desperate need to believe that Jesus was divine, the one and only Son of God. Need does not create truth.

Numerous scholarly books have been written on the ancient culture of myth making. I encourage you to read at least one of them. Burton L. Mack's *Who Wrote the New Testament?* is a good one to start with. Once you understand the historic and universal process by which myths over the millennia were created, embellished, and ultimately converted first into truths and then into articles of religious faith, you will more clearly see the New Testament as the work of fiction it largely is.

I for one do believe — I naturally can't prove it — that a man named Jesus lived and preached in Judea two thousand years ago about life after death (salvation), about the almighty merciful God who created the universe, and about the need to worship God and love oneself and others. But that's all I believe regarding Jesus. I view the stories about his walking on water, curing the sick, and raising people from the dead as worthless myth-made froth nurtured from the beginning by the Church to incite faith in Church dogma and loyalty and obedience to the Church's leaders. An endearing humorous line by cowboy Kevin Costner to his new wife in the movie *Open Range* describes the early Church's position very well: "How will [our marriage] work if you don't do what I say?"

Best of all I have squelched the pervasive and insidious notion that we humans are born sinners, and as sinners we shall die. We are absolutely not born sinners nor are we *lifelong* sinners! If we're not lifelong sinners, then there's no basis for a Final Judgment after we die. Final Judgment, like other Christian beliefs, is a myth. I repeat, there is no Final Judgment. These are beliefs cooked up and pedaled by the Church over the centuries and ingrained in Christians to increase and perpetuate their fear of death and everlasting punishment in the fires of Hell. Fear, of course, is the mechanism by which the Faithful have been and still are controlled by their Church hierarchies and, if you will, held hostage. The greater the fear, the greater the control, the stronger the bonds of captivity.

In that context I have junked the abominable myths of Hell, Purgatory, Limbo, and Satan. As I have convincingly explained, at least I believe it's convincing, these places and the entity called Satan are human-made myths, not God-made realities. You disagree? Then prove that any of these fairy tales are true? You can't, of course. It's all a matter of faith! Save me from faith!

But what's the harm, you ask, in believing in these religious tenets? It is after all, and I firmly agree, each person's right to believe whatever they want to believe. Moreover, I concede and wholeheartedly agree that these beliefs generally arm people with the means and mindsets to live "good Christian" lives, worshiping God, loving one another, loving others, and helping those in need. But the harm comes, and it is indeed an insidious harm, when people are *required, intimidated,* and even *terrorized* to believe in some untenable article of faith and are threatened by their Church with terrible punishments in the afterlife if they don't believe. That requirement arises <u>only</u>...I repeat <u>only</u>...when one becomes a signed and sealed member of a religion. What is more, beliefs imposed under duress are shams which are as malignant as forcing a child, as a disciplinary measure, to believe a monster lurks in a closet.

Every religion, like any organization, by its very human nature and of necessity generates strict rules and hard-line beliefs as well as a range of varying punishments for those who violate those rules or blaspheme those beliefs. For example, in the secular world, if you don't show up for work, your pay is docked. If you steal from a business, you're fired. In the religious world, if you fail to attend Sunday services, you are chastised. If you marry outside your religion, you are excommunicated. If you deride your religion, as I have done in this book, you are condemned to Hell, and in the olden days you would have been burned at the stake. Even now I can imagine a mob of outraged "Christians" gathering outside my door with righteous vengeance on their minds for the statements I have made in this book that blaspheme their religion and its beliefs.

The Puzzle of Secrecy

A lingering and unanswerable question bothers me greatly: If God through Jesus wanted to awaken the human masses to the message and reality of "salvation"... life in Heaven after death...if that was Jesus' purpose on Earth, which I devoutly believe it was (I can't prove it), why then did Jesus appear after his death *secretly* to his disciples in the upper room? Why didn't he parade himself, together with his jubilant disciples, through the Jerusalem streets crowded with Passover celebrants? Word of his crucifixion, death, and resurrection would have spread quickly throughout the city. Why didn't he enter the Temple and display himself alive to the high priests of the Sanhedrin? Doing so would have been a sensation, a real, believable, incontestable miracle, news of which would have spread from village to village, city to city, country to country. Moreover, showing everyone his living proof that he had returned from the dead would not have placed himself or his disciples under threat of punishment from the Sanhedrin, which would have been awed. So why not?

Why didn't Jesus tell his followers to leave his body to rot on the cross like the two men allegedly crucified next to him...irrefutable evidence that he had indeed died? Instead, according to the Gospels, his followers, in what would evidently have been a curious and perhaps unprecedented break with longstanding Roman policy, reportedly took his body down after only six hours on the cross with the express approval of Pontius Pilate, the Roman governor of Palestine, and *secreted* it in a cave. According to the Gospels, instead of making his reappearance from the dead a magnificent memorable public spectacle, which would have been the perfect and historic way to proclaim the miracle of his resurrection and the proof of salvation and life after death, it was kept a *secret*, which predictably sowed the seeds of incredulity and doubt that have dogged Christianity to this very day. Indeed, any number of books have postulated that Jesus' crucifixion was a charade, that Jesus conspired with Pilate to make it appear that Jesus had died, that someone else took his place on the cross, that Jesus escaped from Jerusalem, traveled to Europe, and preached and died there, and so on. If God's purpose through Jesus was to proclaim that there is life after death, why all this *secrecy*, which only cast doubt on the truth of his return from the dead and, more important, on salvation after death? I know what you're going to say. **But, Phil. God's ways are incomprehensible.** No argument there, but just because we can't read God's "mind" doesn't mean He's holding out on us. The fact is the _secrecy_ of which I speak severely undermined the credibility of the resurrection and led directly to the justifiable suspicion that Literalists in the decades immediately after Jesus' alleged death on the cross, needing to believe — and needing the Faithful to believe — he was a deity, the divine and only son of the almighty god of the universe, made up the story of his crucifixion and resurrection to "prove" his divinity. Remember that there is no proof whatever that a prophet and teacher in ancient Israel named Jesus was ever crucified or that he in fact ever lived in the flesh.

Think about it!

The Gospels' Split Personality

More perplexing than the secrecy of Jesus' resurrection is the uncanny impression I get from the teachings attributed to him that I am reading attestations by two different people: one who loves everyone, especially sinners, and mercifully forgives all of them their trespasses; the other who unforgivingly hates all sinners and threatens them with merciless punishment. This perception creates a giant discontinuity. Indeed, the statements attributed to Jesus in the four Gospels make him seem to be afflicted with a split personality. I'm not joking. That's exactly what the statements suggest. See for yourself.

On the one hand, Jesus is reported to have spoken earnestly about love, mercy, turning the other cheek, loving one's enemies, forgiving everyone for their trespasses and then, in what appears to be a complete baffling about-face, he speaks earnestly about _not forgiving_ sinners, punishing them, sending them to Hell, throwing them into the unquenchable fires of Gehenna. Thus his teachings have a sort of split personality, one benevolent, the other malevolent. What gives here?

Do I believe Jesus suffered from a split personality? Of course not. The answer, at least to me, is quite simple and obvious: Jesus didn't say everything attributed to him in the Gospels. More specifically, _he never threatened anyone with an eternity in the unquenchable fires of Hell!_ As my _Encyclopedic Dictionary_ avers, "Jesus proclaimed the unlimited forgiveness of sin by God to all who turn to Him." Note the word "unlimited". And the _Dictionary_ goes on to say, "Regardless of the immensity of the sin, the mercy and forgiveness of God are infinitely greater." Note the word "infinitely". In other words, no matter how sinful the sin (the mistake), God will forgive it.

The Gospels, on the other hand, are replete — overflowing, actually — with threats of punishment of sinners, including eternal violence. Likewise the Catholic Church, as I have explained, is all about punishment. Yes, the Church preaches Jesus' teachings about love, but somewhere along the line — at its formation, I dare say — the Church down pedaled the love stuff and went for the jugular, to punish sinners in order to bring the Faithful and not so Faithful unmercifully in line with Church dogma and under the Church's control, no matter the cost in suffering and death.

As you'll recall from Chapter 3, the Church throughout its early decades was locked in a struggle to survive against the encroachments of Gnostic Christianity, Paganism, and Judaism. In the face of this relentless dire competition the Literalists, reading God's "mind" again, would have said, "Are we not the Jesus-appointed surrogates of God on Earth? We, the very holy Church of Christ on which Christ bestowed the *whatever power*, will hate sinners as God surely does and punish them and the non-believers as God *surely wants us to*. God's will be done!"

And let us not forget that the world in which Christianity was born was brutal and merciless: death by torture and imprisonment was commonplace. Throughout the long history of human civilization, society's rulers had always governed with an iron, ruthless, unforgiving hand. As I have explained, it was the way of the world. So when the Church of believers in Jesus came into power, it naturally adopted the customary proven methods for proselytizing their Faith and maintaining control over the Faithful: fear and punishment. It was the only way they or anyone in that and previous ages knew how to seek and maintain power and govern. True democracy and its incomparable protections of individual freedoms, including freedom of religion and belief, were many centuries away.

What I find remarkable and insightful is that the punishment side of the Gospels fits like a glove with the Church's historic punishing nature. But which, I ask, came first? The Church's punishing nature or the Gospels' statements arguing for punishment? By that I mean, did the Literalists in the early Christian centuries lace Jesus' teachings of love and peace with dire threats of punishment for sins in order to justify the nascent Church's persecution of those who defied what the Literalists deemed was the will of God? As every writer and reader knows, the meaning of a sentence can be changed dramatically with the addition or deletion of one or two words. Indeed, a text can be totally redirected by the addition of one or more carefully worded sentences and paragraphs. As I said earlier, the Church, in a Vatican minute, would have deleted, amended, and altered the language of the books of the New Testament to bring their texts in line with "orthodox" beliefs. And remember that there are no extant originals of any book in the New Testament with which to compare today's versions to discover changes.

Telling examples of Jesus' "split personality", what I would call a Jekyll-and-Hyde syndrome, are Mark 3:23, Matthew 12:31, and Luke 12:10 where Jesus is reported to have said, "Amen, I say to you, every sin and blasphemy will be forgiven men, but the blasphemy against the Spirit will not be forgiven." The first sentence is the kind, loving, and forgiving Jekyll. The second sentence, the evil Hyde, is unforgiving and threatens everlasting punishment. I contend that Jesus never spoke the Hyde sentence, that it was inserted by self-serving Literalists to justify and empower their cruel domination of both the Faithful and the non-believers...the so-called heretics. Another Jekyll example is John 12:44 where Jesus is reported to have said, "And if anyone hears my words and does not observe them, I do not condemn him, for I did not come to condemn the world but to save the world." If that were true, why did Jesus vow to pitch sinners into the unquenchable fire? Answer: He never made such a vow, because he had no vindictive desire to see sinners punished. He came to Earth to proclaim the salvation of everyone, sinners and non-sinners alike.

Perhaps the most meaningful and useful teaching attributed to Jesus was the Lord's Prayer:

> Our Father, who art in Heaven, hallowed be thy name. Thy king-dom come, thy will be done on Earth as it is in Heaven. Forgive us our trespasses as we forgive those who trespass against us. And lead us not into temptation, but deliver us from evil, for thine is the kingdom, the power, and the glory for ever. Amen.

Where in this prayer do we find the threat of punishment for sins? Nowhere. The entire prayer is a pure, comprehensive reflection of Jesus' philosophy of kindness, mercy, and love which, according to the statements attributed to Jesus, mirrors God's.

As I mentioned in Chapter 4 it is the consensus of biblical scholars that the early Literalists purged popular Gnostic works, such as the Acts of Thomas, of their "heretical" content and adapted them to suit a Literalist agenda. My reasoning says the Literalists likewise regarded the teachings attributed to Jesus in the Gos-pels as much too meek and mild, too kind and forgiving, to enable "his Church" to withstand the criticisms and assaults by the Gnostic Christians, Pagans, and Jews. One couldn't create a strong, powerful, stable, ever-lasting church by being nice to the Faithful. That wasn't how things were done in societies...had never been done. Jesus' loving words weren't threatening enough to force believers to obey the Church fathers, who ordained for themselves the role of interpreting those teachings...to rescue "orthodoxy" from the clutches of "heresy". No one knows nor can know how extensively the Church revised Jesus' teachings, but what is a well established fact is that significant elements of the New Testament, as explained in Chapter 4, were substantially altered, deleted, and augmented from Christianity's earliest days onward.

The Church and its theologians and scholars are obviously loath to acknowledge, probably even among themselves in the recessed confines of their theological discussions, that a host of statements attributed to Jesus in the Gospels were never spoken by him. If such an acknowledgement were made public, it would destroy the very foundations upon which Christianity rests.

Nevertheless, is it really a stretch to conjecture that Literalists amended Jesus' teachings in the Gospels to imbue them with a fearsome character...to balance with threats of punishment his "weak" and non-threatening message of love, kindness, peace, and forgiveness? Hardly. As Freke and Gandy state in *Jesus and the Lost Goddess*[1], "The role of the Literalist bishops was to tell people what to believe and to discipline those who disagreed." Discipline was everything, for through it the Church secured the obedience of the Faithful and ensured the Church's preeminence and survival. Jesus' statements promoting love, charity, and kindness were at direct odds with the Church's aims and the despotic methods it employed to achieve them. The very title of Bishop Spong's book, *The Sins of Scripture: Exposing the Bible's Text of Hate to Reveal the God of Love* underscores my point.

But, Phil, why couldn't Jesus' teachings be threatening? Don't you see that God's ways are unfathomable? Things may seem illogical to you, but they aren't to God.

Now why didn't I think of that?

Actually I did, and here's what I think: Every time something about Christian doctrine doesn't make sense, it's because God didn't want it to make sense. Huh? Read that sentence again and tell me it's not pure baloney. Of course, if you're a knowledgeable Catholic theologian with graduate degrees up the kazoo in biblical studies and holding an esteemed academic position, you'll immediately caucus with your colleagues and devise in rebuttal a slippery coil of complex, highly theoretical but thoroughly sourced explanations. Then you'll sit back content and fully satisfied and tell me, "You see, Phil, you're all wet!" This exact scenario has been repeated again and again through the centuries to rationalize and tissue-paper over the gaping fissures in Catholic/Christian dogma. Through this process the Vatican, using its indomitable position and power, has over time erected a seemingly impenetrable, unassailable bulwark around its mountain of dogma, and anyone, like me, who challenged it has been dealt with severely. So deal with me severely, take your best shot, because I surely have penetrated and assailed that mountain of dogma.

The Enigma of Life's Hardships and Horrors — and the Answer

A universal question, repeated several times in this book, is customarily raised when things go tragically wrong — a baby dies, a family is burned to death in an automobile accident, millions of Jews are murdered by the Nazis, and so on. The question voiced by the Faithful each time is: "If God is all-loving and all-merciful, how could He allow this awful thing to happen?" But people don't go the next logical step to find the answer. If these things happen, then God most assuredly lets them happen, else they wouldn't happen at all. He is after all master of our universe. But why would He let them happen? Now that's the real question. Not how could He let these things happen but *why* He would?

The answer again is obvious and unavoidable when you think about it. Since people suffer from these horrific events and since God lets these incidents happen, *He must therefore want people to suffer!* What other reason could there be? The only possible conclusion is not that He wants to punish us — as Augustine contended — but that he wants us during our stay on Earth to have negative experiences, that they are an intentional, inextricable, and often excruciatingly painful part of life: sickness, the pain of losing a loved one, the stress and uncertainty of life, the threat and reality of violence, life-crippling diseases, and so on, even the itching of insect bites — all of the things that make life on Earth miserable. You can sing "It's a Wonderful World" all you want, but it clearly isn't wonderful at all. It's awful!

Take defecating, for example. It's a disgusting, obnoxious, odious act that our God-created humanity requires us to perform one or more times a day every day of our lives! You call that wonderful?

Check out the following abbreviated summaries of a sampling of episodes reported in the daily "Across the USA: News From Every State" page in *USA Today*, August 3, 2007:

Alabama	college president accused of failing to fire a convicted felon
Arkansas	third autopsy of teenager raises questions about the cause of her death
California	raids on medical marijuana dispensers by federal agents
Connecticut	Hartford Diocese sued for sexual abuse
Delaware	drug charge against a former gubernatorial candidate
D.C.	city Housing Authority disbursed $300,000 illegally to homeowners
Illinois	man killed two women and a 6-year-old
Iowa	city celebrates the day gangster Dillinger robbed a bank in 1934
Kentucky	man emailed to himself a campus bomb threat
Louisiana	fifteen more schools designated "academically unacceptable"
Maine	man stabbed a single mother more than fifty times
Minnesota	man illegally sold painkillers via the Internet
Mississippi	father and son charged with growing and marketing marijuana
Nevada	company charged for selling unnecessary repairs and parts to customers

New Jersey	man robbed eighteen banks in a crime spree
New Mexico	state treasurer sent to prison
New York	man and wife accused of giving exam answers for state certifications
Oregon	two hundred people put out of work
Texas	two teenagers kidnapped a baby
Utah	bodies of a man and two children found in a burning jeep
Virginia	man charged for the fifth time for driving on a suspended license
Wisconsin	alderman charged with bribery

The very same kinds of abhorrent episodes are reported every weekday in *USA Today*. Every weekday! And these are only episodes that occurred within the United States that *USA Today* deemed worthy of citing. Imagine what's going on that wasn't reported, not only within the U.S. but among the rest of the Earth's six billion inhabitants.

Look at the staggering statistics for poverty throughout the world, for death from hunger, for rape, for kidnapping, for pedophilia, for incest, for child abuse, for spousal abuse, for fraud, for thievery, for diarrhea, for diabetes, for cancer, for sexually transmitted herpes that reportedly infects one of every five adolescent and adult American males, for mental retardation, for Alzheimer's, for Parkinson's, for other life-crippling diseases, for pestilential allergies of every kind, for physical and mental disabilities, for epidemics that kill thousands of humans and live stock, for deaths from malaria (2.7 million per year worldwide[2]), for terminal illnesses, for aging and all its torments, for menopause, for menstruation, for death by accident, for suicide, for adultery, for embezzlement, for drug addiction, for murder, for brutality of every kind, for corruption at every level of society, for identity thieves, for the 70 percent of all businesses which experience fraud, for pornography, for stalkers, for dishonest malpracticing doctors and lawyers, for arsonists, for plagiarists, for drunk drivers who kill innocent people, for scam artists who bilk people of millions of dollars every year, for corrupt law-enforcement officers, for polluters of the Earth's environment, for fires that destroy homes, businesses, and hospitals, for money-hungry manufacturers oblivious to the dangers of their products, for itchy skin, hangnails, the common cold, toothaches, fleas and other blood-sucking insects, poisonous plants and snakes, and the myriad bruises, cuts, abrasions, and broken bones that typify human existence. And how about headaches and their epitome, the migraine, which is misery personified. Look at the interminable wars humans have always waged and continue to wage against each other, killing, raping, pillaging, burning, laying waste. And how about this for a "wonderful" statistic? One in every 6,000 babies born in the U.S. has spinal muscular atrophy (SMA), a terminal disease that is the leading killer of toddlers and babies. About fifty percent of the infected children die before they turn two-years-old.[3] Wonderful!

And, of course, there is the ceaseless battle with Nature: hurricanes, floods, tornadoes, earthquakes, tsunamis, mudslides, sink holes, ice storms, lightning-ignited forest fires, volcanic eruptions, and so on that kill tens of thousands of people every year and injure scores of thousands more.

And then there's sex. Nothing causes more problems, more pain, more violence, more disease, more stress, more unhappiness than sex. Sex is an unrelenting daily lifelong hunger of members of our species affecting males much more than females. It was Augustine who wrote of the continual "diabolical excitement" of the genitals. As you may recall, it was sex that ultimately drove Henry VIII to separate the English Church from papal authority in 1534.

Thoughts about sex and women assail males constantly. According to a survey I read a couple of years ago in *USA Today* [I regret to say I can't find the issue's date], men think about sex on average every 53 seconds, while women on average think about it only once a day. As a general rule, when a heterosexual male sees a woman's front, his eyes flit quickly from her face to her bosom, then perhaps to her hips and crotch, and then back to her face. It all happens so quickly that many people may well deny it ever happens. But check it out for yourself; see if most men don't behave this way. If the man is behind the woman, his eyes will instantly focus on her rump. This is instinctive, not learned, behavior. These glances at once generate fleeting thoughts in the man's mind of having sex with the woman. If she is reasonably sensual, the thoughts linger; if not, they extinguish themselves in nanoseconds.

In all-male environments — military units, police stations, fire stations, law firms, physicians in operating rooms, etc. — the mere presence of a woman is diverting to the males, leading to the claim that, say, female firefighters weaken the cohesiveness and firefighting capabilities of a station's crew. Over time this claim has proven to be untrue, but only because the male members in such groups have become accustomed to a female's presence and learned to accept her as a capable group member. But the sexual attraction is always there as the countless cases of copulation in such groups attests.

The ever-present allure of sex is as inescapable as its numberless unpredictable consequences. Yes, sex is, I most heartily agree, delightful, but it is also, if you will, a God-given curse. Nothing on Earth has caused more jealousy, infidelity, pain, hardship, abuse, rape, violence, and misery than sex. It is one of the myriad things that make life on this planet unwonderful.

Worsening this situation is Hollywood which, despite its occasional wondrous, spiritually uplifting productions, pumps out a steady stream of sleazy, violent, profanity-ridden, sexually explicit movies... labeled euphemistically "entertainment" and "comedy"... that vicariously lower the standards of our nations morality, encouraging violence and wanton sex, especially among youngsters.

According to an email I received, Ben Stein on CBS Sunday Morning Commentary (the sender didn't cite the broadcast date) said, "Funny how you can send 'jokes' through e-mail and they spread like wildfire, but when you start sending messages regarding God, people think twice about sharing. Funny how lewd, crude, vulgar and obscene articles pass freely through cyberspace, but public discussion of God is suppressed in school and the workplace." But it's not funny at all. It's just one of the unwonderful aspects of life on Earth.

I could go on for pages listing all the things that make this planet of ours a miserable place to live. And don't deny it. You know very well what I'm talking about. (See Annex B for a few more ghastly statistics.)

Sure, you can bury your head in your Bible, focus on your loving spouse, your wonderful children, your best friends, on the truly incomparable beauty of Nature, appreciate wondrous works of art of every kind, read inspiring poetry, sing spiritually uplifting hymns (I've sung them for decades, and they're both soothing and inspiring), hold hands and acknowledge with your fellow worshipers the glory of God, while willfully blinding yourself to Earth's truly evil reality.

John Jakes put it well in his novel, *Heaven and Hell*[4]: "Every day of our lives we live with stupid mischance and clumsy melodrama, cupidity, greed, and suffering. We forget it, we mask it, we try to [blot it out] with our arts and philosophies, numb ourselves to it with diversions and drugs. We try to explain and compensate for it with our religions. But it's always there, very close, like some poor deformed beast hiding behind the thinnest of curtains."

No matter how many verses of "It's a Wonderful World" you sing, the onerous hardships of the world remain, as they always have from the first *Homo sapiens* to our world today, testifying to the fact that ours is a world of endless fear, strife, physical and mental pain, and tears...a veritable hell hole.

And don't tell me I'm painting too gruesome and pessimistic a picture. Every day of the year, morning, noon, and night, the news media in countries around the globe both in print, on the radio, and especially on television report the latest horrors of life on Earth in gory lurid detail, complete with color photos, videos, live shots of the murdered and dismembered, and live interviews with downtrodden victims of disease, violence, and mishap and their mourning relatives and neighbors. The television talk shows year-in-year-out, day and night, parade before the cameras peoples' tear-jerking tales of woe. The fact that millions of people sit in front of their sets for hours absorbing these stories of misery is a sad and, to borrow a word from Catholic dogma, *mysterious* commentary on basic human interests and motivations. Is it that we take comfort that we were not the victims in each horrendous episode? Better thee than me? Viewers say to each other, "Isn't that awful!" Then, because they are so habituated to these miseries, as we all are, they sit contentedly, eat snacks, sip beer, wine, tea, coffee, or cola, maybe smoke a cigarette or cigar, and watch the advertisements during breaks in the "news". If you were a visitor to Earth from another planet and read the newspapers, watched TV news programs, and observed humans' reactions to them, you would ask in astonishment, "What's going on here?"

Consider the Internet, which I regard as humankind's most useful invention to date. It has shrunk the world down to pressing a button on a keyboard, creating, if you will, a "shared world" unlike anything in human history. The Internet bridges geologic and national boundaries, societies, cultures, and religions. Because of the Internet, totalitarian governments can no longer easily deny their populations knowledge of the outside world and its incomparable freedoms. Reports of major events are communicated around the globe instantly via communications satellites. Anyone can communicate in seconds with anyone else in the world who is connected to the Internet. How's that for a miracle!

But every time something new and wonderful is invented, some new life-improving invention like the Internet, some new breakthrough in technology, some new medicine to save lives, there are always dark, sadistic, mean-spirited individuals somewhere in the world who try, and largely succeed, to convert that new beautiful thing into something ugly and evil. It's the nature of our God-created world. It's the nature of humans. For example, out of curiosity I recently searched the wondrous Worldwide Web using the keyword "sex" and got 415,000,000 hits. I assure you, without looking, that a good ninety percent or more of these hits, which are websites (many, of course, the same site), are pure pornography, intended not to uplift the human spirit but to lower it into the muck of human depravity.

Human life is traumatic and fear-ridden. Fear of personal injury. Fear for the safety of one's loved ones. Fear of being robbed. Fear of being raped. Fear of contracting a deadly disease. Fear of being fired from one's job. Fear of dying. Fear, fear, fear. To paraphrase Bishop Spong in *The Sins of Scripture*,[5] humans know the dangers of life on Earth in a way no other creatures ever have. Tell me again "It's a Wonderful World".

I ask you, would you choose to live on this miserable planet if there were as beautiful and peaceful but unevil an alternative? I would jump at the chance. But on this planet we have persons fighting persons, gangs fighting gangs, family fighting family, political party fighting political party, business fighting business, government fighting government, nation fighting nation, all driven by compulsive self-interests that begin with the simple God-created impulse for each of us individually to fight for our and our loved ones' survival, day to day, month to month, year to year, throughout our lives.

Why would God want us human souls to experience this dreadful place? I propose two reasons (I'm sure there are others):

(1) To learn what Love really is. According to those humans who have been to Heaven and returned (believe them or not!), God's incomparable, overwhelming love enfolds Heaven and all of its inhabitants. But until a soul experiences "non-love", one can't fully appreciate what Love means. Since "non-love" doesn't exist in Heaven, the only way for Heavenly souls to experience it is to sojourn in a place like Earth where the full meaning of "love" becomes clear.

(2) To allow us to fully appreciate Heaven. And please don't tell me, echoing the wild rantings of Augustine, that God put us on this miserable planet to punish us for something we did in Heaven. Hello! As you will probably agree, there are by definition no negatives in Heaven. No human vices. No antagonisms. No jealousies. No hate. No violence. And most important of all, no death. Indeed, to have anyone but especially our loved ones die on Earth is traumatic, whether death comes at home, in a hospital, in a hospice, on a battlefield, in a drive-by shooting, in a back alley from a drug overdose, or from suicide. And that's what Earth is: traumatic. Heaven, on the other hand, is pure love, pure peace and serenity permeated with God's unending inundating love. Most important of all, there are no strictures in Heaven. One can do as one pleases. At least that is my unprovable belief. Earth is Heaven's absolute antithesis. Here limitations and dangers abound. How can the souls in Heaven truly appreciate Heaven if they haven't experienced its antithesis — the hardships of life in a place like Earth? For the same reason, we humans don't fully appreciate something until we have experienced its opposite: the raucous trading on the floor of the New York Stock Exchange as opposed to the serenity of a sailboat on a peaceful lake or a bitter relationship filled with anger and cruelty as opposed to a loving relationship filled with kindness and love.

Incidentally, isn't it possible that God made the physical nature of Earth so awesome — snowcapped mountains, rolling meadows, glistening lakes, gurgling brooks, blue sky, green grass, flowers of every color as well as gorgeous birds and butterflies — to constantly remind us of the indescribable beauty of Heaven and sustain our belief in life after death? Just a thought.

After-Life Experiences

Speaking of life after death, there's an enormous blind spot in Christian thinking. Christianity for the most part — I can't, of course, speak for all Christians — pays little attention to the thousands, yes, thousands of recorded cases of after-life experiences. And for one very obvious reason. Those cases don't square with the Christian dogma of sin, salvation, Hell, punishment, the whole works. Indeed, these after-life phenomena poke gigantic holes in Christian theology. If everyone's soul, according to these experiences, travels after death up a music-filled tunnel to the warm loving light at its end in Heaven, how do Final Judgment, Hell, Purgatory, Limbo, and all the rest fit in? They don't! Wouldn't you think this would give Christians pause to reconsider their beliefs? I certainly think so, but as I have said and resaid, Christians are hostage to their beliefs, which place greater store in unverifiable, contradictory, mystical two-thousand-year-old legends than in the testimonies — a great many verified — of sincere intelligent reasonable people living in today's enlightened world.

Religious Freedom

Lastly, my advice, which I offer merely as a courtesy, not a mandate, is to eschew membership in any "organized religion". I realize this is a mind-stopping idea (though I'm certainly not the first person to articulate it) and one you will probably in knee-jerk fashion reject. But I'm serious. Being a member of an organized religion isn't necessary if all you want to be, as I do, is a God-loving, humanity-loving human who is confident of returning to Heaven after death and experiencing once again God's all-embracing love.

As a general rule, we become members of a particular religion by birth, not by choice. The religion of the family into which we are born customarily becomes our Faith. Unless we make what can be a mind-rending decision and break from our birth-established Faith, we are wedded to it for life...and solely because that was the Faith of our parents. Given that happenstance determines our Faith, shouldn't that move us to question the validity and superiority of one Faith over others? I think so. What is more, this happenstance makes me question the logic of one's pledging oneself to a single religion.

Elaine Pagels in a 2003 Public Broadcasting System interview[6] stated, "The Gospel of Thomas speaks of Jesus as the Divine Light that comes from Heaven, but says, 'and you, too, have access to that divine source within yourself' — even apart from Jesus. That might suggest you don't need a church, or a priest, or an institution." And I categorically agree. If you feel more comfortable out of habit praying in a sanctuary dedicated to God, then go alone or with like-minded friends to any church, when no religious service or rite is being performed there, and pray to God. But remember that you don't have to be in a church for God to hear and answer your prayers. You also can join any number of nondenominational religious communities that, eschewing conformity to a particular dogma, gather together only to worship God and to help anyone in need.

History repeatedly shows that religions inevitably and predictably devise dogmas that create needless divisions among people, divisions that generate arrogance, suspicions, fears, and animosities that lead to bigotry, racism, hatred, terrorism, and war. Significantly, unlike the founders of many religions, Jesus didn't specify a canon of rules and punishments that would force us to obey his universal commandment to love one another; the Church did. I'm not convinced he even wanted a Church established in his name. Matthew 16:13 claims that Jesus told Peter, "Upon this rock I will build my church, and the gates of the netherworld shall not prevail against it." But did he really say this? It is well established that Matthew, like the other books of the New Testament, was revised in the Church's early days to conform to the Church's evolving orthodox doctrine. The Literalists could well have created that text, inasmuch as they wanted a church whose members they could control and to whom they could dictate dogma. Consistent with this possibility, they also wanted the more authoritarian Peter, not the laissez-faire Gnostic Paul, to head that church.

So, you will be well-served to forget religion-mandated dogma. It serves no useful purpose other than enforcing conformity, which only illuminates and focuses on the differences among people, separating those "inside" — the favored, the saved — from those "outside" — the unfavored, the condemned. Instead dedicate your life to (a) loving and worshiping God and (b) helping others in need. Thank Him each morning for His gift of another day of life, and thank Him each night for whatever blessings that day has granted you. God is after all your loving Creator.

Love is everything! Jesus, according to Mark 12:30 and Matthew 22:37 taught that "The first commandment is you shall love the Lord your God with all your heart, with all your soul, with all your mind, and with all your strength. The second is this: you shall love your neighbor as yourself. There is no other commandment greater than these." I repeat, No other! What could be simpler? And by the way, has it ever occurred to you that, when you lovingly hug someone, God lovingly hugs that person through you? That the love we share with each other comes directly from God? Think about it. I do.

Again, love is everything. If we love ourselves, others, and our antagonists, the world in which each of us lives can indeed be "wonderful" as the song says. But "wonderful" doesn't mean we can avoid the hardships of life. God obviously meant life on Earth to be hard — really hard — but with His help and the help of our loved ones and others we can work our way through it and return to our home in Heaven ever more appreciative of its wonders.

And no one — no priest, no reverend, no minister — needs to tell you what is right and what is wrong. Our God-created conscience unerringly tells us what is "right". As the Catholic Catechism[7] beautifully states:

"Deep within our conscience we discover a law which we have not laid upon ourselves but which we must obey. Its voice, ever calling us to love and to do what is good and to avoid evil, sounds in our hearts at the right moment...For we have in our hearts a law inscribed by God...Our conscience is our most secret core and our sanctuary. There we are alone with God whose voice echoes in our depths."

We know instantly whether something we or other people have done or plan to do or some thought we have or some action we contemplate is good or evil. So try to do good and pray thanks to God, not through any intermediary but directly to Him, for the goodness of others. Will we make mistakes? Will we "*sin*"? Of course we will. That's how God made us *Homo sapiens* types. We are a flawed, error-prone, "sin-prone" species. And when we do screw up, we can quickly ask His forgiveness and help. He'll surely give it to us because He loves us with "infinite" mercy. He's with us every moment of our lives, even this instant as you're reading this book. It's that simple. It's only the Church that makes it all so complex and fearful.

Guidelines for Life

As Rocco A. Errico eloquently observes in *Let There Be Light, The Seven Keys*[3], "Jesus continues to speak through all the ages. His human personality, his loving nature, and his simple teachings will live forever to enrich and embrace the hearts of the human family everywhere."

So what are the Jesus-inspired guidelines for a happy, God-loving, humanity-loving life? That's easy, too. Follow the beneficent teachings attributed to him. Not the false nonsense ones about punishment in the "unquenchable fires of Hell". Look to the loving, merciful, helpful teachings, whose attributes my Bible's *Encyclopedic Dictionary* lists as follows:

abhorrence of evil	Godliness	peaceableness
abhorrence of violence	honesty	perseverance
benevolence	hopefulness	prayerfulness
charitableness	hospitableness	ready for good works
consideration for others	humility	reliance upon God
devotion to duty	justice	respect for rulers
diligence	kindness	self-denial
faithfulness	love for God	steadfastness
faith in God	love for enemies and others	sympathy
fervency of spirit	mercifulness	thankfulness
forgiving spirit	morality	truthfulness
gentleness	patience	

To make the most of your life on Earth, let these attributes serve as your life's guide. We can never be as good as we want to be, but that shouldn't stop us from trying to be the best we can be in the eyes of God, to honor Him, our Creator.

Most of all keep in mind that we are all immortal souls. There's a spark of God in each of us. We came from Heaven, and to Heaven we shall return. And no matter what we do in life — whether we are good or bad, beautiful or homely, big or small, rich or poor, educated or uneducated, skilled or unskilled, black, white, yellow, or brown — God loves us everyone.

EPILOGUE

I began this literary journey seeking to learn the origins of the Catholic Church and Christianity, but as my research evolved, I came to realize the full extent of Christianity's appalling plague on civilization and how mythical is the foundation of Christian dogma. The resulting text is a sober thought-provoking examination of the underpinnings of that dogma and of the organized religions which base their theology on it. The effect — which I assure you was not intended when I began my research — is a thorough, systematic dismantling of that theology.

I don't wish to engage Catholics/Christians in a congenial theoretical discussion. I want to grab them by the shoulders and shake some enlightened common sense into their slumbering minds. I want to challenge them to read about the history of the Church, both that written by the Church itself and by its critics, to get a balanced perspective. I want to urge them to research each item of Christian doctrine, its origin and rationale, to challenge the observations and assertions made in this book and in others, and to challenge and thoroughly analyze *each word* in each statement as I have done. Does it make common sense? What is its basis? What is its source? Is the source conceivable and reliable? Does it contradict other words and statements? Then reach their own conclusions...not simply accept as true whatever the clergy, I, or other authors tell them.

Read, read, read! Decide for yourself. Stop assuming that whatever the Church decrees has God's imprimatur through the Holy Spirit.

How Will Christian Communities Receive This Book?

I am sure that critics of this book will triumphantly find here and there historical and/or theological errors. I diligently sought to validate the accuracy and logic of every statement in the book, but the text covers so broad a range of issues, most of which are inherently controversial, that my being in error on some key points or other seems inevitable. Nevertheless, when you read or hear criticism of this book, be sure to challenge the critic to separate supportable *fact* from unsupportable *belief.*

And what will the Vatican's reaction be? Outrage, of course. Without even convening a high-level council to deliberate the matter — the book's title alone will be sufficient justification — the Vatican will fall all over itself to ban the book as quickly as emails denouncing it can be broadcast to every Catholic diocese in the world. Then, only if the book receives any public attention (which I regret to say is unlikely), the Vatican, taking a bit more time to gather its ammunition, will disseminate worldwide press releases condemning the book in lofty sober language, claiming that, because the book's conclusions contradict two thousand years of renowned Catholic/Christian theology, tradition, beliefs, and faith, the book obviously cannot be taken seriously.

The Vatican will then focus on me, labeling me a wild, ranting, demonic hater of Christ and the Church. Who is this audacious upstart, they will ask, who lacks the necessary academic credentials of biblical scholarship to write such a book? My conclusions, they will say, about the Bible, the Church, and Catholic/Christian dogma are grossly, even comically flawed and should be dismissed out of hand in their entirety. Furthermore, they will proclaim that, however entertaining the book may be to the unenlightened, it is an heretical, blasphemous, irresponsible attack (which it most certainly is not!) on the holy words of our Savior, Jesus Christ. It's inevitable, to be sure, that Vatican spokesmen will invoke Jesus' name and even the Holy Spirit to lend ineffable authority to their denunciation.

Finally, the Vatican will claim that Philip Charleston, lacking the courage of his convictions to reveal his true identity, hides cowardly behind his pen name. The truth is, as I have explained, I hide behind my pen name (a) to protect myself and my family from harm from fanatic avengers who, urged on by Rome's virulent vituperations, will surely regard me as the flesh-and-blood incarnation of the Anti-Christ and (b) to preserve my professional position and my employer's public reputation, both of which would suffer if my true identity as the author came to light.

Finally, many Catholics will condemn this book as a monstrous emotional diatribe. What else can they say? Well, for one thing, they can do their own research and write their own books challenging my assertions, though I wonder to what they can resort for support of their criticisms other than *faith*. The other thing they can do is, of course, be quiet and ignore that *man behind the curtain*...who happens to be me!

FOOTNOTES

FORWARD

1   Gallup, George & Jem Castilli. The People's Religion. Macmillan Publishing Co., date unknown; Barna Organization poll; and David Gibson, www.beliefnet.com–cited in Leedom and Muroy, *The Book Your Church Doesn't Want You to Read*, page 117.

2   Faulkner, Mary. *Supreme Authority*. Marie Butler-Knight, 2003, page 217.

3   Ibid, page 130.

4   Conference of the Vatican Council–Conferenza Concilio Vaticano, Const. De Fide cath., cap. 1, De Deo rerum omnium creatore.

CHAPTER 1

1   Jackson, John G. *The African Origin of the Myths & Legend of the Garden of Eden*, 1933, www.africawithin.com.

2   Leedom, Tim C. & Maria Muroy. *The Book Your Church Doesn't Want You to Read*. Cambridge House Press, New York 2007, page 60.

3   Ibid page 61.

4   Stanford Online Encyclopedia of Philosophy, Stanford University, *http://plato.stanford.edu/ see "Augustine"*.

5   Pagels, Elaine. *Adam, Eve, and the Serpent*. New York: First Vintage Books, 1989, page xxvi.

6   *New Advent Online Catholic Encyclopedia.org*, see "Pelagius and Pelagian".

7   Ibid see "Pelagian Controversy".

8   Ibid.

9   Ellerbe, Helen. *The Dark Side of Christian History*. Morningstar & Lark, 2004, page 32.

10   Spong, John Shelby. *The Sins of Scripture: Exposing the Bible's Text of Hate to Reveal the God of Love*. HarperSanFrancisco, 2005, page 164.

11   Ellerbe. *The Dark Side of Christian History*, page 106.

12   Spong. *The Sins of Scripture: Exposing the Bible's Text of Hate to Reveal the God of Love*, page 163.

13   *New Advent.org*, see "Original Sin".

14   Faulkner. *Supreme Authority*, page 54.

15   Ibid, page 55.

16   Ibid, page 54.

17   Simon, Bernard. *The Essence of the Gnostics*. New Jersey: Chartwell Books, Inc., 2004, page 21.

18   Faulkner. *Supreme Authority*, page 54.

19   *New Advent.org*, see "virgin birth of Christ".

20   *New Advent.org*, see "immaculate conception".

21   Faulkner. *Supreme Authority*, page 54.

22   Greenberg. Gary. *101 Myths of the Bible: How Ancient Scribes Invented Biblical History,* Sourcebooks, Inc. 2000, page 9.

23   Ibid, page 4.

24   Ibid, page 8.

25   Ibid, page 8.

26   *New Advent.org*, see "Adam".

27   Lawrence, Jill. "Poll shows belief in evolution, creationism." *USA Today*, June 8, 2007, page A1.

28   Crichton, Michael. *Prey*, HarperCollins Publisher, 2002, page 181.

29   *New Advent.org*, see "Evolution".

30   Spong. *The Sins of Scripture*, page 176.

31   Ibid page 176.

32   Haley, Jay. *The Power Tactics of Jesus Christ*, Crown House Publishing, Ltd., 2005.

CHAPTER 2

1   *New Advent.org,* see "Baptism".

2   Freke, Timothy and Peter Gandy. *The Jesus Mysteries: Was the "Original Jesus", a Pagan God?* New York: Three Rivers Press 1999, page 35.

3   Spong. *The Sins of Scripture*, page 177.

4   *New Advent.org*, see "Baptism".

CHAPTER 3

1   Faulkner. *Supreme Authority*, page 163.

2   Browne, Sylvia. *The Mystical Life of Jesus: An Uncommon Perspective on the Life of Christ.* New York: Dutton, 2006, page 109.

3   Faulkner. *Supreme Authority,* page 152.

4   Freke, Timothy & Peter Gandy. *Jesus and the Lost Goddess: The Secret Teachings of the Original Christians.* Three Rivers Press, 2001, page 22.

5   Ehrman, Bart D. *Lost Christianities: The Battles for Scripture and the Faiths We Never Knew.* Oxford University Press, 2003, page 203.

6   Ehrman, Bart D. *Misquoting Jesus: The Story Behind Who Changed the Bible and Why.* HarperSanFrancisco, 2005, page 23.

7   Faulkner. *Supreme Authority*, page 40.

8   Freeman, Charles. *The Closing of the Western Mind: The Rise of Faith and the Fall of Reason.* New York: Vintage Books, 2005, page 77.

9   Strobel, Lee. *The Case for Christ.* Zondervan, 1998, page 343.

10 Freke, Timothy & Peter Gandy. *Jesus and the Lost Goddess*, page 11.

11 Gardner, Laurence. *The Magdalene Legacy.* Element–HarperCollinsPublishers 2005, page 171.

12 Simon. *The Essence of the Gnostics*, page 157.

13 Ehrman. *Lost Christianities,* page 6.

14 Ibid, page 152.

15 Freke, Timothy & Peter Gandy. *The Laughing Jesus: Religious Lies and Gnostic Wisdom.* New York: Harmony Books, 2005, page 67.

16 Hoeller, Stephan A., *Freedom: The Alchemy of a Voluntary Society,* Quest Books,1992. Cited in Leedom and Mulroy, *The Book Your Church Doesn't Want You to Read*, page 71.

17 Freke and Gandy. *The Laughing Jesus: Religious Lies and Gnostic Wisdom*, page 68.

18 Simon. The Essence of the Gnostics, page 72, and Leedom and Mulroy. *The Book Your Church Doesn't Want You to Read*, page 162.

19 Johnson, Paul. *A History of Christianity*, Weidenfeld and Nicolson, 1978, cited in, Tim Wallace-Murphy. *Cracking the Symbol Code: Revealing the Secret Heretical Messages within Church and Renaissance Art.* London: Watkins Publishing, 2005, page 43.

20 Ehrman. *Misquoting Jesus*, page 152.

21 Wallace-Murphy. *Cracking the Symbol Code*, page 82.

22 Ehrman. *Misquoting Jesus*, page 195.

23 Freke & Gandy. *The Jesus Mysteries,* page 3.

24 Ibid pages 3, 24, 25, and 256.

25 Ibid page 23.

26 Ibid page 256.

27 Iles, Greg. *Turning Angel.* Scribner, 2005, pages 261.

28 Ehrman. *Misquoting Jesus,* page 217.

29 www.anakosha.com–Anakosha, a non-profit corporation organized for the purpose of education and exploration of human sexuality and love.

30 Craig, Dr. William Lane. *The Son Rises: Historical Evidence for the Resurrection of Jesus,* Chicago: Moody Press, 1981, page 140.

31   Wikipedia.com, see "Son of Man".

32   Strobel, Lee. *The Case for Christ*, page 101.

33   Graves, Kersey, *The World's Sixteen Crucified Saviors,* Truth Seeker Co., New York, 1875. Cited in Leedom and Mulroy, *The Book Your Church Doesn't Want You to Read*, page 176.

34   Wikipedia.com, see "Krishna".

35   Churchward, Albert. *Book of Religion*, first published in 1924. Cited in Leedom and Mulroy, *The Book Your Church Doesn't Want You to Read*, page 43.

36   http://www.aboutbuddha.org/english/life-of-buddha.htm.

37   http://Wikipedia.com, see "Mithras".

38   Freke and Gandy. *The Laughing Jesus: Religious Lies and Gnostic Wisdom*, page 57.

39   Freke & Gandy. *Jesus and the Lost Goddess*, page 55.

40   Freke and Gandy. *The Laughing Jesus: Religious Lies and Gnostic Wisdom*, page 67.

41   Feather, Robert. T*he Secret Initiation of Jesus at Qumran: The Essene Mysteries of John the Baptist.* Bear & Company, 2005, page 114.

42   Ibid page 55 and Ehrman. *Lost Christianities*, page 15.

43   Osman, Ahmed. *Christianity: An Ancient Egyptian Religion.* Bear & Company. 2005, page 200.

44   Freke & Gandy. *Jesus and the Lost Goddess,* page 39.

45   Pagels. *Adam, Eve, and the Serpent*, page xxv.

46   Harpur, Tom. *The Pagan Christ: Recovering the Lost Light.* New York: Walker & Company, 2004, page 29.

47   Freke & Gandy. *The Jesus Mysteries,* page 5.

48   Ibid page 47.

49   Ibid page 31.

50   Harpur. *The Pagan Christ*, page 29.

51   Freke & Gandy. *The Jesus Mysteries*, page 27.

52   Tim Wallace-Murphy. *Cracking the Symbol Code*, page 60.

53   Freke & Gandy. *The Jesus Mysteries*, page 80.

54   Ibid page 42.

55   Ehrman. *Lost Christianities*, page 233.

56   Tim Wallace-Murphy. *Cracking the Symbol Code*, page 76.

57 White, Michael L. *From Jesus to Christianity: How Four Generations of Visionaries & Story-tellers Created the New Testament and Christian Faith.* HarperSanFrancisco, 2004, page 96.

58 Ibid page 97.

59 Osman, Ahmed. *Christianity: An Ancient Egyptian Religion*, page 117.

60 Feather, Robert. *The Secret Initiation of Jesus at Qumran*, page 47.

61 Freke & Gandy. *The Laughing Jesus*, page 68.

62 Eisenman, Robert. *James the Brother of Jesus.* Penguin Books 1998, page xxiii.

63 Osman, Ahmed. *Christianity: An Ancient Egyptian Religion*, page 238.

64 White. *From Jesus to Christianity,* page 96.

65 Schweitzer, Albert. *Quest of the Historical Jesus: A Critical Study of Its Progress from Reimarus to Wrede.* Johns Hopkins University Press 1998, page 398.

66 Harpur. *The Pagan Christ*, page 166.

67 Ibid page 161.

68 Ibid page 169.

69 Osman, Ahmed. *Christianity: An Ancient Egyptian Religion*, page 108.

70 Ibid page 112.

71 Ibid page 116.

72 Ibid page 112.

73 Ehrman. *Lost Christianities,* page 206.

74 Harpur. *The Pagan Christ,* page 163.

75 Ibid page 164.

76 Ibid page 162.

77 Ibid page 24.

78 Ibid page 166.

79 Ibid page 121.

80 Osman, Ahmed. *Christianity: An Ancient Egyptian Religion*, page 121.

81 Stanton, G. *Gospel Truth*, HarperCollins, 1995, page 130.

82 Freke & Gandy. *The Jesus Mysteries*, page 151.

83 Harpur. *The Pagan Christ*, page 168.

84   Ibid page 166.

85   Freke & Gandy. *The Laughing Jesus,* page 69.

86   Freke & Gandy. *Jesus and the Lost Goddess*, page 21.

87   Freke & Gandy. *The Jesus Mysteries*, page 134.

88   Ibid page 136.

89   Ibid page 136.

90   Ibid page 148.

91   Ibid page 157.

92   Ibid page 135

93   Eisenman. *James, the Brother of Jesus,* page 65.

94   Ibid, page 27.

95   Ibid, page 8.

96   Ibid, page 95.

97   Freke & Gandy. *The Laughing Jesus*, page 68.

98   Ehrman. *Lost Christianities*, page 250.

99   Ibid page 249.

100   Harpur. *The Pagan Christ*, page 83.

101   Freke & Gandy. *The Laughing Jesus,* page 77.

102   Freke & Gandy. *The Jesus Mysteries,* page 236.

103   Freeman. *The Closing of the Western Mind*, page 202.

104   Freke & Gandy. *The Jesus Mysteries*, page 250.

105   Ehrman. *Lost Christianities*, page 250.

106   Ellerbe. *The Dark Side of Christian History*, page 16.

107   Spong. *The Sins of Scripture*, page 165.

108   Faulkner. *Supreme Authority*, page 152.

109   Ellerbe. *The Dark Side of Christian History,* page 100.

110   Spong. *The Sins of Scripture*, page 165.

111   Silva, Daniel. *The Kill Artist.* Random House, 2000, page 94.

112   Spong. *Jesus for the Non-Religious,* page xv.

113   Faulkner. *Supreme Authority*, page 198.

114   Tim Wallace-Murphy. *Cracking the Symbol Code*, page 50.

115   Freke & Gandy. *Jesus and the Lost Goddess*, page 58.

116   Harpur. *The Pagan Christ*, page 161.

117   Freke & Gandy. *The Jesus Mysteries,* page 246.

118   Osman, Ahmed. *Christianity: An Ancient Egyptian Religion*, page 240.

119   Ellerbe. *The Dark Side of Christian History,* page 41.

120   Ibid page 2.

121   Ibid page 42.

122   Ibid page 44.

123   Ibid page 44.

124   Ibid page 80.

125   Ibid page 50.

126   Tim Wallace-Murphy. *Cracking the Symbol Code*, page 53.

127   Ibid page 87.

128   Penman, Sharon Key. *When Christ and His Saints Slept.* NY: Henry Holt and Company, Inc., 1995, page 138.

129   Ellerbe. *The Dark Side of Christian History*, page 86.

130   Ellerbe. *The Dark Side of Christian History*, page 86.

131   Spong. *Jesus for the Non-Religious*, page 407.

132   Whitehead, Alfred North (cited by William Edelen in Leedom and Mulroy. *The Book Your Church Doesn't Want You to Read*, page 268).

133   Leedom and Mulroy. *The Book Your Church Doesn't Want You to Read,* page 281.

CHAPTER 4

1   Strobel. *The Case for Christ*, page 54.

2   White. *From Jesus to Christianity*, page 98.

3   Ibid, page 99.

4   Ibid, page 8.

5   Leedom and Mulroy. *The Book Your Church Doesn't Want You to Read,* page 142.

6   Freke & Gandy. *The Jesus Mysteries,* page 67.

7   Harpur. *The Pagan Christ*, page 33.

8   Thompson, Thomas L. *The Messiah Myth: The Near Easter Roots of Jesus and David.* Basic Books, 2005, page 11.

9   Harpur. *The Pagan Christ*, page 165.

10   Prophet, Elizabeth Clare. *The Lost Years of Jesus.* Summit University Press, 1987, page 13.

11   Feather. *The Secret Initiation of Jesus at Qumran*, page 163.

12   Ibid page 183.

13   Ibid page 64.

14   Ibid page 163.

15   Ibid page 171.

16   Ibid page 163.

17   Ibid page 180.

18   Ibid page 180.

19   Ibid page 151.

20   Ibid page 156.

21   Ibid page 157.

22   Ibid page 179.

23   Ibid page 386.

24   Ehrman. *Lost Christianities*, page 248.

25   Strobel, page 25.

26   Ehrman. *Lost Christianities*, page 235.

27   *New Advent.org*, see "Gospel".

28   Ehrman. *Lost Christianities*, page 235.

29   Freke & Gandy. *The Jesus Mysteries*, page 224.

30   Ellerbe. *The Dark Side of Christian History,* page 16.

31   Osman, Ahmed. *Christianity: An Ancient Egyptian Religion,* page 213.

32   Freke & Gandy. *Jesus and the Lost Goddess*, page 22.

33   Freke & Gandy. *The Jesus Mysteries*, page 225.

34   Schweitzer, Albert. *Quest of the Historical Jesus*, page xvi.

35   Eisenman, page 56.

36   Ibid, page xxiii.

37   Ibid, page 93.

38   Spong. *Jesus for the Non-Religious*, page 51.

39   Harris, Robert. *Imperium.* Simon & Schuster 2006, page 299.

40   Leedom and Mulroy. *The Book Your Church Doesn't Want You to Read,* (Rabbi Tovia Singer's *Resurrection Evidence Chart*) page 244.

41   Spong. *Jesus for the Non-Religious*, page 44.

42   Ibid, page 39.

43   Wallace-Murphy. *Cracking the Symbol Code*, page 59.

44   Ibid page 64.

45   Osman, Ahmed. *Christianity: An Ancient Egyptian Religion*, page 121.

46   Leedom and Mulroy. *The Book Your Church Doesn't Want You to Read*, page 386.

47   Strobel, Lee. *The Case for Christ*, page 79.

48   Ehrman. *Misquoting Jesus*, page 74.

49   Ehrman. *Lost Christianities*, page 219.

50   Gardner. *The Magdalene Legacy*, page 140.

51   Breslin, Jimmy. *The Church That Forgot Christ.* Free Press, 2004, page 36.

52   Freke & Gandy. *The Jesus Mysteries,* page 145.

53   Ibid page 145.

54   Ellerbe. *The Dark Side of Christian History*, page 16.

55   Freke & Gandy. *The Laughing Jesus,* page 70.

56   Spong. *Jesus for the Non-Religious,* page 34.

57   Ibid, page 30.

58   *Dialogue of Justin, Philosopher and Martyr, with Trypho the Jew.* Published in many collections of the early fathers of the Church.

59   Spong. *Jesus for the Non-Religious*, page 31.

60   Spong. *The Sins of Scripture*, page 40.

61   Baigent, Leigh, and Lincoln. *The Messianic Legacy,* page 32.

62   *New Advent*, see "Trinity".

63   Wikipedia.org, see "Trinity".

64   Freeman. *The Closing of the Western Mind*, page 190.

65   *New Advent*, see "Trinity".

66   Ibid.

67   Jackson, Wayne. "Defending the Faith with a Broken Sword, Part 3". *Christian Courier,* October 31,2003. www.christiancourier.com/articles.

68   Ibid.

69   *New Advent*, see "Trinity".

70   Ehrman. *Misquoting Jesus*, page 96.

71   Gardner. *The Magdalene Legacy*, page 105.

72   Freke & Gandy. *The Jesus Mysteries*, page 145.

73   Ibid page 169.

74   Freke & Gandy. *The Laughing Jesus*, page 73.

75   Ehrman. *Misquoting Jesus*, page 235.

76   Harpur. *The Pagan Christ*, page 192.

77   Freke & Gandy. *The Laughing Jesus*, page 71.

78   Ehrman. *Misquoting Jesus*, page 190.

79   Eisenman. *James, the Brother of Jesus,* page 51.

80   Spong. *The Sins of Scripture,* page 185.

81   Ehrman. *Lost Christianities*, page 20.

82   Ellerbe. *The Dark Side of Christian History,* page 68.

83   Spong. *The Sins of Scripture,* page 81.

84   Cornwell, John. *Hitler's Pope: The Secret History of Pius XII.* Penguin Books, 2000, page 46.

85   Spong. *The Sins of Scripture,* page 81.

86   "Highlights of Pope John Paul II's papacy" Associated Press, April 2, 2005.

87   Silva, Daniel. *The Confessor.* Thorndike Press, 2003, page 92.

88   *National Catholic Reporter,* December 17, 1999.

89   Spong. *The Sins of Scripture*, page 24.

CHAPTER 5

1   Freke & Gandy. *Jesus and the Lost Goddess*, page 52.

2   Freeman. *The Closing of the Western Mind*, page 278.

3   Ibid page 5.

4   Strobel, Lee. *The Case for Christ*, page 355.

5   *The Catechism of the Catholic Church*, Doubleday, 1995, page 91, paragraph 309.

6   Ibid page 180, paragraph 632.

7   http://jackmansystems.com/jesusartorg.

8   www.istockphoto.com, #8833462, marble statue of Christ.

9   Pew Forum on Religious and Public Life, "U.S. Religious Landscape Survey", May-Aug 2007.

10   Osman, Ahmed. *Christianity: An Ancient Egyptian Religion*, page 148.

11   http://en.wikipedia.org/wiki/Gehenna.

12   Smith, Wilbur. *Heaven and Hell.* Harcourt Brace Jovanovich, 1987, page 592.

13   Breslin, Jimmy. *The Church That Forgot Christ*, page 53.

14   Freke, Timothy & Peter Gandy. *The Jesus Mysteries*, page 81.

15   *New Advent*, see Augustine.

16   Science Beat, Berkely Lab, "The truth about Earth's core?"
     www.lbl.gov/Science-Articles/Archive/Phys-earth-core.html.

17   *New Advent* (see Hell).

18   *USA Today* article in 2006 (but I can't find the date of publication).

19   Pagels, Elaine. *The Origin of Satan.* New York: Random House, 1995, page 39.

20   *The Catechism of the Catholic Church*, page 110, paragraph 391.

21   Ibid page 394.

22   Ellerbe. *The Dark Side of Christian History*, page 39.

23   Thomas, Keith. *Religion and the Decline of Magic* (cited in Ellerbe. The Dark Side of Christia history, page 39).

24   Pagels. *The Origin of Satan*, page xvi.

25   Ibid page 48.

26   Ibid page 39.

27   Ellerbe. *The Dark Side of Christian History,* page 110.

28   http://en.wikipedia.org: "Roman Catechism".

29   *New Advent*, see "Purgatory".

30   Ibid, see "Baptism".

31   www.catholicfaithandreason.org/depositoffaith.htm.

32   http://en.wikipedia.org/wiki/Veneration.

33   Ibid.

34   www.catholic.org, see "Saints".

CHAPTER 6

1   Ratzinger, Cardinal Joseph. *In the Beginning.* Eerdmans, 1986, page 7.

2   Ibid page 37.

3   Center for Applied Research in the Apostolate. "Sacraments Today: Belief and Practice Among the U.S.", February 2008.

4   http://Wikipedia.com, see "Evolution of the Roman Catholic Church".

5   Ratzinger. *In the Beginning*, page 41.

6   Allen, John L. Jr. "Benedict's thinking on creation and evolution," *National Catholic Reporter,* September 1, 2006, www.nationalcatholicreporter.org.

7   Ratzinger. *In the Beginning,* page 57.

8   Ibid page 72.

9   Ingman, Max (an Australian geneticist). "Mitochondrial DNA Clarifies Human Evolution." www.actionbioscience.org/evolution/ingman.

10   *Fidei Depositum*. Libreria Editrice Vaticana (October 11, 1992).

11   *Catechism of the Catholic Church*, Doubleday, 1995, paragraph 263.

12   Ratzinger. *In the Beginning,* page 7.

13   Ibid, page 73.

14   *Catechism* paragraph 306.

15   Ratzinger. *In the Beginning,* page 73.

CHAPTER 7

1   Freke & Gandy. *Jesus and the Lost Goddess,* page 39.

2   www.junkscience.com/malaria.

3   Levine, Brittany, article "Assistance dog, 12-year-olds make 'Marvelous' pair", *USA Today,* September 27, 2007, page 9D.

4   Jakes, John. *Heaven and Hell,* Harcourt Brace Jovanovich, New York, 1987.

5   Spong. *The Sins of Scripture,* page 34.

6   Pagels, Elaine. Public Broadcasting System interview, October 10, 2003, www.pbs.org/wnet/religionandethics/week706/profile.html.

7   *The Catechism of the Catholic Church,* page 490, paragraph 1776.

8   Errico, Rocco A., *Let There Be Light, The Seven Keys.* DeVorss & Company, 1994 (cited in Leedom and Mulroy, *The Book Your Church Doesn't Want You to Read,* page 191).

ANNEX A: SURVEYS RESULTS

Source: Gallup Poll in 2006 of 1,002 adults nationwide. Margin of Error ± 3.

"Which of the following statements comes closest to describing your views about the Bible?

(a) The Bible is the actual word of God and is to be taken literally, word for word.
(b) The Bible is the inspired word of God, but not everything in it should be taken literally.
(c) The Bible is an ancient book of fables, legends, history, and moral precepts recorded by man".

(percentages)	Actual Word of God	Inspired Word of God	Fables	Unsure
2006	28	49	19	3
2005	32	47	18	3
2004	34	48	15	3
2002	30	52	15	3
2001	27	49	29	4
1998	33	47	17	3
1980	40	45	10	6
1976	38	45	13	5
Average	34	48	16	4

Newsweek Poll conducted in 2004 by Princeton Survey Research Associates of 1,009 adults nationwide. Margin of Error ± 3.

Do you believe that every word of the Bible is literally accurate – that the events it describes actually happened?

Those Surveyed	Believe	Do Not Believe	Unsure
All	55	38	7
Evangelical Protestants	84	12	5
Non-Evangelical Protestants	47	48	5
Catholics	45	46	9

ANNEX B: STATISTICS

United States

Every two and a half minutes someone is sexually assaulted.[1]

In 1994, women with disabilities were raped and abused at twice the rate of the general population.[2]

Only 26 percent of all rapes or attempted rapes are reported to law enforcement officials.[3]

In a 1994 study of 6,000 students at 32 colleges, one in four women had been the victim of rape or attempted rape.[2]

Leading causes of death from illness: heart attack, cancer, stroke, emphysema, chronic bronchitis, diabetes, flu, pneumonia, Alzheimer's disease, kidney disease, systemic infection, liver disease, and high blood pressure.[4]

There are close to 6,000 work-related fatalities each year.[4]

Every year 16,000 are murdered, more than 20,000 people die from the common flu and its complications, and 42,000 people are killed in car accidents.[5]

Medication errors kill an estimated 7,000 people a year and injure at least 1.5 million, nearly one-third in hospitals.[6]

16 people die each day for lack of a kidney transplant.[7]

Over 13,700 people over the age of 65 die each year from injuries related to falls.[19]

Suicide is the fourth leading cause of death for ages 15 through 24.[8]

2,300 people of all ages are reported missing every day.[9]

Of the 850,000 people reported missing every year 7,000 are murdered or never heard from again.[10]

Every day in the United States five children are killed by other children with guns.[11]

A man serving a life sentence in Colorado Springs, Colorado for murdering a teenage girl claimed responsibility for as many as 48 slayings across the country dating back more than three decades.[12]

One in every 150 children have an autism disorder. On average 48 percent of autistic children are mentally retarded.[13]

42,642 people die in traffic deaths in 2006, lowest rate in more than a decade.[14]

As of December 31, 2006, U.S. federal and state prisons and local jails held 2,300,000 prisoners.[15]

Russia

Domestic violence kills one woman every 40 to 60 minutes.[16]

An average of 14,000 women a year were killed by their husbands from 1995 to 2000. In the U.S.

about 1,200 women are killed annually by their partners.[17]

United Kingdom

In the United Kingdom two women are killed by their partners every week.[18]

Indian Ocean

The death toll from the 2004 tsunami in the Indian Ocean killed 170,000 people with another 130,000 listed as missing.[19]

Peru

More than half of all Peruvian women over the age of 15 have suffered sexual or physical violence by men during their lifetime as a direct consequence, experts say, of poverty. Since 2003, more than 300 have been killed by men committing sexual violence.[20]

India

More than 18,000 rape cases are reported against women every year in India. Some 8,800 women are killed in India every year in dowry disputes.[21]

Statistics Sources

1   RAINN: Rape, Abuse, Incest National Network.

2   University of California Santa Cruz.

3   National Crime Victimization Survey. Bureau of Justice Statistics, U.S. Department of Justice.

4   Fitzgerald, Nora. Article "Center helps free battered women: Campaign works to change attitudes in Russia," *USA Today*, June 14, 2006.

5   Centers for Disease Control, National Transportation Safety Board, FBI Crime Index.

6   "Rx for medication error?," editorial, *USA Today*, July 26, 2006.

7   TNT's the *Law and Order* TV program.

8   CDC.

9   TNT's *Without a Trace* TV program.

10   Healy, Michelle. Article in *USA Today*, November 28, 2006.

11   *The Selected Works of Jack W. Gresham*, 2007.

12   Sarche, Jon. Undated article in the *Associated Press Writer.*

13   Szabo, Liz. Article "Roots of autism more complex than thought" in *USA Today*, February 18, 2007.

14   Copeland, Larry. Article "Lowest fatality rate ever on roads in '06" in *USA Today*, July 24, 2007.

15   U.S. Department of Justice, Bureau of Justice Statistics, www.ojp.usdoj.gov.

16 Amnesty International report released in December 2005.

17 CDC and National Transportation Safety Board.

18 Friederike Behr, one of the authors of the Amnesty International report.

19 CNN.

20 Ordonez, Isabel. Article "Peru confronts escalating violence against women," *USA Today*, July 24, 2006.

21 Shankar, Jay. Undated article in *Agence France- Presse (AFP)*: India's National Crime Records Bureau.

22 Brophy-Markus, Mary. Article "Seniors vulnerable to taking a tumble," *USA Today*, April 23, 2007.

BIBLIOGRAPHY

Alexander, Pat ed. *Encyclopedia of the Bible.* Lion Publishing Corporation 1978.
Ardrey, Robert and Berdine. *African Genesis.* Delta 1963.
Armstrong, Karen. *The History of God.* Alfred A. Knopf 1993.
Atwill, Joseph. *Caesar's Messiah.* Ulysses Press 2005.
Baigent, M. & R. Leigh. *The Dead Sea Scrolls Deception.* Touchstone Book 1991.
Baigent, M., R. Leigh, & H. Lincoln. *Holy Blood, Holy Grail.* Delta Trade Books 2004.
Baigent, M., R. Leigh, & H. Lincoln. *The Messianic Legacy.* Delta Trade Books 2004.
Baigent, Michael. *The Jesus Papers.* HarperSanFrancisco 2006.
Bargeman, Lisa A. *The Egyptian Origin of Christianity.* Blue Dolphin Publishing 2005.
Barnes, Harry Elmer. *Twilight of Christianity.* [publisher unknown] 1929.
Bidstrup, Scot. *What the Christian Fundamentalist Doesn't Want You To Know:
    a Brief Survey of Biblical Errancy.* www.bidstrup.com.
Breslin, Jimmy. *The Church That Forgot Christ.* Free Press 2004.
Brown, Dan. *The Da Vinci Code.* New York: Doubleday 2003.
Browne, Sylvia. *The Mystical Life of Jesus.* Dutton 2006.
Catechism of the Catholic Church. Image Book Doubleday 1995.
Cayce, Edgar. *Modern Prophet.* Gramercy Books 1989.
Collins & Evans. *Christian Beginnings and the Dead Sea Scrolls,* Baker Academic, 2006.
Complete Idiot's Guide to Understanding Catholicism. Alpha Penguin Group 2006.
Cornwell, John. *Hitler's Pope: The Secret History of Pius XII.* Penguin Books 2000.
Cornwell, John. *Thief in the Night.* Penguin Books 1989.
Crichton, Michael. *Prey.* HarperCollins 2002.
Djilas, Milovan. *The New Class.* A Harvest/HBJ Book 1993.
Eisenman, Robert. *Dead Sea Scrolls and the First Christians.* Castle Books 2006.
Eisenman, Robert. *James the Brother of Jesus.* Penguin Books 1998.
Ellerbe, Helen. *The Dark Side Christian History.* Morningstar & Lark 1995.
Encyclopedia of the Bible. *A Lion Book.* Reader's Digest Association Inc. 1986.
Erhman, Bart D. *Lost Christianities: The Battles for Scripture and the Faiths We
    Never Knew.* Oxford University Press 2003.
Erhman, Bart D. *Misquoting Jesus.* HarperSanFrancisco 2005.
Erhman, Bart D. *Peter, Paul, and Mary.* Oxford University Press 2006.
Faulkner, Mary. *Supreme Authority: Understanding Power in the Catholic Church.*
    Marie Butler-Knight 2003.
Feather, Robert. *The Secret Initiation of Jesus at Qumran: The Essene Mysteries of
    John the Baptist.* Bear & Company 2005.
Follan, John. *City of Secrets.* HarperCollins 2003.
Foster, David. *Renegade's Guide to God.* Faith Words 2006.
Freeman, Charles. *The Closing of the Western Mind: The Rise of Faith and the Fall
    of Reason.* New York: Vintage Books 2005.
Freke, Timothy & Peter Gandy. *Jesus and the Lost Goddess: The Secret Teachings
    of the Original Christians.* Three Rivers Press 2001.
Freke, Timothy & Peter Gandy. *The Jesus Mysteries: Was the "Original Jesus" a Pagan
    God.* New York: Three Rivers Press 1999.
Freke, Timothy & Peter Gandy. *The Laughing Jesus: Religious Lies and Gnostic
    Wisdom.* New York: Harmony Books 2005.
Gardner, Laurence. *The Magdalene Legacy: The Jesus and Mary Bloodline
    Conspiracy.* Element–HarperCollins 2005.
Graves, Kersey. *The World's Sixteen Crucified Saviors.* New York, Truth Seeker 1875.
Greenberg, Gary. *One Hundred One Myths of the Bible.* Sourcebooks Inc. 2000.
Greenberg, Gary. *The Moses Mystery.* Birch Lane Press Book 1996.
Harpur, Tom. *The Pagan Christ: Recovering the Lost Light.* New York: Walker &
    Company 2004.
Iles, Greg. *Turning Angel.* Scribner 2005.
James, E.O. *Ancient Gods.* Phoenix 1999.
Kasser, Meyer, & Wurst eds. *The Gospel of Judas.* National Geographic Society 2006.
Knight, Christopher & Robert Lomas. *The Hiram Key.* Element Books Inc. 1997.

Krosney, Herbert. *The Lost Gospel*. National Geographic 2006.
Laughlin, P. *Remedial Christianity: What Every Believer Should Know*. Polebridge 2000.
Lockerbie, D. Bruce. *Apostle's Creed: Do You Really Believe It?* Victor Books 1977.
Lost Books of the Bible. Bell Publishing 1979.
Mack, Burton L. *Who Wrote the New Testament?* HarperSanFrancisco 1996.
Malloch, Douglas.K. *Christ and the Tauroboleum: Lord Mithras in the Genesis of Christianity*. Lochan Publisher, early-to-mid 1900s.
Martin, Michael. *The Case Against Christianity*. Temple University Press, 1993.
McKinsey, C. Dennis. *The Encyclopedia of Biblical Errancy*. Prometheus Books, 1995.
Mercer, Jerry L. *Being Christian*. Discipleship Resources 1993.
Meyer, Marvin. *The Gospels of Mary*. HarperSanFrancisco 2004.
Monks of Mount Angel Abbey. *The New Order of the Mass*. The Liturgical Press 1970.
New American Bible. Catholic Bible Publishers 1994-1995 edition.
Notovitch, Nicolas. *The Lost Years of Jesus: The Life of Saint Isa*. (Publisher?) 1890.
Osman, Ahmed. *Christianity: An Ancient Egyptian Religion*. Bear & Company 2005.
Pagels, Elaine. *Adam, Eve, and the Serpent*. New York: First Vintage Books 1989.
Pagels, Elaine. *The Origin of Satan*. New York: Random House 1995.
Pelikan, Jaroslav. *Whose Bible Is It?* Penguin Books 2006.
Picket, Lynn. *Mary Magdalene*. Carroll & Graf Publishers 2003.
Picknett, Lynn & Clive Prince. *The Templar Revelation*. Touchstone 1998.
Prophet, Elizabeth Clare. *The Lost Years of Jesus: Documentary Evidence of Jesus' 17-Year Journey to the East*. Summit Beacon International 1993, 1988.
Prophet, Elizabeth Clare. *The Lost Years of Jesus*. Summit University Press, 1987,
Prophet, Elizabeth Clare. *The Missing Link in Christianity*. Summit Publications, 1997.
Ratzinger, Joseph. *In the Beginning: Creation and the Fall*. Eerdmans, 1986.
Robinson, J. A.T. *The Difference in Being a Christian Today*. Westminster Press 1972.
Schweitzer, Dr. Albert. *The Quest for the Historical Jesus: A Critical Study of Its Progress from Reimarus to Wrede*. Johns Hopkins University Press 1998.
Seward, Desmond. *Monks of War: The Military Religious Orders*. Penguin Books 1995.
Simon, Bernard. *The Essence of the Gnostics*. New Jersey: Chartwell Books, Inc. 2004.
Smith, Wilbur. *Heaven and Hell*. Harcourt Brace Jovanovich, 1987.
Spong, John Shelby. *Jesus for the Non-Religious*. HarperCollins 2007.
Spong, John Shelby. *The Sins of Scripture: Exposing the Bible's Text of Hate to Reveal the God of Love*. HarperSanFrancisco 2005.
Stanton, G. *Gospel Truth*. HarperCollins 1995.
Starbird, Margaret. *The Goddess in the Gospels*. Bear & Company 1998.
Starbird, Margaret. *The Woman with the Alabaster Jar*. Bear & Company 1993.
Strobel, Lee. *The Case for Christ*. Zondervan, 1998.
Sweeting, George. *How to Begin the Christian Life*. Moody Press 1975.
Thomason, Bill. *Real Life Real Faith*. Judson Press 1994.
Thompson, Thomas L. *The Messiah Myth: Near Eastern Roots of Jesus & David*. Basic Books, 2005.
Van Praagh, James. *Talking to Heaven*. Signet Book 1999.
Wallace-Murphy, Tim. *Cracking the Symbol Code: Revealing the Secret Heretical Messages within Church and Renaissance Art*. London: Watkins Publishing 2005.
Wallace-Murphy, Tim & Marilyn Hopkins. *Rosslyn*. Barnes & Noble Books 2000.
Weiss, Brian L. *Many Lives, Many Mansions*. A Fireside Book by Simon & Schuster, 1988.
Weiss, G. Christian. *On Being a Real Christian*. Moody Press 1951.
White, L. Michael. *From Jesus to Christianity: How Four Generations of Visionaries & Storytellers Created the New Testament and Christian Faith*. HarperSanFrancisco 2004.
Wise, M., M. Abegg, and E. Cook. *The Dead Sea Scrolls*. HarperCollins, 2005.
Williams, Larry. *The Mountain of Moses*. Wynwood Press 1990.

SUBJECT INDEX

Acts of the Apostles
      – diminished Paul vice Peter, 96
      – Gnostic Christians claimed Acts was a crude forgery, 97
      – Irenaeus and Tertullian considered Acts to be holy scripture, 80
      – originally a Gnostic text, 80
Acts of Thomas was adapted to Literalism, 80
Adam
      – and death, 8
      – father of the human race, 17
      – never existed, 21
adultery survey, 38
anti-Semitism, 97
      – God's vengeance upon the Jews for killing Christ, 99
      – Hitler: the Pope asked German-Jew converts be spared, 100
      – Holocaust, 62, 101-102
      – Jerusalem: its destruction was God's punishment of Jews, 99
      – Jesus: never told Jews "you belong to your father the devil", 97
      – Jews' historic admission of guilt, 99
      – Kalwaria, Poland: Easter attack on Jews, 100
      – Luke: "forgive them father" was a forgery, 97
      – Pilate: absolved by the Gospels of guilt for Jesus' death, 97
      – Pope John Paul II: Church's "sons and daughters" were the guilty ones, 101
      – Pope John Paul II: visited Jewish synagogue, 101
Augustine
      – disbelief in remission of Original Sin by baptism condemns the Church, 127
      – faith over reason: humans can't think for themselves, 104
      – hardliner on punishment, 127
      – heresy: defined by Augustine, 65
      – his concept of punishment became a pillar of Catholic dogma, 12
      – his doctrine on Original Sin had far-reaching impact on Church dogma, 12
      – his writings became the cornerstone of Christian doctrine, 9
      – on Limbo, 127
      – on sex, 11
Augustus, Caesar (27 BC-14 AD), 47
Bacon, Sir Francis: "We prefer to believe what we prefer to be true", 104
baptism
      – anathema on those who don't believe baptism removes all sin, 24
      – baptism serves no purpose, 24, 137
      – cleanses Original Sin, 13
      – disbelief in remission of Original Sin by baptism condemns the Church, 127
      – door to Church of Christ, 23
      – in ancient religions, 23
      – indistinguishable from Pagan baptism, 23
      – Jesus: on baptism, 23
      – Jesus: why baptized? 23
      – necessity of infant baptism, 10
      – quietus of baptism, 23
      – Sacrament of Baptism, 13, 23
belief in tenets is insidiously harmful if required, 139
belief: there is no substance to it, 107
Bible
      – canon: by vote, 76
      – canon: selection criteria–credibility and compatibility with beliefs, 82
      – Catholics are biblically illiterate, 2

Tertullian
- considered Acts of the Apostles holy scripture, 80
- Gnostics filled "the whole universe", 32
- thirst for knowledge replaced by the virtue of blind faith in scripture, 104
Theophilus (see Trinity)
Third Council of Carthage (397): agreed on canon, 80
Thoreau, Henry David: "quiet desperation", 61
Tiberius, Claudius Nero aka Claudius Augustus (AD 14 to 37), 46
Tree of Knowledge of Good and Evil in the Garden of Eden, 7, 8, 21
Trent Catechism (1545), 125
Trinity
- *Comma Johanneum*–the John Clause, 92
- doctrine: never if another religion had won, 76
- first reference to Trinity was in Theophilus, 92
- scriptural evidence was inconclusive, 92
- Trinity dogma by way of revelation, 94
- two cunningly inserted phrases, 92
Turkana Boy, 19
Valley of Hinnom's Son: garbage dump, 112
virgin birth, 90
"whatever" power, 25-30,36-38, 54-59, 61, 66-67, 91, 130-132
- big news, 28
- canonizing saints, 130
- citations in the Gospels, 29
- concocted by the author of Matthew, 30, 38, 91
- greatest controlling influence, 59
- intimidation–a natural by-product of the "whatever" power, 59
- Luke and John didn't mention the "whatever" power, 26
- Matthew cited the "whatever" power, 25
- no mention in Mark, 27
- two all-important effects, 55
- why early Christians needed a mechanism, a hook, 34
- would Jesus have done it? 36
Wilson, Flip: "the devil made me do it", 124
wise men at Jesus' birth, 84
witch trials, 65
women at Jesus' tomb, 85
women: role in Christianity, 11, 33, 26
Word of God
- any suggestion that the Bible is not the Word of God frightens the Faithful, 68
- belief that the NT is the Word of God is purely a matter of faith, 103
- Creationists distort incontrovertible scientific facts, 17
- despite its contradictions, say diehard Faithful, NT still the Word of God, 102
- not claiming that this book is the Word of God, 80
- televangelists, 105
- that the Faithful need the Bible to be the Word of God doesn't mean it is, 76